BIOGRAPHY AND CRITICISM

General Editors
A. NORMAN JEFFARES
R. L. C. LORIMER

4
HENRY JAMES
and the Modern Reader

D. W. JEFFERSON

HENRY JAMES
and the Modern Reader

OLIVER & BOYD

EDINBURGH AND LONDON

1964

OLIVER & BOYD LTD
Tweeddale Court
Edinburgh 1

39A Welbeck Street
London W1

813.4
J35h
73521

February, 1971

First published 1964

Preface

THE time is now ripe for a much more general recognition of the greatness and also of the readability of James's work. The epithet "difficult" has too long been used to segregate him from other writers, with the effect also of segregating his readers from other readers. The difficulties he presents are not on the scale that we have become accustomed to in works like *Ulysses*, to say nothing of *Finnegan's Wake*. Those in Faulkner are, for some readers, greater and harder to bear. And, after all, difficulty does not always mean inaccessibility. A writer's humour, personal rhetoric, and charm may be very evident in passages where the meaning itself raises problems, so that a reader can be on good terms with him even if he is occasionally rather lost. The difficulties in James are often the result of idiosyncrasies in themselves admirable and delightful.

Most of his work, including everything of the early and middle periods, cannot be described as difficult at all by twentieth-century standards: but its readability has not yet been sufficiently recognised. The secret of its attraction often lies in a certain Jamesian point of view and manner, a special version of something profoundly national; and this may have to be identified if he is to be fully enjoyed. With the contemporary development of interest in the Americanness of American literature, James's Americanness will, no doubt, become increasingly more appreciated.

The modern reader has the advantage of inheriting the progress in understanding achieved by two or three generations of critics. The intellectual climate for readers of James has completely changed. *The Portrait of a Lady*, relatively little read in the nineteen-thirties, has become widely accepted as one of the great classics of our fiction; and this is only the most conspicuous example of a development of critical interest from which almost all the novels have benefited. It now seems incredible that books of the quality of *The Europeans* and *What Maisie Knew* were so long ignored. The reader of to-day receives every encouragement to regard them as the masterpieces they are from critics well qualified to reveal their excellence. The re-issue of works long out of print, including some of his most entertaining pieces—short stories; travel sketches; criticisms of the arts, as amiable as they are acute—adds to one's general impression of favourable prospects.

But one cannot be sure that this wider acceptance of James will develop as it might. In some places where James is studied the emphasis falls almost everywhere but on the things that make him readable. It has become a habit with many of his critics to read between the lines, ignoring the experience that the writing itself can give. Problematic implications are discussed with inadequate reference to the factors most likely to be of help where problems arise: the mood, the tone, the point of view, and James's uses of language in relation to all these things. Some interpretations of the novels and stories are strangely unsympathetic, the critic's moral approach being so much more unsparing than James's text would seem to invite. For example, Basil Ransom is seen as a ruthless egoist who will certainly make Verena unhappy. But the passage on the last page about Verena's tears does not really justify this. To make possible such an interpretation the good-humoured, chivalrous side of Ransom (his gentleness towards Miss Birdseye, his appreciation of Dr Prance) and the charm of his meetings with Verena are played down; and the novel appears less attractive. Mr Terence Martin, in an article on "The Pupil," claims, but quite arbitrarily, that the expression "seeing 'through,'" used by James of his exploitation of the point of view, has here a double meaning, and that Pemberton, the tutor, is "seen through" (in the moral sense) by his pupil in the final episode.[1] On any fair estimate, Pemberton is an exceptionally good person. How much more he would

---

[1] Mr Martin calls to his aid a textual ambiguity which must be disallowed. Morgan, we read, is "beyond their wildest recall" (*i.e.*, dead) before the look of dismay passes between Pemberton and another person; and there can be no doubt of the other person's being Mrs Moreen. The two "they's" in this sentence must refer to the same people—the alternative would be perverse—and in the first instance Mrs Moreen and Pemberton are too clearly indicated for any question to arise.

actually have done for Morgan, had the boy lived, we are in no
position to know: but up to this point he has behaved admirably, and his startled look at the sudden prospect of being
saddled with permanent responsibility for him does him no
real discredit. The suggestion that James terminates their
relationship with Morgan's despairing recognition of his lack
of love gives the story a morbid stringency that is quite alien
to it. But James's scrupulous recognition of limits in his
characters exposes him to such interpretations. There are
many other places where this disconcerting technique could be
applied, if the reader were so minded. Much more could
be done with the faults of Isabel Archer. Evidence may be
found in the text of *The Ambassadors* that the sight of a distinguished aristocratic Frenchwoman in tears is one of those
things that an especially privileged American cherishes among
his experiences in Europe; and an odd view of Strether's
character could be developed from such material, if one chose
to be sufficiently unjust to all the things that make him sympathetic. Some of these ungenerous readings have the effect
of associating James more closely with the moral frustration
and pessimism of the Puritan tradition than the truth warrants.
Other interpreters try to associate him with exalted and complicated schemes of quasi-religious allegory, the terms of which
have to be imposed from outside because his text does not
contain them. The image of James as a rather forbidding
writer may be kept alive artificially by these schools of criticism.

Even in his late phase he is a simpler writer than much of
this work would lead one to expect. Or, at least, his com-
plexities are organic, not intellectual. One must learn, of
course, to *read* him, to become familiar with his idiom, his
manner, his characteristic gestures, and this may take time.
But the experience of reading late James is that of sensing
situations in their wholeness: sensing, admittedly, rather than
seeing clearly, if it is the first attempt of a reader not unusually
gifted. This sense of the situation as a whole sustains one
through the intricacies, the necessary intricacies, of the
presentation. The spellbinding quality of the prose is the
unifying force. The readability of the late prose consists in
its power to subdue and beguile, to charm the reader into an

acceptance of the oneness of the experience that the work unfolds.

The readability of James will be one of the themes of this study. In designing the book I have tried to avoid repeating material from my short introduction to James in the paperback *Writers and Critics* series. The chapters in Part II deal with a similar kind of subject-matter to that of certain chapters in my earlier volume, but the illustrations are not the same, and the fuller treatment allows scope for different emphases. Having already dealt briefly with aspects of the first part of *The Golden Bowl* I limit myself here to the second part; and my two treatments of *The Ambassadors* are equally distinct from each other. Some of the novels and short stories discussed here received only the briefest mention or none at all in the earlier volume. Statements which had to be cut to an extreme brevity in the paperback are now illustrated at greater length.

My chief indebtedness is to Professor A. N. Jeffares, who encouraged me to write the book, and made valuable criticisms of the manuscript.

Leeds   D. W. J.
June 1963

Acknowledgments

For permission to quote from the works of Henry James acknowledgments are due to the Trustees of Henry James's Estate, to John Farquarson Ltd., and to Rupert Hart-Davis Limited.

Acknowledgments are also due to the following for permission to quote from the works mentioned: Cambridge University Press (Dorothea Krook, *The Ordeal of Consciousness in Henry James*); Chatto and Windus Ltd. (F. R. Leavis, *The Great Tradition*); Chatto and Windus Ltd. and Oxford University Press Inc. (Richard Poirier, *The Comic Sense of Henry James*); Oxford University Press and Houghton Mifflin Co. (W. D. Howells, *The Rise of Silas Lapham*); Charles Scribner's Sons (Edith Wharton, *The Custom of the Country*).

Some of the material in Chapter Three first appeared, in a different form, as part of a Third Programme broadcast, and acknowledgments are made to the British Broadcasting Corporation for permission to use it again.

Contents

		PAGE
Preface		v

PART I

INTRODUCTORY : APPROACHES TO JAMES

| I | Questions of Tone | 3 |
| II | Questions of Moral Content | 22 |

PART II

JAMES AND HIS WORLD

III	Sense of Place	41
IV	Sense of Type	63
V	American Themes	93
VI	English Types	114

PART III

JAMES'S ART : THE CULMINATING PHASE

VII	Method and Style	129
VIII	Short Stories	146
IX	Two English Novels	164
X	The Later Novels: I	188
XI	The Later Novels: II	206

APPENDIX

A Description of the Standard Edition of the Novels and Stories of Henry James, edited by Percy Lubbock	227
Bibliography	229
Index	237

PART I

INTRODUCTORY: APPROACHES TO JAMES

I

Questions of Tone

In his Preface to *The Tragic Muse*, James confesses to a difficulty in achieving structural balance in a novel, so that his work is liable to suffer "the disgrace of legs too short, ever so much too short, for its body." In very few of his compositions, he admits, is the organic centre in the proper position:

> Time after time, then, has the precious waistband or girdle studded and buckled and placed for brave outward show, practically worked itself . . . to a point perilously near the knees—perilously I mean for the freedom of these parts. In several of my compositions this displacement has so succeeded, at the crisis, in defying and resisting me, has appeared so fraught with probable dishonour, that I still turn upon them, in spite of the greater or less success of final dissimulation, a rueful and wondering eye.[1]

He referred to the same failing many years before in a letter to W. D. Howells, where the reference is to "Lady Barbarina."[2] The note of amusement, and the pleasantly absurd image used to express his artistic plight, are recurring features of James's Prefaces. There is a remarkable sequence of images in the Preface to the volume containing "The Author of Beltraffio," where he recalls his painful efforts to restrict the length of certain stories. Of "The Middle Years" he writes:

> . . . I scarce perhaps recall another case . . . in which my struggle to keep compression rich, if not, better still, to keep accretions compressed, betrayed for me such community with the anxious effort of some warden of the insane engaged at a critical moment in making fast a victim's straitjacket.[3]

---

[1] *The Art of the Novel. Critical Prefaces by Henry James* [= *A.N.*], ed. R. P. Blackmur (1934), pp. 85-6.
[2] *The Letters of Henry James* [= *L.*], ed. P. Lubbock, I. 104.
[3] *A.N.*, p. 232.

The same operation is then seen in culinary terms:

> . . . after boilings and reboilings of the contents of my small
> cauldron, after added pounds of salutary sugar, as numerous as
> those described in the choicest recipe for the thickest jam, I
> well remember finding the whole process and act (which, to the
> exclusion of everything else, dragged itself out for a month)
> one of the most expensive of its sort in which I had ever
> engaged.[4]

Part of the problem was to disguise the fact that the story
really called for fuller treatment; and here, referring to "The
Abasement of the Northmores" and "The Tree of Knowledge," which he describes as "developmental with a vengeance," he makes the witty remark that "the need for an
apparent ease and a general congruity" enforced "——as on
behalf of some victim of the income-tax who would minimise
his 'return'——an almost heroic dissimulation of capital."[5]
The same situation is charmingly expressed, towards the
end of the Preface to the "Altar of the Dead" volume, where he
portrays himself as, for many years, "astride the silver-shod,
sober-paced, short-stepping, but oh so hugely nosing, so tenderly
and yearningly and ruefully sniffing, grey mule of the 'few
thousand words'. . . ."[6]

A happy note of excess may transform for us his exposition
of technique. In the Preface to *The Awkward Age*, one of his
more extreme experiments in the novel, he refers to his method
as pumping the air "gaspingly dry, dry not only of superfluous
moisture, but absolutely (for I have encountered the charge)
of breathable air";[7] which expresses a by no means unpleased
awareness of where his idiosyncrasies could lead him. He brands
the work, "but ever so tenderly,"[8] as monstrous. Fully conscious of how little *The Awkward Age* would appeal to most
tastes, he admits undismayed that for him it is completely
successful: "The thing carries itself to my maturer and
gratified sense as with every symptom of soundness, an insolence of health and joy":[9] words which convey an insolence
of artistic well-being in the teeth of common opinion.

[4] *A.N.*, p. 233.   [5] *A.N.*, pp. 234-5.   [6] *A.N.*, p. 266.
[7] *A.N.*, p. 114.   [8] *A.N.*, p. 99.   [9] *A.N.*, p. 117.

It is characteristic of the way James is viewed by many of his greatest admirers that R. P. Blackmur's Introduction to the Prefaces makes no reference to these elements of humour and extravagance. James said of his father that "his philosophy was his tone"; and it may be said of James's own ideas about literature that they lose much of their significance when the personal tone is ignored, as it is in a summarised version giving only the abstract principle. Blackmur goes as far as anyone could wish in his recognition of the greatness of the Prefaces, which he describes as "the most eloquent and original piece of literary criticism in existence," and he writes admirably of the many technical issues they raise: but in emphasising the dedicated artist and the logical theorist in James he not only misses human elements in the writing but is also liable to get the theory out of focus.

In a passage from the Preface to the volume containing *The Aspern Papers*, where the effect of incontinent invention is compared with the "absolute singleness, clearness and roundness" resulting from artistic severity, it is neither irrelevant nor out of character that James should do justice—it would take James to do justice—to the wanton pleasures as well as to the perils of the former way of writing:

> Nothing is so easy as improvisation, the running on and on of invention ; it is sadly compromised, however, from the moment its stream breaks bounds and gets into flood. Then the waters may spread indeed, gathering houses and herds and crops and cities into their arms and wrenching off, for our amusement, the whole face of the land—only violating by the same stroke our sense of the course and the channel, which is our sense of the uses of a stream and the virtue of a story. Improvisation, as in the Arabian Nights, may keep on terms with encountered objects by sweeping them in and floating them on its breast ; but the great effect it so loses—that of keeping on terms with itself.[10]

This passage gives the piquant and satisfying impression of an artist acquainted with profusion, for whom economy has nothing to do with natural meagreness. In the Preface to *Roderick Hudson* he refers to "the ache of fear," which was to

---

[10] *A.N.*, pp. 171-2.

recur again and again, of being excessively tempted by "developments." "Really, universally, relations end nowhere," but it is the exquisite problem of the artist to make them "happily *appear* to do so."[11] The idea of economy excites sympathy and delight when we are reminded of this conflict with an inveterate lavishness. Writers on James often ignore the latter aspect of him when they quote his views on form, and the result is a misleading and rather unattractive impression of his critical outlook.

"Clumsy life again at her stupid work"[12]—his comment when the story heard in conversation goes beyond the point of true suggestiveness—is precisely the kind of phrase, quoted in isolation and by a reader who has not caught the note of James's humorous rhetoric, which creates the false legend: that is, of a novelist whose commitment to art and selection involves a fastidious preciosity inimical to "living values." But the following passage (also from the Preface to *The Spoils of Poynton*), which says much the same thing, says it in such a way as to represent art as an intensely living activity, a means of laying life under contribution so that its treasures may be appropriated:

> Life being only inclusion and confusion, and art being all discrimination and selection, the latter, in search of the hard latent *value* with which alone it is concerned, sniffs round the mass as instinctively and unerringly as a dog suspicious of some buried bone. The difference here, however, is that, while the dog desires his bone but to destroy it, the artist finds in *his* tiny nugget, washed free of awkward accretions and hammered into a sacred hardness, the very stuff for a clear affirmation, the happiest chance for the indestructible. It at the same time amuses him again and again to note how, beyond the first step of the actual case, the case that constitutes for him his germ, his vital particle, his grain of gold, life persistently blunders and deviates, loses herself in the sand. The reason is of course that life has no direct sense whatever for the subject and is capable, luckily for us, of nothing but splendid waste. Hence the opportunity for the sublime economy of art, which rescues, which saves, and hoards and "banks", investing and reinvesting

---

[11] *A.N.*, pp. 4-5.   [12] *A.N.*, p. 121.

these fruits of toil in wondrous useful "works" and thus making up for us, desperate spendthrifts that we all naturally are, the most princely of incomes.[13]

It is unfortunate that James, in a letter to Howells,[14] provided authority for the view that the Prefaces are little treatises on method, a manual for aspirants. They are not really systematic or doctrinaire enough for this, but they are also a great deal more. For some readers their greatest charm may be in the autobiographical passages: for example, in the numerous evocations of the places where the books were composed. He associates the writing of *Roderick Hudson* with memories of the Piazza Santa Maria Novella, Florence;[15] and this is linked in his mind with the problem of portraying Northampton, Massachusetts, the early environment of his hero. *The American* he wrote partly in Paris itself, and in recalling its sights and sounds he refers to the difficulty of writing about a place when one's impression of it is too immediate and powerful. The Preface to *The Portrait of a Lady* begins with an account of Venice and its distractions, to which he often had recourse, "in the fruitless fidget of composition," to see whether it could not help him out with the right phrase or stroke. He draws a humorous moral. Italy does not help an artist to concentrate, when Italy is not the immediate subject of his composition. What it has to give is so much out of proportion to the scale of his problems that it is like "asking an army of glorious veterans to help him to arrest a peddlar who has given him the wrong change."[16] *The Spoils of Poynton* was composed in a cottage on a cliff-side; "A London Life" in an old Venetian palace, with a Tiepolo ceiling; "The Chaperon" in an Irish inn, with a table of "an equilibrium so vague that I wonder to-day how any object constructed on it should stand so firm."[17] "Lady Barbarina" is associated with rooms near Piccadilly, a region with a rich Thackerayan atmosphere. These vivid and intimate little sketches of the place of composition are in James's surest manner. He had been a master of this kind of writing for nearly forty years.

The Prefaces often begin with a history, richly retrospective

[13] *A.N.*, p. 120.   [14] *L.*, II. 102.   [15] *A.N.*, p. 7.
[16] *A.N.*, pp. 40-1.   [17] *A.N.*, p. 138.

and imaginative, of the composition in question. In some cases this opens with an account of the first hint, the story overheard, which provides the germ of the subject. Slight though the suggestion may be—the slighter the better, in James's view—"the novelist's imagination winces,"[18] as at the prick of a needle; and here is the beginning of a process of incubation, of gestation, which he describes in a manner that combines critical acuteness with so many other elements—humour, poetry, rhetorical extravagance—that any attempt to say briefly what he is conveying can only be a poor travesty. At a certain decisive stage in the process a point of principle may emerge. For example, an important moment in the development of *The Spoils of Poynton* is his recognition that the situation, already partially formulated in his mind, must be presented as the experience of one character peculiarly equipped to appreciate it; that is, Fleda Vetch. Similar moments occur elsewhere; for example, in his account of *What Maisie Knew*. References to his use of a "point of view" are quite frequent in the Prefaces, and it is now universally known as a common Jamesian principle of composition: but it is most desirable that his discussion of it in each instance should be read in its autobiographical context. In the first place, he is describing an individual solution to a particular problem. If James is occasionally inspired to generalise, it is under the influence of some emotion excited by the special problem or achievement he is depicting. Though full of implications for the theorist, these parts of the Prefaces are primarily records of his own imaginative experience and have a fullness of interest that goes far beyond the abstract questions of method which they may raise. His delight in the experience itself may indeed be of more value than the mere point of technique, considered theoretically. He expresses it in a variety of engaging ways. "Once the germ had been transferred to the sunny south window-sill of one's fonder attention . . . .":[19] this is his turn of phrase as he approaches an important point in the progress of *The Spoils of Poynton*. "Once 'out'," he writes of a novelist's theme, in the Preface to *What Maisie Knew*, "like a house-dog of a temperament above confinement, it

<hr/>

[18] *A.N.*, p. 119.   [19] *A.N.*, p. 127.

defies the mere whistle, it roams, it hunts, it seeks out and 'sees' life. . . ."[20] It is in conveying the solicitations to which "life" exposes him that he writes most imaginatively in his Prefaces. His idea for *The Princess Casamassima*, he confesses, was "unmistakeably the ripe round fruit of perambulation," in a London full of beckoning themes. "Possible stories, presentable figures, rise from the thick jungle as the observer moves, fluttering up like startled game, and before he knows it indeed he has fairly to guard himself against the brush of importunate wings. He goes on as with his head in a cloud of humming presences. . . ."[21] What follows is a most moving and beautiful account of how the subject of Hyacinth Robinson first suggested itself.

That James is the most serious and subtle of artists is fundamentally true, but in literary discussion he is too often quoted as the representative of a supersubtle intensity in contrast to writers who are credited with a broader, more human approach. The emphasis needs to be placed elsewhere. The traditional image of him is misleading, unless he is seen also as buoyant, relaxed, even rather irresponsible at times. He is, in fact, an American humorist on a generous scale, and some of his more conscientious modern admirers may occasionally be worried by his drolleries, which are often pleasantly gratuitous. The Preface to *The Golden Bowl*, which actually contains very little of theoretical interest, has an amusing passage about the revision of works written many years before ("the first-born of my progeny"). It pleases his fancy to see the process

> . . . as a descent of awkward infants from the nursery to the drawing-room under the kind appeal of enquiring, of possibly interested, visitors. I had accordingly taken for granted the common decencies of such a case—the responsible glance of some power above from one nursling to another, the rapid flash of an anxious needle, the not imperceptible effect of a certain audible splash of soap-and-water ; all in consideration of the searching radiance of drawing-room lamps as compared with nursery candles. But it had been all the while present to me

---

[20] *A.N.*, p. 144.   [21] *A.N.*, pp. 59-60.

that from the moment a stitch should be taken or a hair-brush applied the *principle* of my making my brood more presentable under the nobler illumination would be accepted and established, and it was there complications might await me.[22]

He is much given to broad, homely metaphors and similes:

> . . . a compactness into which the imagination may cut thick, as into the rich density of wedding-cake.[23]

> . . . any free plunge of the speculative fork into the contemporary social salad.[24]

These flourishes exist only to testify to the author's good spirits and imaginative superfluity. It is worth while to stress that the James of the Prefaces, so often represented—and, of course, with much truth—as suffering acutely from lack of appreciative recognition, could nevertheless address himself with this colloquial expansiveness, eloquence and humour to such readers as he had. James's personal sense of privation is a matter for the biographer, and need not concern us here. It would need a good deal of assurance on the part of a critic to claim that the Prefaces actually convey any hint of defeat or frustration.

As for James's teaching on the novel: we do him an injustice and spoil our own and other people's reading of his work, by associating him with abstractions such as "method," "form," "art," and the like. He was, of course, passionately concerned with the things these words signify, but he did not use the words in this dry academic way; and he is very far removed from the pedantries or *clichés* with which discussions of such terms are ridden. Above all—there is really no escape from this—what James says cannot be understood except in the language in which he says it. Attempts to present his ideas at second-hand—yet how can we avoid it, if we are critics or teachers?—can only lead to thinner, less generous, less sympathetic, and perhaps seriously distorted versions.

The purpose of this chapter is to examine a number of the ways in which an enjoyment of James can be hindered. We begin with the later James, because this is the James of the

---

[22] *A.N.*, pp. 337-8.   [23] *A.N.*, p. 88.   [24] *A.N.*, p. 91.

theorists and also the James of the legend. Most of the *clichés*
associated with him—literary discussion runs mainly to *cliché*,
even among the highly qualified—relate to it. Of these *clichés*,
some are actually misleading; others are merely unfortunate
in that they do not place the facts in the best order or in the
happiest relation to each other. The order in which a writer's
qualities are stated can be very important. If we say of Ben
Jonson, first, that he was a great comic genius, with a prodigious capacity for poetic extravagance, and then, that his
imagination could do wonders with the materials of his learning,
we can have some hope of awakening interest in his works.
If we begin by saying how learned he was we kill him stone
dead. To begin an account of Swift by emphasising the
plainness of his prose is a similar piece of maladroitness.

It would be amusing to experiment with a different set of
clichés for James. One might begin by stressing the hugeness
of his output. The very thought of such lavishness combined
with great care over each single composition might well, in
Jamesian phrase, make one ache. It is as well to realise
that, careful though he was, there was not much time for
lingering scrupulosity. Little harm would be done if exuberant
energy and expansiveness were the first qualities to be associated
with his name. In a letter of 1911 to Edith Wharton he writes
of *The Golden Bowl*: "The vague verbosity of the Oxus-flood
. . . terrifies me—sates me," and he goes on to express his
preference for the "steel structure" of his more recent (and
very poor) production *The Outcry*:[25] perhaps not a statement
to be taken too seriously, but it is charming to think of his
having a conscience about this tendency to overflow like a
river in flood. The image in the Preface to *The Aspern Papers*
will be remembered. Fortunately his conscience did not
prevent him from writing in his most expansive manner in
his last great works, the autobiographies. Terms like "expansiveness" need, of course, to be qualified: but so also do
the other terms which suggest economy and precision of
method. In the world where *cliché* is pitted against *cliché*
the idea of James as primarily a writer of abounding generosity
and richness would serve a purpose.

[25] *L.*, II. p. 217.

Again, we might emphasise his generosity to the work of others, expressed sometimes in letters of the most sprawling exuberance. A notable example of how he can be misunderstood, and insufficiently appreciated as a man, may be found in the Introduction by Leon Edel and Gordon N. Ray to their most useful volume of letters and other materials illustrating the relationship between James and H. G. Wells. The most important of the letters are those in which James acknowledges recently published works by Wells, recording his admiration together with certain reservations and criticisms. There are about a dozen of them, extending over fifteen years, the most successful of Wells's career. Briefly, it may be said that the editors fail to do justice to the pleasure that James expresses time after time in these cordial outpourings. The reason seems to lie in a preconceived idea that, James's artistic principles and susceptibilities being what they were, he could not have enjoyed Wells's books as much as he said; from which it would follow that his expressions of delight may be attributed to a "mandarin politeness," or regarded as a "cushioning" for what he really meant: that is, for attacks on Wells's method or lack of it.

The question of what James "really" thought of Wells is, of course, rather complex. No doubt his praises in the letters are somewhat inflated by the generous mood in which they were written. Allowance could be made for some inflation, since the praises are about as enthusiastic as they could be. Like many readers of Wells, James probably read the books with great enjoyment and then thought less highly of them on reflexion. The critical note is more prominent in his comments on Wells in the celebrated 1914 essay on "The New Novel" than it had been in the letters, but even here the flavour of the enjoyable and indeed of the irresistible is present in James's account of him. The point on which it is reasonable to differ from Edel (who, of the two editors, is presumably responsible for the opinion on James) simply concerns his general sincerity in these letters.

A certain amount of documentation is necessary here. It is difficult to bring out the extent and consistency of James's attitude without what must seem to be an excessive piling-up of quotations. Quantity is indispensable since the editors also quote from his expressions of admiration, but in such a way as to do less than justice to their total effect.

From an early stage in the correspondence James tended to sandwich his reservations between liberal slices of praise. For instance, in the first letter acknowledging *When the Sleeper Awakes* (1899), he says "You fill me with wonder and admiration," and then makes a few detailed criticisms of Wells's conception of the future: but brushing aside further points of this kind as "irrelevant and ungracious," he adds the full-blooded tribute: "Your spirit is huge, your fascination irresistible, your resources infinite. *That* is much more to the point."[26] His comments on *Anticipations* (1902) follow the same pattern. "I gave myself up—utterly, admirably up—to the charm," he writes. He refers to certain "reserves and reactions," but again puts the main stress on the positive factor: "that the main source of interest never failed: which main source was simply H.G.W. himself. You, really, come beautifully out of your adventure, come out of it immensely augmented and extended, like a belligerent who has annexed half-a-kingdom, with drums and trumpets and banners all sounding and flying." That Wells himself is the main source of interest is a limitation, by James's standards—the point is more explicitly made in the comments on later books— but at least it "never failed." Further tentative criticisms follow, but are again countered by remarks in a positive strain, and the general tone of the letter is fairly represented by the comment towards the end: "I am under the charm. My world *is*, somehow, other; but I can't produce it. Besides, I don't want to. You can and do produce yours—so you've a right to talk. Finally, moreover, your book is full of truth and wit and sanity."[27] Writing of *Mankind in the Making* (1904) he again makes the point that Wells himself is central to his books: "I mean that it has affected me . . . as a record of romantic adventure of which you are the Hero. As such *Mankind in the Making* thrills and transports me. . . ." He

[26] *Henry James and H. G. Wells* . . . ed. Leon Edel and Gordon N. Ray [= *H.J. and H.G.W.*] (1958), p. 62.

[27] *H.J. and H.G.W.*, pp. 75-7.

praises its humane purpose: "I found myself singularly sub-
jugated by your volume and in abject agreement with its main
theses. . . . And the humanity and lucidity and ingenuity, the
pluck and perception and patience and humour of the whole
thing place you before me as, simply, one of the benefactors of
our race."[28] These books, after all, are not among those by which
Wells is now chiefly remembered. When James writes about *A
Modern Utopia* and *Kipps* (1905) his praises go further. "Let me
tell you, however, simply that they have left me prostrate with
admiration, and that you are, for me, more than ever, the most
interesting 'literary man' of your generation—in fact, the only
interesting one." It may be true, as the editors suggest, that
James's repeated use of the word "cheek" in this letter annoyed
Wells, but surely the tone of the letter as a whole is so laudatory
that we must take the word to signify a careless audacity
which, in combination with so many gifts, is a matter for
admiration. ("Indeed, your Cheek is positively the very sign
and stamp of your genius.") If the word is double-edged, the
fact that in the same letter Wells is described as "the satirist
with *irony*—as poor dear old Thackeray was the satirist without
it," and hailed for coming to "save" an epoch "starving in our
enormities and fatuities," (there are other splendid compli-
ments), might be said to mitigate its sharpness. Wells is again
praised for his humane attitudes: "Meantime you set a
magnificent example—of *caring*, of feeling, of seeing, above all,
and suffering from, and with, the shockingly sick actuality
of things." His comment on *Kipps* is worthy of full quotation:

> And now, coming to Kipps, what am I to say about Kipps but
> that I am ready, that I am compelled, utterly to *drivel* about
> him? He is not so much a masterpiece as a mere born gem—
> you having, I know not how, taken a header straight down into
> mysterious depths of observation and knowledge, I know not
> which and where, and come up again with this rounded pearl of
> the diver. But of course you know yourself how immitigably
> the thing is done—it is of such a brilliancy of *true* truth. I
> really think you have done, at this time of day, two particular
> things for the first time of their doing among us. (1) You

---

have written the first closely and intimately, the first intelli-
gently and consistently ironic or satiric novel. In everything
else there has always been the sentimental or conventional
interference, the interference of which Thackeray is full. (2)
You have for the very first time treated the English "lower
middle" class, etc. without the picturesque, the grotesque, the
fantastic and romantic interference, of which Dickens, e.g. is so
misleadingly, of which even George Eliot is so deviatingly, full.
You have handled its vulgarity in so scientific and historic a
spirit, and seen the whole thing all in its own strong light.
And then the book has, throughout, such extraordinary life;
everyone in it, is so vivid, and sharp and *raw*. Kipps himself is
a diamond of the first water, from start to finish, exquisite and
radiant; Coote is consummate, Chitterlow magnificent (the
whole first evening with Chitterlow, perhaps the most
brilliant thing in the book—unless that glory be reserved for the
way the entire matter of the *shop* is done, including the admirable
image of the boss). It all in fine, from cover to cover, does you
the greatest honour. . . .[29]

The editors single out for attention the expression "not so
much a masterpiece as a mere born gem," apparently implying
that it involves a limiting judgment; which it does, perhaps,
but only very remotely.

It is difficult to justify the reference in the editors' Introduction to "the rising curve of James's exasperation." The
element of criticism does, no doubt, become more explicit
in the later letters, as James sees the same Wellsian characteristics recur, but his enthusiastic reception of the books, faults
and everything, continues unabated. James's letter on *The
Future of America* (1906), which includes some mild criticism
relating to over-simplification (but he immediately refers to
himself as "accursedly born to touch nothing save to compli-
cate it"), has, like all the others, a preponderance of praise.
Ann Veronica (1909) he confesses to have taken "in deep rich
draughts," and adds: "I never vibrated under anything of
yours, on the whole, I think, *more* than during the intense
inglutition. . . ." The letter oscillates several times between
positive and negative comments: "lucidity and logic" do not,

[29] *H.J. and H.G.W.*, pp. 103-5.

he finds, reign supreme so far as definition of subject is concerned, and there is a lack of "clearness and *nuances*" in the treatment of the heroine: but it is fair to claim that the document as a whole is a panegyric.[30]

The letter acknowledging *The New Macchiavelli* (1911) again contains both types of comment. The reference to "that accurst autobiographic form which puts a premium on the loose, the improvised, the cheap and the easy," is James's strongest expression of this particular objection: but elsewhere in the letter, confronted with Wells's "big feeling for life" he asks himself, "what the devil, in the way of effect and evocation and general demonic activity, one wants more. He has acclaimed Wells earlier as "the most interesting and masterful prose-painter of your English generation (or indeed of your generation unqualified)"; and in closing the letter, he states his wish to send "across the wintry sea" nothing but his "expressed gratitude for the immense impressionistic and speculative wealth and variety" of the book.[31] The last two letters of this kind, acknowledging *Marriage* (1912) and *The Passionate Friends* (1913) respectively, resemble each other and their predecessors in the distribution of praise and criticism. The chief criticism relates again to the autobiographical method and to the fact that Wells himself outshines his other characters: "I see you 'behave' all along, much more than I see them even when they behave (as I'm not sure they behave *most* in *Marriage*) with whatever charged intensity or accomplished effect; so that the ground of the drama is somehow most of all in the adventure for *you*—not to say *of* you. . . ." But to the very end of their correspondence James acknowledged the power and spell-binding quality of his fellow novelist, and confessed with his humorous rhetoric that, as he read him, principles went by the board:

> I have read you, as I always read you, and as I read no one else, with a complete abdication of all these 'principles of criticism', canons of form, pre-conceptions of felicity, references to the idea of method or the sacred laws of composition, which I roam, which I totter, through the pages of others

---

[30] *H.J. and H.G.W.*, pp. 121-3.   [31] *H.J. and H.G.W.*, pp. 127-9.

attended in some dim degree by the fond yet feeble theory of,
but which I shake off, as I advance under your spell, with the
most cynical inconsistency.[32]

This is not wholly true: he cannot keep his critical spirit
quiet: but he returns to his constant affirmation that Wells's
work is " more convulsed with life and more brimming with
blood than any it is given me nowadays to meet." The final
words of the last letter before the breach between James and
Wells are true to the spirit in which all his comments had been
written:

> Go on, go on and do it as you like, so long as you *keep* doing
> it; your faculty is of the highest price, your temper and your
> hand form one of the choicest treasures of the time; my offen-
> sive remarks are but the sign of helpless subjugation and
> impotent envy. . . .[33]

In his Introduction to *Selected Letters of Henry James* (1956)
Edel refers to James's habit, in dealing with certain people,
of resorting to "verbal ambiguity and ironic shadings," and to
"an encircling process by which he manages to be candid
while relying on the vanity of his correspondents to read only
that which would please them." He refers also to "cushion-
words" which "surround the expression of the truth or act as an
immediate palliative to the administered shock. . . ." For the
cushioning process, James had his special phrase. It was the
"mere twaddle of graciousness."[34] The phrase occurs in a
letter to Sarah Orne Jewett. Edel's view is that the letters to
Wells contain a certain amount of this kind of language.

It was James's privilege to use the phrase "mere twaddle
of graciousness" of his own epistolary style, but as a heading
for a group of letters in Edel's volume it is open to objection,
and any general use of it by critics or editors involves com-
promising and hazardous reflexions on James's attitude to his
correspondents and on his character as a man. Edel's reading
of the letters printed in this section of the *Selected Letters* may
perhaps be near enough to the truth: but in any case the letters

---

[32] *H.J. and H.G.W.*, pp. 166-7.
[33] *H.J. and H.G.W.*, p. 176.
[34] *H.J. and H.G.W.*, Introd. pp. 22, 24.

to Wells are very different. They are much more enthusiastic. James commits himself much more boldly and specifically.

Why should we not simply accept the view that James enjoyed Wells's novels as much as he said he did? With his feeling for the prodigious, he must have responded to Wells as a remarkable phenomenon, as a vehicle of restless, irresistible energy. With his American's feeling for England—one is reminded of his avid response to even the commonest manifestations of "Englishness" in the sketches reprinted in *English Hours*—he must have found both Wells and his books full of the national flavour and character. The fact is that James's tastes in literature do not on the whole reflect the kind of rigour with which so many of his admirers prefer to associate him. He was brought up in a mental world saturated with the influence of Dickens, and in the autobiographical books he testifies in splendid terms to the latter's power: "There has been since his extinction no corresponding case—as to the the relation between benefactor and beneficiary, or debtor and creditor; no other debt in our time has been piled so high, for those carrying it, as the long, the purely 'Victorian' pressure of that obligation."[35] Not that the early experience of reading Dickens lends itself to renewal, yet it has gone so deep that "criticism, roundabout him, is somehow futile and tasteless. His own taste is easily impugned, but he entered so early into the blood and bone of our intelligence that it always remained better than the taste of overhauling him. . . . Happy the house of life in which such chambers still hold out, even with the draught of intellect whistling through the passages."[36] He kindled to the greatness of Balzac, and he kindles his readers too: "We most of us aspire to achieve at the best but a patch here and there, to pluck a sprig or a single branch, to break ground in a corner of the great garden of life. Balzac's plan was simply to do everything that could be done. He proposed to himself to 'turn over' the great garden from north to south and from east to west; a task—immense, heroic, to this day immeasurable. . . ."[37] His essay on Zola (1903) could win

[35] *Autobiography*, ed. F. W. Dupee (1956), p. 388.
[36] *Op. cit.*, p. 68.
[37] *Notes on Novelists* (1914), p. 88.

converts to that novelist. Again it is his feeling for the inordinate that qualifies him almost uniquely for the task; that is,
of conveying the peculiar value and fascination of the brute
facts which Zola chose for treatment:

> There was a great outcry, as we all remember, over the rank
> materialism of *L'Assommoir*, but who cannot see today how much
> a milder infusion of it would have told against the close
> embrace of the subject aimed at? *L'Assommoir* is the nature
> of man—but not his finer, nobler, cleaner or more cultivated
> nature; it is the image of his free instincts, the better and the
> worse, the better struggling as they can, gasping for light and
> air, the worse making themselves at home in darkness, ignor-
> ance and poverty. The whole handling makes for emphasis
> and scale, and it is not to be measured how, as a picture of
> conditions, the thing would have suffered from timidity.
> The qualification of the painter is precisely his stoutness of
> stomach, and we scarce exceed in saying that to have taken
> in and given out again less of the infected air would, with such
> a resource, have meant the waste of a faculty.[38]

He recognises Zola's capacity "to make his characters swarm,
and to make the great central thing they swarm about 'as
large as life,' portentously, heroically big. . ." and his image
of this "great central thing" as "some seated Moloch of custom,
of commerce, of faith, lending itself to portrayal through its
abuses and excesses, its idol-face and great devouring mouth
. . ."[39] (he refers piquantly to the portrayal of Les Halles in
Le Ventre de Paris), is in the vein of one who, in spite of immense
differences, has some fellow-feeling with the maker of such
creations.

Critical judgments as such are not easy to find in his
essays. He was concerned less with expressing an opinion than
with describing an object and his response to it. He had the
amiable gift of being able to find at least some pleasure-giving
quality in a very wide range of literary objects. He probably
enjoyed Wells more keenly than most civilised readers have
done, in addition to being more keenly aware of his faults.
He seems, in a certain sense, to have enjoyed Hugh Walpole;
and his comment on *The Duchess of Wrexe*, though in one

---

[38] *Op. cit.*, p. 30.   [39] *Op. cit.*, p. 33.

respect it amounts to a charge of incompetence, manages somehow to be handsome: "All of which does not mean, we hasten to add, that the author of *The Duchess of Wrexe* has not the gift of life; but only that he strikes us as having received it, straight from nature, with such a concussion as to have kept the boon at the stage of violence—so that, fairly pinned down by it, he is still embarrassed for passing it on. On the day he shall have worked himself free of this primitive predicament, the crude fact of the convulsion itself, there need be no doubt of his exhibiting matter into which method may learn how to bite."[40] The essay on "The New Novel" (1914), in which this engaging comment occurs, can easily be misrepresented, if James's attitude is not conveyed in James's own words: a difficult requirement to satisfy in a critical study, since he expresses himself very copiously, with an abundance of felicitous and attractively turned images. It is, of course, true that James salutes Conrad as a solitary "votary of the way to do a thing that shall make it undergo most doing," and delights in *Chance* as an example of supreme devotion to method: such views are in keeping with the James of the legend. But it must also be said that, in raising questions about Conrad's method, he refers to it as "desperate and eccentric." He describes Conrad's use of narrators in terms which make it seem extravagant, though in fact he accepts it as justified:

> Mr. Conrad's first care . . . is expressly to posit or set up a reciter, a definite responsible intervening first person singular, possessed of infinite sources of reference, who immediately proceeds to set up another, to the end that this other may conform again to the practice, and that even at that point the bridge over to the creature, or in other words to the situation or the subject, the thing 'produced', shall, if the fancy takes it, once more and yet once more glory in a gap.[41]

The tone is not unlike that in which he refers to his own extravagance in *The Awkward Age*. Method is prized here because it produces prodigies, and especially cherished when its triumphs hover in the region of the absurd. But it is not true to say that he sees Conrad as a master sees a disciple. He did

---

[40] *Op. cit.*, p. 270.   [41] *Op. cit.*, p. 275.

not often play this game of narration within narration. In saluting Conrad, he salutes someone in many ways different from himself, which is what he does continually in his critical essays.

The only obligation to which all novels are subject, he insists, is that they should be " interesting," and the ways of achieving this end are "innumerable." This is his affirmation in the 1884 essay on "The Art of Fiction," and in his last letter to Wells he eloquently reasserts his belief in inexhaustible variety. His own increasing attachment to certain means in preference to others, and his habit in later life of mentally rewriting the books of his friends, are idiosyncrasies which need to be seen against this background.

II

Questions of Moral Content

THE theme of the last chapter was that enjoyment of James is often impeded by failure to do justice to his own capacity for enjoyment. His most devoted admirers may do him a disservice by saddling him with solemn attitudes as critic and theorist, or as moralist, or by attributing to him the wrong virtues. The phrase "unvarying courtesy and moderation of statement,"[1] in the introduction to the James-Wells letters, is in that context unfortunate. "Courtesy" is right, but James often preferred immoderate statements. His courtesy goes mainly with humour and expansiveness, rather than with disingenuous caution and ceremonious civility.

James's novels and stories are not about Innocence and Experience, the Individual in Collision with Society, Emotional Cannibalism, or any other moral themes, whatever speculations on these lines they may suggest. Critics who discuss him in terms of these abstractions usually add that, of course, James is not overtly didactic (he is "a novelist, not a moralist"), but this is an insufficient corrective to the use of the thematic formulae as chapter headings or in classifications of subject-matter. This approach is, on the whole, less justifiable with James than with other novelists, many of whom do moralise directly. Jane Austen and E. M. Forster do so habitually. But James does not concern himself with recommending or censuring ways of living. If his situations are rich in what we call moral implications, the shape they take for our delight as readers of fiction is not the shape of a moral theme. They may provide illustrations of themes such as those labelled above, but this is incidental and not the central point about the story in question; and the attempt to describe his stories in this manner is one of the commonest ways of making James seem less rich as an artist.

[1] *H.J. and H.G.W.*, Introd., p. 34.

A distinction must be made here between such attempts by literary critics, and a work like R. W. B. Lewis's *The American Adam*, which traces the historical development of the national ethos, with its themes of innocence and experience, drawing upon James's works among others for illustrations. The ethos and themes that he expounds are real enough, as facts of history, and examples of them can legitimately be abstracted from James. Lewis does this sensitively, when he says that the qualities under consideration are "actualised (by James) with every conceivable variety of ethical weight."[2] He is not pretending to deal with works of literature in and for themselves: James's novels and stories are cited principally as symptoms of a sociological phenomenon: but being masterpieces, they are referred to with discrimination and respect. It is in works of literary criticism *per se* that this reduction to themes is open to objection.

In J. A. Ward's article "*The Ambassadors*: Strether's Vision of Evil,"[3] not only is the thematic formula given too much prominence: it is manifestly the wrong kind of formula, quite untrue to James's idiom or, more specifically, to Strether's. The word "evil," used repetitively here in relation to both America and Europe, has no such place in Strether's vocabulary. It is not to Strether's vision or James's that "Waymarsh, whose provincialism is at first comic, emerges in the course of the novel as sinister"; and nothing could be further from the spirit of the book than observations like: "Jim Pocock is the American business man blighted and dehumanised, made bestial through his activity in industry." Strether's response to Chad and Mme. de Vionnet is referred to in such terms as "self-surrender," "personal renunciation," "rejection of personal pride"—pretentious abstractions which give a false sublimity to his behaviour, taking away its charm and naturalness.

A similar distortion is produced by exaggerating the role of allegory and symbol. The critic, using this approach, seizes upon what looks like a key image and brings the whole novel within the pattern of meanings furnished by its ramifications.

---

[2] *The American Adam* (1955), p. 152.
[3] "The Ambassadors : Strether's Vision of Evil," *Nineteenth Century Fiction*, XIV., 1, June 1959, pp. 45-58.

This is one of the many ways, and not one of the best, of uniting James with the American literary heritage. *The Golden Bowl*, for example, is really a very different kind of book from *The Scarlet Letter*. Though in a few places the image in the title is used ominously and lavishly enough, one cannot say that, in the novel as a whole, either the author or any of the characters is much obsessed by it. For nine-tenths of the way it can be forgotten; so that when James L. Spencer refers to it as "the controlling principle" of the work, claiming that "all that happens . . . is in some way brought under [its] governance,"[4] he is imposing a narrowness and concentration of design upon it which are alien ; and, by implication, he is bringing James into quite the wrong relationship with his great predecessor and with the allegorical tradition in American literature.

Spencer's interpretation of the symbolism is interesting, but a little too complicated. He tells us that the flaw in the crystal is "the Prince's lack of a moral sense." If this were so, why should the Prince be so uncannily aware of the crack when Charlotte and he visit the Bloomsbury shop? Spencer tries to get round this by giving the bowl a different meaning for the Prince, and then argues that this in itself is a manifestation of his lack of awareness of the primary meaning. He rejects the bowl "on the basis of superstitition. If he and Maggie accepted the bowl as a gift from Charlotte, the Prince would be afraid for his marriage—indeed 'for everything'. The Prince would think of the bowl, if accepted, as a symbol of marriage. The bowl would be imperfect: it might mean that his marriage was imperfect. But we must remember the Prince's concept of perfection: it is perfection in manners, not in the morals which underlie manners. The prince is still in the dark concerning the morals which are expected of him. Thus, in the larger context of the novel as a whole the Prince's *interpretation* of the flaw becomes the objective correlative of the flaw itself." A symbol should operate directly, and it is difficult to see how it can do so if its meaning calls for such deciphering. If the symbolism of the bowl is to be so conscientiously analysed,

---

[4] "Symbolism in James's 'The Golden Bowl,' " in *Modern Fiction Studies*, Winter 1957-8, III. 4, pp. 333-44.

why should Mrs Assingham be singled out for the distinction of
dramatically destroying it? This lady at no time takes the lead
in forcing matters into the open. Equally objectionable is the
suggestion that all the morality is on the Verver side, and that
this is a straight case of graceful, amoral Europe contrasted with
the American awareness of right and wrong. Too tight an
interpretation of symbols tends to be accompanied by moral
over-simplification.

The bowl, of course, *has* symbolic value, but not of the most
important kind. Merely as a "property" it is well chosen.
In a novel where human relations become so mixed up with
wealth and connoisseurship, it is appropriate that an *objet
d'art* should play a suggestive role in the drama. The bowl,
unlike the Verver treasures, was cheap: it was to have been
Charlotte's present to Maggie, the gift of the poor to the rich:
but, what with its imperfection and the Ververs' plenty—
Maggie has all she needs, and she has the Prince—it serves to
emphasise that there is really nothing that the unfortunate
Charlotte can give to Maggie—except trouble, and that is to
come later. When the flawed bowl comes into Maggie's
possession, the very fact of her buying it is in keeping with
what we know of her: that she is one of the unsuspecting, one
of the humble who may be imposed upon; and its flaw, together with its secret, does embody for her the secret flaw in her
marriage. But after her two scenes, with Fanny and then
with Amerigo, in which she develops the bitter ironies provoked
by the bowl, what further purpose does it serve? To attach great
importance to such a feature of James's art (to say nothing of
misconstruing it), is a way of belittling him. It deflects attention from the incomparably more interesting things in the book,
and from its generally expansive and varied quality.

The claim that James is not a moralist in the sense in which
Jane Austen or Forster is, calls for detailed discussion. A good
example of what it implies may be found in one of the early
novels, *The Europeans* (1878), which used to be rather neglected
but is now in high reputation, largely owing to F. R. Leavis's
valuable appraisal of it.[5]

The Europeans is morally interesting, morally delightful, but

[5] *Scrutiny*, xv. 3 (1948), pp. 209-21.

also morally elusive. A long passage from the third chapter where Felix tells his sister Eugenia of his visit of reconnaissance to their New England cousins, the Wentworths, illustrates all these qualities. Felix and Eugenia, newly-arrived from Europe, are having their first contact with native American ways:

"... No splendour, no gilding, no troops of servants; rather straight-backed chairs. But you might eat off the floors, and you can sit down on the stairs."

"That must be a privilege. And the inhabitants are straight-backed, of course."

"My dear sister," said Felix, "the inhabitants are charming."

"In what style?"

"In a style of their own. How shall I describe it? It's primitive; it's patriarchal; it's the *ton* of the golden age."

"And have they nothing golden but their *ton*? Are there no symptoms of wealth?"

"I should say there was wealth without symptoms. A plain, homely way of life; nothing for show, and very little for—what shall I call it?—for the senses; but a great *aisance*, and a lot of money out of sight, that comes forward very quietly for subscriptions to institutions, for repairing tenements, for paying doctor's bills; perhaps even for portioning daughters."

"And the daughters?" Madame Münster demanded. "How many are there?"

"There are two, Charlotte and Gertrude."

"Are they pretty?"

"One of them," said Felix.

"Which is that?"

The young man was silent, looking at his sister. "Charlotte," he said at last.

She looked at him in return. "I see. You are in love with Gertrude. They must be Puritans to their finger-tips; anything but gay."

"No, they are not gay," Felix admitted. "They are sober; they are even severe. They are of a pensive cast; they take things hard. I think there is something the matter with them." [6]

---

[6] *The Europeans* [= *Eur.*], pp. 34-5.

His remarks are not all on the same note, so that a shorter quotation would have been misleading, and it would have required some skill in a summary to do justice to the total impression. His response to the Wentworths, upon which our view of them will to a large extent depend, is personal, variable, coloured by generosity or gaiety of mood, or sharpened to a more critical assessment partly by his sister's questioning. One remark is modified by another, the references to the "golden age" gaining in charm by the shrewdness of what follows, and softening the later comments on their Puritan constraint. The moral for the reader, and it holds good more or less for the novel as a whole, is that we are not invited to arrive at a firm and settled opinion of how these various ingredients are combined in anything so stodgy or unlike James as the "total reality of the Wentworth way of life." Felix likes the Wentworths: he likes people generally. His view of his cousins is lively and hopeful; it is his nature to respond to the best in others, and the artist in him takes pleasure in displaying it to advantage. Through Felix's view of him we see Mr Wentworth at his best—a sympathetic combination of Puritanical gravity and American tolerance and accommodation:

> The tall gentleman came to meet her, looking very rigid and grave. But it was a rigidity that had no illiberal meaning. Mr. Wentworth's manner was pregnant, on the contrary, with a sense of grand responsibility, of the solemnity of the occasion, of its being difficult to show sufficient deference to a lady at once so distinguished and so unhappy. Felix had observed on the day before his characteristic pallor; and now he perceived that there was something almost cadaverous in his uncle's high-featured white face. But so clever were this young man's quick sympathies and perceptions that he had already learned that in these semi-mortuary manifestations there was no cause for alarm. His light imagination had gained a glimpse of Mr. Wentworth's spiritual mechanism, and taught him that, the old man being infinitely conscientious, the special operation of conscience within him announced itself by several of the indications of physical faintness.[7]

---

[7] *Eur.*, p. 38.

Much of our knowledge of the characters in this novel is
conveyed by similar personal impressions and comments.
There is not much examination of their background and development, such as we find in books like *Middlemarch*, *The
Portrait of a Lady* and *Lord Jim*, and many facts are withheld.
For example, in another sort of book Gertrude's feeling
"restless" on Sunday morning and absenting herself from
church, and her being "an object of extreme concern"[8] to her
father, could have been a matter for more specific treatment.
What is happening to Gertrude or, for that matter, to her
world? Is she another of those nineteenth-century reflective
young women who are turning away from the traditional
faith? If so, in what direction? What exactly are "the great
questions of life"[9] to which Mr Brand refers when he speaks
bitterly of Felix's levity; and what does Gertrude mean by her
reply that she doesn't care for the great things of life, and that
Mr Brand has made her talk "a great deal of nonsense," but
that there are "some things" she cares for?[10] Nothing precise
is indicated, and this is no weakness. Somehow the impression
is finely given that here we have a little moment in the history
of New England. The sense, though light, of social actuality
is conveyed by the tone of the characters towards each other,
not by any of those factual revelations that are liable to thicken
the texture of certain other novels without achieving any more
imaginative truth. "The great things of life," and their place
in a person's development, are hazardous material for novelists.
Need we regret that Gertrude's thoughts are not more fully
recorded? It seems enough for us to know what Felix thinks
of her. Similar comments might be made about the alcoholic
exploits of Clifford: another ominous sign, if we wished to be
speculative, of cracks in the Wentworth system of living.
His awkwardness, his lack of manners, in which he so differs
from his father, make him as suggestive a phenomenon as
Gertrude—that is, if the novel encouraged this kind of
curiosity, which it does not. After some clumsy ventures in the
direction of Eugenia, Clifford suddenly settles his life by
marrying Lizzie Acton, a decision concerning which we receive no inside knowledge. We are merely left with the

---

[8] *Eur.*, p. 192.   [9] *Eur.*, p. 123.   [10] *Eur.*, p. 123.

indication, derived from the attitude of the other characters, that this settles the matter for us too.

It is characteristic, in general, of the relationships in the novel that moral question are not forced to an issue. Within the Wentworth family itself there is a firmly established freedom and forbearance, modifying their Puritanism, and giving an almost relaxed quality to scenes where solemnity is also present. In the passage where Mr Wentworth, faced with the visit of the cousins, warns Gertrude of the need for care and self-control, she pauses "in deference to her father's speech," and then openly expresses a very different kind of interest in the newcomers' way of life with its intriguing points of novelty: "When we go over there it will be like going to Europe. She will have a boudoir. She will invite us to dinner— very late."[11] These words bring no comment from her father, but a little later he asks her to promise him something: "not to get excited." She confesses that she cannot do this, since she is already excited, and to this he says nothing. The scene thus foreshortened may appear to be one almost of disharmony, but read in full it is not so. Parental influence does not hang heavy in this New England atmosphere. The daughter is simply speaking frankly of her attitude, with no intention of hurting or provoking her parent, who is clearly neither hurt nor provoked. Nor are the "Europeans" (they are, of course, Americans too—returned expatriates) aiming at strident contrasts between their way of life and that of their hosts. This element of accommodation—to put the virtue at its lowest— is part of what is being portrayed: it is an American value, though James does not openly display it as such. And it has the effect, as an artist's resource, of keeping the action and its crises within bounds, and of facilitating a lightness in the portrayal of the characters which is one of the graces of the novel. They do not apply too much pressure to each other, and James does not apply too much pressure (either of curiosity or moral probing) to them.

He does not take sides, or use his characters as vehicles for his own opinions; and though we may sympathise with some characters more than others, this does not place their attitudes

[11] *Eur.*, p. 54.

in clear-cut divisions of right and wrong. Felix and Eugenia,
we note, are not always in agreement about New England
manners.   Felix is delighted with the freedom of relations
between young men and girls:

> He had never had any cousins, and he had never before found
> himself in contact so unrestricted with young unmarried
> ladies. He was extremely fond of the society of ladies, and it
> was new to him that it might be enjoyed in just this manner . . .
> he liked so much knowing that he was perfectly at liberty
> to be alone for hours, anywhere, with either of them. . . .[12]

Felix has the American naturalness and good faith, combined
with a European sophistication and vivacity of mind.   It
might be claimed that his quickness and subtlety in discrimination are the characteristic *American* contribution to his equipment, though perhaps it takes Europe to give them their chance;
and, as for the Europeanised surface, what form of embellish-
ment could be more essentially American? Felix's temperament reminds one of that passage in James's celebrated early
letter to Perry, where he comments on the "spiritual lightness"
that accompanies the American's moral consciousness, and
also on his genius for happy dealings with "forms of civiliza-
tion not his own."[13]   Felix, the expatriate returning home,
takes naturally to American qualities which for him are quite
new. His pleasure may remind one of those admirable passages
in the autobiographies where James himself, also in a position
to appreciate contrasts, describes the good faith and naturalness
of the young people of his own circle in the eighteen-sixties.
Felix is a case of the American in whom the American qualities
have not been extinguished but subtilised and improved by
Europe, so that when he visits the States again he greets with
joy something that answers to his own spirit.

Eugenia's response to the Wentworths is, in some scenes
and especially the earlier ones, in harmony with Felix's:
but from the beginning there is a difference. Her recognition,
partly aesthetic, partly sentimental, of their charm, is more
governed by mood; and the mood is transient. After all her

[12] *Eur.*, pp. 61-2.
[13] *Selected Letters of Henry James*, ed. Leon Edel (1956), p. 52.

vexations and humiliations in Europe, she succumbs to her first encounter with the Wentworths:

> There were tears in her eyes. The luminous interior, the gentle, tranquil people, the simple, serious life—the sense of these things pressed upon her with an overmastering force, and she felt herself yielding to one of the most genuine emotions she had ever known.[14]

A touch of worldly connoissuership enters into her appreciation:

> With her lively perception and her refined imagination, she was capable of enjoying anything that was characteristic, anything that was good of its kind—the Wentworth household seemed to her very perfect of its kind—wonderfully peaceful and unspotted; pervaded by a sort of dove-coloured freshness that had all the quietude and benevolence of what she deemed to be Quakerism, and yet seemed to be founded upon a degree of material abundance for which, in certain matters of detail, one might have looked in vain at the frugal little court of Silberstadt-Schreckenstein.[15]

Unlike Felix, she dislikes the relations of the sexes in America. No doubt her embitterment, as a not very young woman who has suffered some of the disadvantages of women in Europe, expresses itself in impatience and possibly jealousy. There is perhaps an element of sheer cultural snobbery in her preference for the ways of old Europe; and also a defensiveness about her own position, so dubious to New England eyes:

> "But in this country, you know, the relations of young people are so extraordinary that one is quite at sea. They are not engaged when you would quite say they ought to be. Take Charlotte Wentworth, for instance, and that young ecclesiastic. If I were her father, I should insist upon his marrying her; but it appears to be thought there is no urgency. On the other hand, you suddenly learn that a boy of twenty and a little girl who is still with her governess—your sister has no governess? Well, then, who is never away from her mamma—a young couple, in short, between whom you have noticed nothing beyond an exchange of the childish pleasantries characteristic of their age, are on the point of setting up as man and wife. . . ."[16]

---

[14] *Eur.*, p. 47.   [15] *Eur.*, pp. 57-8.   [16] *Eur.*, p. 148.

Eugenia dislikes Lizzie, and reflects that American girls have
no manners.   "Lizzie struck her as positive and explicit
almost to pertness."[17]

   We can be sure that James is much nearer to Felix's way of
thinking, and of course Felix is a happier person than his sister
and in a better position to respond generously, but if we are
trying to attribute specific preferences to James we must be
careful.   James knew what the American girl was capable of,
in the way of uncomely positiveness and sheer rudeness.   Within
a year or so he was to create the charmless Miranda Hope and
the appalling Sophy Ruck.   Whether Eugenia's irritation at
Lizzie's manners was in any degree justified, we do not know,
since no full account is given of the latter.   F. R. Leavis writes
that "James largely approves of the social order that enables
young men and girls to mix with such innocent freedom—
for it *is*, for all its informality, an order, embodying a number
of positive values";[18] and there are good reasons for accepting
this, as we have seen: but we may also welcome Leavis's
correction of his own statement: "Perhaps it would be better
not to refer, in this way, to James himself.   When we elicit
judgments and valuations from the fable . . . we don't think of
them as coming from the author."   It is far better to think of
them as coming from the characters responsible for them;
and although we may sympathise with certain characters, and
find their ideas especially congenial, to attempt to extract a
way of life from them would be a crude moralistic misreading.
What, after all, is the moralistic reader to make of the passage
in which Felix discusses the erring Clifford with the latter's
father?   "The best thing for Clifford . . ." he says, "is to become
interested in some clever, charming woman. . . .   You see, I
believe greatly in the influence of women.   Living with women
helps to make a man a gentleman."[19]   When he adds that, "if
he could fall in love with her a little, so much the better,"
Mr Wentworth, who is a remarkably good listener, still utters
no protest.   Felix makes some interesting remarks on the
civilising—indeed, sobering—influence that a "charming, witty
woman" can exercise, "especially if she is a little of a coquette,"
and suggests that Clifford should be recommended to be nice

[17] *Eur.*, p. 98.   [18] *Scrutiny*, xv. 3 (1948), p. 218.   [19] *Eur.*, p. 108.

to Eugenia. The conversation is now too enigmatical for Mr
Wentworth, and as it proceeds it does not become less so:

> "Do I understand," asked the old man, "that I am to suggest
> to my son to make a—a profession of—of affection to Madame
> Münster?"
>
> "Yes, yes—a profession!" cried Felix sympathetically.
>
> "But as I understand it, Madame Münster is a married
> woman."
>
> "Ah," said Felix smiling, "of course she can't marry him.
> But she will do what she can."[20]

It would be difficult to make any comment on this passage
without being heavy-handed. Certainly we know that James
is not using Felix as a mouthpiece for European enlighten-
ment and graciousness, to challenge the Puritan code and
make it appear stiff and absurd. Certainly we think no worse
of Mr Wentworth for being at a loss. Felix's words are the
expression of Felix's special personal sense of fitness, his light-
heartedness, good humour and good faith. Uttered by another
speaker in another context, and with a little rewording, what
he says could have quite a different effect. And indeed much
the same tradition does look different when Eugenia invokes
it for the benefit of the unteachable Clifford: "My dear child
. . . there is no agreeable man who has not, at some moment,
been to school to a clever woman—probably a little older than
himself."[21] She is not proposing a *liaison*, but being the kind
of American she is, Eugenia is probably rather proud of having
belonged to a society which cultivates this institution. Her
attempts to tell Clifford about her former world make excellent comedy. Like Jane Austen's Emma instructing Harriet
on the nature of a gentleman and the privileged status of an
unmarried gentlewoman of independent fortune, Eugenia
says much that is true and acute: but in both cases we note
the over-ripe complacency of the speaker with her untaught
companion:

> "A young man of importance ought to learn to bear obser-
> vation—to carry himself as if he were quite indifferent to it.
> I won't say, exactly, unconscious. . . . No, he must seem to

---

[20] *Eur.*, pp. 109-10.   [21] *Eur.*, p. 134.

know he is observed, and to think it natural he should be;
but he must appear perfectly used to it. . . ."[22]

"You should go to Europe and make the tour," she said to
him one afternoon. "Of course, on leaving college, you will
go."

"I don't want to go," Clifford declared. "I know some
fellows who have been to Europe. They say you can have
better fun here."

"That depends. It depends upon your idea of fun. Your
friends probably were not introduced."

"Introduced?"

"They had no opportunity of going into society; they
formed no *relations*." This was one of a certain number of
words that the Baroness pronounced in the French manner.

"They went to a ball, in Paris; I know that," said Clifford.

"Ah, there are balls and balls; especially in Paris. No,
you must go, you know; it is not a thing from which you can
dispense yourself. You need it."

"Oh, I'm very well," said Clifford. "I'm not sick."

"I don't mean for your health, my poor child. I mean for
your manners."[23]

A true European, like Strether's Mme de Vionnet, would
have known how to be simple. Eugenia makes a parade of the
European tone and *mystique*: " I have the honour of knowing
more distinguished men, my poor child, than you are likely
to see in a lifetime. I see very few women; but those are
women of rank."[24] With all her *savoir-faire*, Eugenia is heading
for a misunderstanding and a setback—like Emma. Part of the
comedy is due to the incongruity of the relationship. With a
young man so callow and wondering, she is betrayed almost
inevitably into overdoing the doctrine and discipline. She
poses. And her tendency to overdo it betrays her in other
situations. Her fib to Mrs Acton about her son's filial speeches
is tell-tale: the European mother-son tradition is part of her
repertory of cultured snobbery.

Some characters impress themselves upon the reader as
happier, more generous, more interesting than others, and this
may affect our opinion of their opinions: but James is not in-

viting the reader to take a side, or make judgments concerning the various ways of life shown in this novel. Richard Poirier seems to me to be on the wrong wave-length when he says that, in so far as James "is positively disposed to the pastoral qualities of the Wentworths and their society, he is satirical about the sophistication of Eugenia, but to the extent that he regrets their incapacity to appreciate her, he adopts Eugenia's sophistication of tone in order to satirise the inadequacies of New England."[25] *The Europeans* is not a satirical work. James regrets nothing, and the inadequacies of this or that society are not directly a part of the subject-matter. (Indirectly, yes, in that some of the characters have phases of slight irritation or alarm at their cousins' ways.) As for his being "positively disposed," that is rather a stiff phrase. Expressions like "he is far from being entirely committed to the virtues of Eugenia," "If James is making a sour commentary on New England," and "the departure of Eugenia is a loss of something valuable,"[26] are in the same key. When Poirier refers to Eugenia's "charm and the significance of her art,"[27] her "contrived richness of tone,"[28] and the community's being "too simple to appreciate her full powers,"[29] he is surely missing her type: that is, the American expatriate who takes her Europe, and her own Europeanness very seriously.

Much of the spirit of the novel is conveyed in the following passage in which the two ways of life are not seen as competing for our approval, but simply as interesting in themselves and in juxtaposition:

> Felix had a confident, gaily trenchant way of judging human actions which Mr. Wentworth grew little by little to envy; it seemed like criticism made easy. Forming an opinion— say on a person's conduct—was with Mr. Wentworth a good deal like fumbling in a lock with a key chosen at hazard. He seemed to himself to go about the world with a big bunch of these ineffectual instruments at his girdle. His nephew on the other hand, with a single turn of the wrist, opened any door as adroitly as a house thief.[30]

---

[25] *The Comic Sense of Henry James* (1960), p. 101.
[26] *Op. cit.*, p. 105.
[27] *Op. cit.*, p. 122.
[28] *Op. cit.*, p. 122.
[29] *Op. cit.*, p. 123.
[30] *Eur.*, p. 102.

The humility, the tentativeness of the older man, is attractive. So is the quickness of Felix, though it is only in relation to other qualities that it escapes being coxcombical.

Robert Acton has fallen away more than the other New England characters from the traditions of his community, to which nevertheless he firmly belongs. The scene in which Eugenia produces her lying piece about his references to his mother shows him as having the moral fastidiousness of his race. Travelled as he is, he is disturbed by this touch of dishonesty. But in a later passage, as he repeats to himself, " She is not honest," he finds that he is less shocked than before. "He almost wished that he could make her lie and then convict her of it."[31] He has a slight touch of that perversion of Puritanism which expresses itself in curiosity and a desire to tamper with other lives: the quality more morbidly developed in the central character of James's story "The Liar" (1888), and in other figures in American fiction. Acton is a mixed and uncertain person. In most situations he does not quite know where he is. But the clue to his nature seems to lie in an analytical and experimental habit of mind, combined with something of the New England disease of self-frustration —"Maule's curse." It is characteristic of the lightness of this novel that when, in the last sentence, we read that he "married a particularly nice young girl," we cannot really judge whether this reversion to the American tradition, after the adventure with Eugenia, will be a success or not; that is, whether he has become a little too desiccated, or is healthy and adaptable enough, more or less, to make the adjustment.

Whatever *The Europeans* is not, it seems reasonable to describe it as a "novel of manners," a term which loses some of its flatness when we realise that at this period (the eighteen-seventies), the American novel of manners was new and fresh, a poetic creation. It was virtually James's own creation, though Howells' contribution also has its element of poetic fineness. There is nothing heavy and stereotyped, nothing mechanically sociological, about it. The sense of what is American, the recognition of types and of individual manifestations within a type, are all on a high imaginative level.

[31] *Eur.*, pp. 178-9.

James conveys most delightfully, mainly through the role of Felix, the thought that New England manners *are* poetically satisfying: but he conveys it in such a way as to imply that this depends in some measure on a happy sensibility in the observer. Felix has the artist's instinct to *make* poetry of his first encounter with Gertrude:

> "Ah, my dear young lady," he said, clasping his hands a little, "if you could give me, in charity, a glass of wine."[32]

Gertrude smiles and nods, and as she goes away for the wine and cake, she is reminded of Mr Brand, whose partiality to cake had seemed gross to her earlier in the morning. Felix, with his glass of wine and "huge morsel" of cake, is a comely figure. People and situations become poetic because someone finds them or makes them so. To describe a novel of manners by James is a delicate task, since the essence of it lies in the poetry; to give a mere abstract of the "social content" would be just another of the ways of cheating the reader. But at least the social content is there; it has an objective existence; and its extent and interest, in the work of James as a whole, are on a scale scarcely recognised. It is there in a way that moral themes and patterns are not there. James was consciously, endlessly, interested in the "documentary," the "illustrational." These words are central to his vocabulary.

To say that he is not a moralist may be just another way of saying that, as an American in a good tradition, he has the gift of intellectual and moral hospitality: something not altogether foreign to that "deference toward every sort of human manifestation" which he found in Emerson.[33] Flavoured with humour, we recognise it as the quality that Strether shows when he realises that Chad is a pagan, and reflects that a pagan may be what ("at the pass they had come to") they most wanted at Woollett.[34] Curiosity, delight in identifying the type, are important aspects of this prevailing attitude of mind, but the essential one is generosity; so that, while no

[32] *Eur.*, p. 28.
[33] Review of "The Correspondence of Thomas Carlyle and Ralph Waldo Emerson," reprinted in *The American Essays of Henry James*, ed. Leon Edel (1956), p. 43.
[34] *The Ambassadors* [= *Amb.*], i. 137-8.

D

moral conclusions are being enforced, the interest promoted is humane and enriching and therefore moral in a special sense.

James developed this basic subject-matter in his early and middle periods, and was developing it to the end. If we study his career more or less chronologically we begin with the bias of our interest towards the establishing of the material itself, while the late works are chiefly remarkable for a greater fineness and intensity of treatment: but this difference is one of degree. In any case the two aspects cannot usefully be separated. An examination of the subject-matter will fail if it is not also one of treatment; and treatment cannot be considered without continual reference to what is treated.

The view held here is that James improved with the years, not only in technical refinement but also in his power to move and delight. The earlier periods are full of brilliant achievement—*The Europeans* is a masterpiece in its small-scale way—but we do James a dubious service if we refer to the works of this phase as his best. Even *The Portrait of a Lady* and *The Bostonians*, impressive though they are, are not the height of his achievement. In some of the early and middle books he is clearly not quite sure of his method; they contain crudities of construction, examples of which will be cited later. To put these works forward as his chief claim to greatness is simply to represent him as less great that he really is: another way in which very eminent and otherwise admirable critics have failed him.

Part II

JAMES AND HIS WORLD

III

Sense of Place

In his review of *Middlemarch*, published in 1873, James wrote:

> English readers may fancy they enjoy the "atmosphere" of *Middlemarch*; but we maintain that to relish its inner essence we must—for reasons too numerous to detail—be an American.[1]

His sketch of Chester of the previous year had contained a similar remark, occasioned by a sermon in the cathedral by Canon Charles Kingsley: a sermon not quite worthy of its setting:

> . . . our poor sentimental tourist begins to hold up his head again and to reflect that so far as we *have* opportunities we mostly rise to them. I am not sure indeed that in the excess of his reaction he is not tempted to accuse his English neighbours of being impenetrable and uninspired, to affirm that they do not half discern their good fortune, and that it takes passionate pilgrims, vague aliens and other disinherited persons to appreciate the "points" of this admirable country.[2]

Many years later, writing on Henry Harland, he said that this capacity to respond to European things was, "almost the sharpest American characteristic."[3] It was a supremely important part of James's equipment as an American novelist, whether his subject is American or European manners.

The relation between the American novel and the literature of travel during this period cannot be overestimated. Hawthorne, Howells and James all excelled as writers of travel books. Awareness of Europe heightened awareness of America, and *vice versa*, and these interactions were important for the

---

[1] Reprinted in *The House of Fiction*, ed. Leon Edel (1957), p. 266.

[2] "Chester," in *English Hours* [= *E.H.*], pp. 67-8.

[3] "The Story-teller at large: Mr Henry Harland" (1898), reprinted in *The American Essays of Henry James*, ed. L. Edel (1956), p. 189.

development of a sense of place and of type that was necessary for American fiction at this time. The combination of freshness and acuteness with which this sense manifests itself in James's work has no parallel in the English and French novel: for the Old World, with its long established features and traditions, presented no such stimulating challenge to the imagination of its literary artists.

The emergence of these qualities, in any serious degree, may be said to date from James's crucial visit to Europe in 1869-70, which was followed by further visits culminating in the decision to settle in England in 1876. But in the interests of strict accuracy we must not altogether ignore the stories written before 1869. After all, James had had earlier experiences of Europe in his adolescence, and was therefore in a position to profit from the contrasts, if only in an immature way, from the outset of his career. But the sense of place is not much in evidence in these stories. The New England impressions of the artist narrator in "A Landscape-Painter" (1866) lack the sharpness, the note of character, that they would have had if the story had been written after 1870. The Newport of "Osborne's Revenge" (1869) is featureless compared with the Newport of James's sketch published in the next year. As for the portrayal of a distinctively American society, it must be admitted that there are beginnings, but they are slight. As one might expect, it is the American girl who is the first type to appear, and several of the early stories have heroines with some of the national traits.

If we note the chronological order of his publications after 1869 we see that the travel essays on Saratoga, Newport and Niagara appeared a year or two earlier than the first essays on English and European places. There is an appropriateness in this. The experience of Europe first quickened his art as a portrayer of his own world. These American sketches, to which we shall turn later, are of remarkable quality. They are the first of his works for which no allowance needs to be made on grounds of immaturity. But in the writings of the next year or two it is the American sensibility succumbing to Europe that provides the main topic, and here we must concentrate our attention for the greater part of this chapter.

The immense susceptibility of the American is an opportunity for eloquence and also wit, for James's attitude is mixed. In his description of Chester he enjoys not only the place itself, but the very idea of how anything so exotic must appeal to "a vision benumbed with brown-stone fronts." "An American," he writes, "is born to the idea that on his walks abroad it is perpetual level wall ahead of him, and such a revelation as he finds here of infinite accident and infinite effect gives a wholly novel zest to the use of his eyes."[4] In "A Passionate Pilgrim" he delights in describing Americans overwhelmed by Hampton Court, by the elementary points of an English village and by the colleges of Oxford.

The American narrator of "The Madonna of the Future" (1873) notes of his companion, the hapless expatriate painter, with whom he shares the wonders of Florence, that as a critic of the arts he has "all our native mistrust for intellectual discretion and our native relish for sonorous superlatives . . . his recognitions had a generous publicity, his discriminations were all discoveries";[5] and American characters in other stories are endowed with the same characteristic fulness of response, amounting sometimes to intemperance. The young tourist-narrator in "Travelling Companions," an early example of this type of story in which seeing Europe is the main part of the action, begins his description of the Veronese "Rape of Europa" with the words: "I steeped myself with unprotesting joy in the gorgeous glow and salubrity of that radiant scene. . . ."[6] And James himself, in an account of his first full view of Compton Wynyates, writes that, "here surely we had arrived at the farthest limits of what ivy-smothered brick-work and weather-beaten gables, conscious old windows and clustered mossy roofs can accomplish for the eye."[7]

James is usually regarded as, first and foremost, a very sophisticated writer, but the tradition of American writings on England and Europe to which he belongs has an attractively elementary side to it. Robert E. Spiller has surveyed a wide range of American comment on England during the

---

[4] "Chester," in *E.H.*, p. 55.   [5] xviii. 410.
[6] *The Collected Tales of Henry James*, ed. Leon Edel [= *C.T.*], ii. 206.
[7] "In Warwickshire," in *E.H.*, p. 208.

period before James's lifetime, much of it shrewd, realistic and critical: but it is the romantic, affectionate strain, represented supremely by Washington Irving's English essays in the *Sketch Book*, that has most relevance when we try to place James. The two writers are so different that what they have in common needs a little emphasis. From a list of Irving's titles —"Rural Life in England," "The Country Church," "Christmas," "Christmas Eve," "Christmas Day," "The Christmas Dinner," "The Boar's Head Tavern, Eastcheap," "Stratford-on Avon," "The Stage-Coach," "John Bull"—it is manifest that these essays present the English popular tradition in its most rudimentary form. The points of the tradition are assembled with a curious completeness. In the descriptions of Christmas at Bracebridge Hall, what with the Yule log, the candles, the games, the mummers, the boar's head, the wassail bowl, and the distribution of beef, bread and ale to the decent peasantry, to say nothing of the Christmas sentiments expressed with the utmost fervour, the old festive theme receives the most lavish treatment imaginable. Details which an English writer might have taken for granted, Irving gives in all fulness. Dickens's Mr Wardle is a relatively diffident traditionalist compared with Squire Bracebridge. It is interesting that Irving, a romantic American with yearnings for the picturesque Old World, writing for other Americans with the same hunger, was extremely popular with English readers too. It took an American, it would seem, to convey the England of popular myth with such simple explicitness and freshness of feeling. Irving's account of the stagecoachman and the kitchen of an English inn are exactly what one would expect. We know without looking that the essay on the Boar's Head Tavern will contain rhapsodies on "old Jack Falstaff!—kind Jack Falstaff!—sweet Jack Falstaff!" And in his essay on John Bull he tells us everything we ever knew about that emblematic figure.

Irving did a great deal to establish certain American attitudes to England which recur, though with a difference, in Hawthorne, James and others. The later writers are less simple in feeling and expression. Their emotional attachment is liable to be modified by sceptical and critical attitudes, perhaps by an element of humorous self-recognition. The objects of their attachment are less broadly obvious. But they have the same feeling for the legendary features of English life, for the things that give it traditional colouring. Hawthorne is far removed from Irving when he devotes a whole chapter of *Our Old Home* to English poverty, and when he describes the squalor of the Thames water-front: but when he writes of a visit to Greenwich Fair, with its pugilists, jugglers and other attractions, not omitting that "ancient and hereditary pastime called 'Kissing in the Ring'," he recalls Irving's essay on Little Britain, where an account is given of the great bell of St Paul's, the giants in the Guildhall, Bartholomew Fair, the Lord Mayor's Day, Shrove Tuesday and other popular London institutions. Hawthorne is intrigued by the phenomenal number of weighing machines, and wonders whether it is a symptom of the materialism of the English that they are so bent on knowing "how solid and physically ponderous they are."[8] He was a shy and uncertain traveller, slow to adjust himself to new environments and not given to extravagant sentiments, but he could say of Kensington on a summer afternoon that it was "as delightful as any place can or ought to be, in a world which, some time or other, we must quit."[9] He gradually achieved an affection for English weather.

What is true of Irving and Hawthorne is true also of James: England, for all of them, was an experience to be appropriated at the most basic level. Whatever their differences, they are united in this: they write primarily as Americans, coming to terms with a country to which they cannot be indifferent: and in writing for their fellow countrymen they make common ground with them. James is interested in what would interest other Americans—old castles, country houses, cathedrals and such places as Stonehenge—and for the usual reasons: that is, because of their glamour. But his enjoyment is flavoured, as we have seen, by a special self-awareness. He takes pleasure in seeing this romantic addiction as a kind of national ailment, recognising himself as quite an advanced case, though not so advanced as some of the passionate pilgrims of his stories.

[8] *Our Old Home* (1864 edn.), p. 214.   [9] *Op. cit.*, p. 201.

Irving and Hawthorne wrote eloquently about Warwickshire, the Shakespeare country, but James is even more eloquent, sometimes with a sort of humorous wildness or lightheadedness. The sheep of Warwickshire are the theme of an absurd conceit: they "were by no means mere edible mutton; they were poetic, historic, romantic sheep; they were not there for their weight or their wool; they were there for their presence and their compositional value, and they visibly knew it."[10]   With his keen eye for the "illustrational" and the "documentary," he could make a vivid and pointed little scene of the most everyday English phenomenon.   Extolling the variety of human types afforded by London (it is "one of the bribes by which London induces you to condone her abominations"), he mentions railway stations as an especially favourable opportunity for observing them, and this brings him to consider W. H. Smith's railway bookstalls: "a feature not to be omitted in any enumeration of the charms of Paddington and Euston. It is a focus of warmth and light in the vast smoky cavern; it gives the idea that literature is a thing of splendour, of a dazzling essence, of infinite gas-lit red and gold."[11]   Descriptions of popular English entertainments are not common in James, but his impressions of Derby Day are entirely in the tradition of Irving and Hawthorne.   Much more frequent is his use of the familiar local colour of English fashionable life: riding in Hyde Park and Rotten Row, the routines of the "season" and country-house visiting.   Of this we shall see a good deal when we consider the novels and stories with English settings.

James's sketches of Italy should also be seen in their tradition, in which Hawthorne and Howells are his chief predecessors. James reviewed Howells's *Italian Journeys* in 1868 and Hawthorne's posthumous *French and Italian Journals* in 1872, and his own work shares some general qualities with them: qualities akin to those already noted in the writings about England.   Again the interest lies often in elementary impacts. The writers are frankly tourists, and their readers, it is assumed, are compatriots who will wish to follow them to the great

---

[10] "In Warwickshire," in *E.H.*, p. 205.
[11] "London," in *E.H.*, pp. 35-6.

centres of pilgrimage, curious about those matters of atmosphere and detail that give places their special character and appeal. These books are therefore very "helpful," not only in the sense of being informative on points of history, architecture and so forth (which they sometimes are, though in moderation) but in the personal and pictorial charm of the impressions they present. It is not to be taken for granted that a book of travel will serve its readers in this way. In the sixteenth and eighteenth chapters of *Eothen*, Kinglake treats only those particular things in Jerusalem and Cairo—pilgrims, victims of plague—that happened to loom large for him at the time. We prize the book for certain strong personal qualities, but if we turn to it after reading Hawthorne, Howells and James, hoping for some account of how the places looked and what they had to offer to visitors, we shall be disappointed. A reader with a similar bias may be disappointed also with Stevenson's *Inland Voyage*, where the pictorial element, though pleasing so far as it goes, is rather scanty and elusive, and the treatment of episodes reveals little interest in the general ways and conventions of the communities where they took place. There is an abundance of Stevensonian reflexion and comment, but not much of it suggests that the object of his "voyage" was to discover Belgium or that the object of the book was to satisfy readers with any such curiosity. Some travel writers, like D. H. Lawrence, are liable to manipulate their material for didactic purposes; and others, like Ruskin, have specialised aesthetic criteria which separate them from the ordinary civilised traveller. Civilised though these Americans are, what counts for most in their travel writings is their participation in a common interest. They are mainly concerned with what the places have to say to Americans. Since the American sees himself as something of a provincial, his tone tends to be modest and unassuming. These writings have, in fact, a disarming quality that makes them very attractive to the provincial, untravelled type of reader, American or otherwise. One of the endearing features of Hawthorne's impressions of France and Italy is his recognition of the limits of his own receptive faculty. To any tourist who is not enjoying things as he thinks he ought, Hawthorne is an assuaging author.

His book is full of quaint Americanisms. Coming out of St Peter's in winter he sees urchins sliding on the ice round a fountain, and he takes a slide with them, "just for the sake of doing what I never thought to do in Rome."[12] Having seen the Pope, he is glad that he can cross him out of the list of sights to be seen. After a charming description of the little Jesuit church of San Andrea, he expresses the wish that he could "pack it in a large box and send it home."[13]

Here is Howells's impression of the Roman ruins: a good example of the pictorial treatment which directly meets the reader's need to know how things look. Independent American attitudes prevail, but do not overshadow the composition:

> I knew that they could only be mere fragments and rubbish, but I was not prepared to find them so. I learned that I had all along secretly hoped for some dignity of neighbourhood, some affectionate solicitude on the part of Nature to redeem these works of Art from the destruction that had befallen them. But in the hollows below the level of the dirty cowfield, wandered over by evil-eyed buffaloes, and obscenely defiled by wild beasts of men, there stood here an arch, there a pillar, yonder a cluster of columns crowned by a bit of frieze; and yonder again, a fragment of temple, half-gorged by the facade of a hideous rococo church; then a height of vaulted brick-work, and, leading on to the Coliseum, another arch, and then incoherent columns overthrown and mixed with dilapidated walls. . . ."[14]

Howells's temperament as a traveller was easier than Hawthorne's. In his greater readiness to enjoy he is nearer to James, and *Italian Journeys* contains many attractive descriptions.

Perhaps the most characteristic note in James's travel sketches, whether of Italy or elsewhere, is a sense of the felicity of appropriating a place, accompanied by an ever-varying grace in the sharing of the experience. Among the many virtues involved is that of courtesy, shown first in an attentive and generous concern for the object itself, expressed in words that enhance it and communicate pleasure, but also in the touches of lightness and humour which not only express his

[12] *Complete Works*, ed. G. P. Lathrop (1893), x. 62.   [13] *Op. cit.*, p. 93.
[14] *Italian Journeys* (1901 edn.), p. 130.

own pleasure, but also serve to put the reader at his ease and mitigate the element of sheer description. He manages to convey the impression that, complex though his composition may be with its unique combination of shades and details, the total effect has a simplicity before which one can relax. In the essay "Roman Neighbourhoods" he achieves this apparent effortlessness in a description of a convent garden:

> But my peculiar pleasure was the thick-shaded garden which adjoins the convent and commands from its massive artificial foundations an enchanting view of the lake. Part of it is laid out in cabbages and lettuce, over which a rubicund brother, with his frock tucked up, was bending with a solicitude which he interrupted to remove his skull-cap and greet me with the unsophisticated sweet-humoured smile that every now and then in Italy does so much to make you forget the ambiguities of monachism. The rest is occupied by cypresses and other funereal umbrage, making a dank circle round an old cracked fountain black with water-moss. The parapet of the terrace is furnished with good stone seats where you may lean on your elbows to gaze away a sunny half-hour and, feeling the general charm of the scene, declare that the best mission of such a country in the world has been simply to produce, in the way of prospect and picture, these masterpieces of mildness.[15]

His descriptions depict not only places or objects, but situations for the traveller; and it is largely in his sense of situation that he makes common ground with his reader. In "Italy Revisited" he can dwell on the mere satisfaction of being in Italy again. It is only Turin, but it is nevertheless Italy: "I roamed all the morning under the tall porticoes, thinking it sufficient joy to take note of the soft, warm air, of that local colour of things that is at once so broken and so harmonious, and of the comings and goings, the physiognomy and manners, of the excellent Turinese. I had opened the old book again; the old charm was in the style; I was in a more delightful world."[16] In another passage, in the essay on "The Old Saint-Gothard," he is on an even more elementary level. Starting on a journey, he reflects on the pleasure that this simple fact in itself can

---

[15] "Roman Neighbourhoods," in *Italian Hours* [= *I.H.*], (1909), p. 183.
[16] "Italy Revisited," in *I.H.*, p. 109.

afford: "I don't envy people, at any rate, who have outlived or outworn the simple sweetness of feeling settled to go somewhere with bag and umbrella. If we are settled on the top of a coach, and the 'somewhere' contains an element of the new and strange, the case is at its best."[17]

Many scenes are agreeably introduced as having a special value for the inveterately romantic American. One essay begins with the tempting sentence: "I made a note after my first stroll at Albano to the effect that I had been talking of the 'picturesque' all my life, but that now for a change I beheld it."[18] A page or so later he begins a dense and vivid little description with the words: "Questioned, as a cherisher of quaintness, as to the best 'bit' hereabouts, I should certainly name. . . ."[19] He is "never weary of staring into gateways, of lingering by dreary, shabby, half-barbaric farm-yards, of feasting a foolish gaze on sun-cracked plaster and unctuous indoor shadows."[20] The function of the personal here is to heighten the sense of place, never to deflect our attention away from the place to the author. The place, we feel, is being allowed to sound its own note.

He could achieve adjustments of manner for a wide range of occasions. The Leonardo *Last Supper* was a great occasion, and he produces an eloquent comment which nevertheless had its touches of amiable familiarity:

> The cathedral is good for another thousand years, but we ask whether our children will find in the most majestic and most luckless of frescoes much more than the shadow of a shadow. Its fame has been for a century or two that, as one may say, of an illustrious invalid whom people visit to see how he lasts, with leave-taking sighs and almost death-bed or tiptoe precautions. The picture needs not another scar or stain, now, to be the saddest work of art in the world; and battered, defaced, ruined as it is, it remains one of the greatest . . . Every painter ought once in his life to stand before the Cenacolo and decipher its moral. Mix with your colours and mess on your palette every particle of the very substance of your soul,

---

17 "The Old Saint-Gothard," in *I.H.*, p. 100.
18 "Roman Neighbourhoods," in *I.H.*, p. 171.
19 *Op. cit.*, p. 172.   20 "Roman Rides," in *I.H.*, p. 165.

and this lest perchance your "prepared surface" shall play you a trick! Then, and then only, it will fight to the last—it will resist even in death.[21]

The same essay ("From Chambéry to Milan") provides a very different example, the theme of which is the "mummified corpse" of San Carlo Borromeo, exhibited in his canonical robes with a profusion of jewels. James's account of the unveiling of this dubious tableau does no injustice to its incongruities, but when one thinks—and it is all too easy—of what Lytton Strachey would have made of it, one admires the graver and finer piquancy which a touch of respect can contribute: "You see I am forced to agree after all, in spite of the sliding shutter and the profane swagger of the sacristan, that a certain pastoral majesty saved the situation, or at least made irony gape."[22] Sometimes admiration is expressed by a humorous throwing to the winds of all caution or right thinking. Thus, in an account of Mondragone, now a Jesuit college for boys, he declares that if he had a little son he would send him there to receive their "crooked teachings"—for the sake of the other memories (of Geoge Sand, for example), and "the avenues of cypress and ilex, the view of the Campagna, the atmosphere of antiquity. . . . But," he continues, "when a sense of 'mere character', shameless incomparable character, has brought one to this it is time one should pause."[23]

His habitual attitude is one of accommodation. He is usually willing to be pleased; he rarely quarrels, and then only reluctantly, with what Italy has to offer. Thus, on the subject of hackney-coaches and omnibuses stationed at the foot of Giotto's tower, he agrees that this is lamentable, but cannot feel as strongly about it as Ruskin: "the sensitive stranger who has been walking about for a week with his mind full of the sweetness and suggestiveness of a hundred Florentine places may feel at last in looking into Mr. Ruskin's little tracts that, discord for discord, there isn't much to choose between the importunity of the author's personal ill-humour and the incongruity of horse-pails and bundles of hay."[24] He goes on to

[21] "From Chambéry to Milan," in *I.H.*, pp. 91-2. [22] *Op. cit.*, p. 90.
[23] "Roman Neighbourhoods," in *I.H.*, p. 189.
[24] "Italy Revisited," in *I.H.*, p. 126.

comment, but partly with amusement, on Ruskin's drastic judgment on the frescoes in Santa Maria Novella and his insistence on the right and wrong ways of seeing Florence.

James recognises, in more than one passage, that his way of enjoying Italy may involve a moral indifference to much that is unpleasant: "To travel is, as it were, to go to the play, to attend a spectacle; and there is something heartless in stepping forth into foreign streets to feast on 'character' when character consists simply of the slightly different costume in which labour and want present themselves."[25] And he adds that the sweet smile of the grateful recipient of twopence may hide the ugliest states of mind. James admits that, as a mere visitor, he is often superficial in his impressions.

It is one of his idiosyncrasies to depict himself as just another loafing, idling, dawdling American, gazing and gaping in a prolonged state of easy receptiveness. He delights—sometimes, perhaps, to excess—in reducing the experience to its most unexacting terms: in taking his Italy without question and without qualms. In an essay on Venice he writes:

> Almost all the pleasures of the place are simple. . . . There is no simpler pleasure than looking at a fine Titian, unless it be look-ing at a fine Tintoret or strolling into St. Mark's—abominable the way one falls into the habit—and resting one's light-wearied eyes upon the windowless gloom; or than floating in a gondola or than hanging over a balcony or than taking one's coffee at Florian's.[26]

It almost seems a little depraved. But this passage may be taken as a piece of amiability in an essay intended for readers to whom adjustment to Europe was by no means a facile matter. The pleasantly shameless expression of the holiday-making mood is another way of making common ground with the audience.

This relation between writer and audience, in James's writings and in those of his American predecessors, is well illustrated in passages where works of art are described. No introduction to a picture or a statue could be on easier terms. The reader may be stimulated to look at the work for himself,

[25] *Op. cit.*, p. 116.   [26] "Venice," in *I.H.*, p. 4.

but even if he does not he will still have been entertained. The description may in some cases show critical discrimination, but its primary object is to convey something of human or pictorial interest. Other writers may have described pictures more knowledgeably, but it may be doubted whether any have done it more engagingly. The style of the description is governed by the pleasant unspoken convention that one takes one's culture not without humour and sometimes with scepticism, and that an American confronted with Europe is privileged to give a turn or a twist to his response. Hawthorne, Howells and James are a long way from the open irreverence of Mark Twain, but sometimes one feels that the difference between them is mainly one of degree. Hawthorne describes Carlo Dolce's picture of the Eternal Father as

> . . . a miracle and masterpiece of absurdity. . . . It is the All-powerless, a fair-haired, soft, consumptive deity, with a mouth that has fallen open through very weakness. He holds one hand on his stomach as if the wickedness and wretchedness of mankind made him qualmish; and he is looking out of heaven with an expression of pitiable appeal, or as if seeking somewhere for assistance in his heavy task of ruling the universe.[27]

He adds that if the painter knew what he was doing, he would be chargeable with blasphemy. The picture is a satire on all incompetent rulers, and "against the rickety machine and crazy action of the universe." Howells, describing a Pompeian fresco, produces a pleasant piece in the gentle half-humorous manner which we encounter later in James:

> One of these is the wounded Adonis cared for by Venus and the Loves; in which the story is treated with a playful pathos wonderfully charming. The fair boy leans in the languor of his hurt towards Venus, who sits utterly disconsolate beside him, while the Cupids busy themselves with such slight surgical offices as Cupids may render: one prepares a linen bandage for the wound, another wraps it round the leg of Adonis, another supports one of his heavy arms, another finds his own emotions too much for him and pauses to weep.[28]

[27] *Complete Works*, ed. G. P. Lathrop (1893), x. 369.
[28] *Italian Journeys* (1901 edn.), p. 89.

E

James combines humour with sensuous fulness in his account
of a Tintoretto picture in the Ducal palace:

> "Pallas chasing away Mars" is, I believe, the name that is
> given to the picture; and it represents in fact a young woman
> of noble appearance administering a gentle push to a fine
> young man in armour, as if to tell him to keep his distance.
> It is of the gentleness of this push that I speak, the charming
> way in which she puts out her arm, with a single bracelet on it,
> and rests her young hand, its rosy fingers parted, on his dark
> breastplate. She bends her enchanting head with the effort—
> a head which has all the strange fairness that the Tintoret
> always sees in women—and the soft, living, flesh-like glow of
> all these members, over which the brush has scarcely paused
> in its course, is as pretty an example of genius as all Venice
> can show.[29]

The following description of a landscape is an object lesson
in the translation into words of a pictorial impression without
any of the straining of visual vocabulary which makes what is
called "word-painting" so often repellent:

> It represents half a dozen cows, driven through a field by a
> young girl on a late summer day. The happy, crooked,
> scattered movement of the cattle; the sweet midsummer whisper
> which seems to lurk in the meadowside copse; the rare and
> natural luminosity, without *recherche*, without a hint of that
> cunning *morbidezza* which marks the corresponding portion
> of the small Decamps near by, in the tender sky, dappled at
> cool intervals—make of the work a genuine pastoral. It is,
> perhaps, as a whole, a little blank and thin; but it is inde-
> finably *honnête*.[30]

His account of some Dutch pictures, purchased by the New
York Metropolitan Museum in 1871, is full of humour. Of a
Rubens *Return from Egypt* he says that the "real success of the
picture is in the free and sweeping contour of Mary, and
in her extremely handsome head. . . . Rubens alone, too,
could have made his Virgin so gracefully huge and preserved
the air of mild maternity in such massive bulk. His Mary is a

---

[29] "Venice," in *I.H.*, p. 24.
[30] Reprinted in *The Painter's Eye* [= *P.E.*] ed. J. L. Sweeney (1956), p. 44.

gentle giantess."[31] Referring to Van Dyck's *St Martha interceding for the Cessation of the Plague at Tarascon* he notes "the lovely flesh-glow of the tumbling cherubs who uplift the pretty postulant into the blue."[32] But Jan Van der Heyden's *Quay in Leyden* is the occasion for a more serious and sustained exercise in interpretative description:

> We doubt whether 'touch' has ever achieved a more signal victory than in this compact pictorial sonnet, as we may call it, to the homely charms of brick-work. A narrow canal divides the picture; on each side of it rise a row of plain high-gabled dwellings. On the left, in the shade, stretches a footway, along which a woman in a ruff and a hoop leads a little girl; opposite, the tall red houses dip their feet into the sluggish moat. A sort of antique, palpable stillness seems to pervade the scene; the perspective is so delicate and perfect that you fancy the very genius of geometry having retired thither from the academic hum near by, to revolve a proposition. The poetic strain resides in a ruddy golden exhalation from the plumbed and measured surfaces of brick, and in the infinite patience of the handiwork. The picture tells more of Dutch conscience than all its neighbours together. Each individual brick is laid with mathematical tenderness, squared and nicked and enriched with its proper particle of damp from the canal; and yet in this aggregation of minute touches, space and unity and harmony are cunningly preserved.[33]

If one had any quarrel with these descriptions, it would not be that James is too much the aesthete, but rather that in his affable way he sometimes overdoes the vein of levity. But if the best way to write about pictures for a general audience is to mediate between aesthetic insight and other levels of pleasure, as far as possible suggesting the subtleties of art while giving the untutored reader something humanly and tangibly interesting, it would be difficult to find anyone who does this on a higher level than James.

In writing stories dominated by the European setting and atmosphere, James was following an illustrious if rather strange example. It is doubtful whether any novel has been

[31] *P.E.*, p. 53.   [32] *P.E.*, p. 55.   [33] *P.E.*, pp. 63-4.

more influenced by its author's feelings for a place than *The Marble Faun* is by Hawthorne's feeling for Rome. To a reader not already prepared for it, it is a tedious book: the space taken up by descriptions of *Sehenswürdigkeiten*, by any ordinary standards of economy, is excessive. We must accept it, if at all, as a monument to a phase of American sensibility, a tribute to the spellbinding power of Rome over members of a race so utterly foreign to it. As such it is on a noble scale. It opens in the Capitol, with the four central characters standing in the sculpture gallery containing the Dying Gladiator, the Antinous, the Lycian Apollo and so forth, from a window of which there is a view of the arch of Septimius Severus, the Forum ("where Roman washerwomen hang out their lines") and the Colosseum. With his characteristic openness the novelist says that, by beginning in this way, he hopes to put the reader "into that state of feeling which is experienced oftenest in Rome . . . a vague sense of ponderous remembrances; a perception of such weight and density in a bygone life, of which this spot was the centre, that the present moment is pressed down or crowded out. . . ."[34] As the novel develops it would seem that incidents are contrived largely for the sake of the places where they occur. Miriam's ghastly pursuer makes his first appearance in the catacomb of St Calixtus, which is atmospherically described. Her extraordinary meeting with Donatello culminating in the Sylvan Dance takes place in the Villa Borghese. Kenyon's stroll with Hilda on the Pincian is an opportunity for a survey of all the notable sights visible from this point. The Moonlight Ramble is a little tour of Rome: the friends pause at the Fountain of Trevi, move on to Trajan's Forum, the Colosseum, the Arch of Constantine and so on until they reach the statue of Marcus Aurelius in the piazza of the Campidoglio. He dwells quite lengthily upon some of these places. The Tarpeian Rock, inevitably, is chosen as the point from which Donatello hurls Miriam's tormentor to his death. It is in the church of the Capuchins, with its daunting burial chamber, that they are confronted by the sight of the dead man laid out on his bier. In each of these passages and many others, Hawthorne's own feelings about Rome are

[34] *Complete Works*, ed. G. P. Lathrop (1893), vi. 20.

decisive in giving the episode richness or at least strength of
décor, whether the narrative satisfies us in other ways or not.
Two of the characters are Americans. By causing their story
to be placed in so dense a setting of Old World associations,
he achieves a bold if rather simple contrast. Hilda and Kenyon
are pure and uninitiated—their Americanness is not developed
much beyond this—and their environment is the most con-
gested theatre of experience the world has known. The wicked
streets of Rome are an ominous background for the disappear-
ance of Hilda; St Peter's is an impressive site for her capitu-
lation to the irresistible consolation of the confessional. Kenyon's search for Hilda and her reappearance take place amidst
the distractions of a Roman carnival.

The Marble Faun stands by itself: but it could be said of
Howells's very slight early novel, *Their Wedding Journey*, that it
also exists very largely for the sale of the places visited by the
characters. It is indeed a mere fictionalised travel book, an
exercise in the portrayal of American and Canadian scenes,
following upon his early achievements in the Italian travel
books of the eighteen-sixties. The wedded pair, Basil and
Isabel March, are very alive to significant differences between
places. As soon as they arrive in New York they compare
it with Boston, and the descriptions of New York that follow
are quite pointed and effective. They go up the Hudson,
and there are pleasant passages of river scenery and impressions of Dutch farms. Howells is at his best in the chapters
about Canada; for example, in the account of Bonsecours
Market, Montreal, and his reflexions on the hybrid character—
so French yet so painfully northern—of Quebec. He has some
of James's gift for the delicate documentary touch in a pictorial
composition. Basil and Isabel respond to points of manners.
It is noted, for example, that costume becomes more informal
as one goes east: "on a westering line, the blacking fades
gradually from the boots, the hat softens and sinks, the coat
loses its rigour of cut. . . ." Basil is amused and Isabel rather
displeased by the tendency further west for loving couples to
sleep in public on each other's shoulders. *A Chance Acquaintance*, also of Howells's early period as a novelist, contains
excellent scenes of Quebec; and *A Foregone Conclusion*, a novel

about Americans in Venice, has plenty of local colour, as one
would expect. Howells had a consulate post in Venice as a
young man. But the topographical interest is less dominant
than in *Their Wedding Journey*.

It is only in the stories of the early eighteen-seventies that
James allows this element to predominate. "Travelling Companions," the first of his stories in which a young American
tourist-narrator appears, begins in Milan with a visit to the
Last Supper, which he describes, and then we are treated to a
series of similar visits, now in the company of an American
girl, to places in Milan, Vicenza, Venice, Padua and so forth.
The story is dated 1870, only a year after James's great initia-
tion. The young narrator is still in an early stage of *his* initia-
tion: the days in Milan are "the sweetest, fullest, calmest
of his life";[35] he rejoices in Italy as only an American can.
The story is slight enough, but interesting as an example not
only of his shameless indulgence in the sense of place, but also
of his rediscovery of his compatriots in a setting that enhances
national differences. If the narrator's delight in Italy occupies
inordinate space, it is in the company of an American girl,
"an American to perfection"[36] in freedom, that he enjoys it.
He gets the best of two worlds.

With "Madame de Mauves," a few years later (1874), a
further stage is reached. The European place, Paris, is no
longer explored for itself, but he uses it most expressively as a
setting for American experiences. The story opens with the
hero, Longmore, placed and poised, ready for something to
happen to him, something in keeping with both the French
idiom and his own, the kind of adventure that James's Americans
come to Europe for:

> The view from the terrace at Saint-Germain-en-Laye is
> immense and famous. Paris lies spread before you in dusky
> vastness, domed and fortified, glittering here and there through
> her light vapours and girdled with her silver Seine. Behind you
> is a park of stately symmetry, and behind that a forest where
> you may lounge through turfy avenues and light-chequered
> glades and quite forget that you are within half an hour of

---

[35] *C.T.*, II. 184.   [36] *C.T.*, II 207.

the boulevards. One afternoon, however, in mid-spring,
some five years ago, a young man seated on the terrace had
preferred to keep this in mind. His eyes were fixed in idle
wistfulness on the mighty human hive before him. . . .[37]

He has his adventure: it is as French as it could be—that is,
within the limits of an equally typical New Englandism—and it
is at the crisis of his emotional drama that again, this time more
emphatically, the setting plays its part. He walks into the
country, in a state of excitement, and finds himself in a place
of peculiar charm and expressiveness: "He thought he had
never seen anything so characteristically French; all the French
novels seemed to have described it, all the French landscapists
to have painted it. . . ."[38] In this soothing atmosphere his
thoughts undergo a change, and he is ready for the very French
little episode that follows: the arrival of the painter and his
mistress, the embodiment, it seems, of a naturalness quite the
opposite of the ethos that has hitherto governed his outlook
and behaviour. James treats the scene with considerable
lavishness of detail; every point that could contribute to its
rich typicality and persuasiveness is used; and the effect
upon Longmore is complete. One might say of the whole
episode that we have too strong a concentration on the typical,
were it not an episode of American sensibility. It is one of the
recurring *motifs* in James's fiction that Americans have this
uncanny sense of type, and that, being themselves at a forma-
tive stage, they are liable to be decisively influenced by
significant places and their *moeurs*.

From Europe seen by Americans we turn now to America
seen either by Europeans, or by Americans returning with
sharpened awareness after a period in Europe. *The Europeans*
calls only for brief mention here: Felix's impressions of Boston
in the first chapter are pointed, but they are subdued. The
story, after all, is set in the past, and it would not have served
James's purpose to insist much on the illustrative points of a
particular phase in the development of Boston and its neighbourhood. But another story of the same year (1878), almost
of novel length, "An International Episode," provides a first-
rate example of the American scene as viewed by strangers.

[37] XVIII. 193.   [38] XVIII. 266.

We begin with the arrival in New York of two well-born
Englishmen, Lord Lambeth and Percy Beaumont, and from
the first page the descriptions of their impressions have the
characteristic notation with which James, Howells and others,
whether in travel books or fiction, catch the sharp, distinctive
features of new places. "Of quite other sense and sound from
those of any typical English street was the endless rude channel,
rich in incongruities, through which our two travellers advanced. . . ."[39] This is Broadway, with its "high-coloured
heterogeneous architecture," white marble facades that seemed
to glare in the "strong crude light," the awnings, banners,
streamers, immense quantities of horse-drawn public transport,
vendors of cooling drinks, and the general air of "brightness,
newness, juvenility." But it is in the hotel, where a crowd
of people waiting dejectedly in a large open space are identified
as "American citizens doing homage to an hotel-clerk,"[40]
that James has freest play with the bizarreness of day-to-day
American phenomena to the innocent patrician English eye.
A brown-stone house, complete with stoop, is, almost as a
matter of piety, specifically described: but the journey in an
elevator to Mr Westgate's office in the ten-storey building is
rather more characteristic of the contemporary flavour of the
whole episode. Stepping to the window of the office, Lord
Lambeth observes, level with his eyes, "the weather-vane of a
church-steeple."[41] The office itself, the phenomenon of an
American at work, is local colour enough. They journey on to
Newport, where they are to enjoy the hospitality of Mrs
Westgate. Their hotel has the same quality of the fabulous
with its "gigantic verandah on which an army might have
encamped—a vast wooden terrace with a roof as high as the
nave of a cathedral,"[42] peopled mainly by pretty young girls.
When they walk down later to the rocks with their new ac-
quaintances, they note that the "little coast-line . . . lacked
presence and character."[43] With the introduction of Mrs
Westgate and Bessie Alden, the story becomes a study in
American types and Anglo-American situations and will be
more conveniently discussed in the next chapter.

[39] XIX. 245.   [40] XIX. 249.   [41] XIX. 253.
[42] XIX. 264.   [43] XIX. 277.

If the dominant quality of James's European scenes is one of saturation in all that makes for "type," often with a density of notation and richness of effect that almost intoxicates the American sensibility that is exposed to them, these impressions of American settings have a charming spareness and lightness.

Occasionally James makes play with the impressions of characters who enjoy some degree of aesthetic training, such as Florimond Daintry in "A New England Winter" (1884), a story quite rich in documentary points, if not in other features. Florimond has returned to Boston from an artistic life in Paris; and the charm of Boston is not lost upon him. He turns his head this way and that, freely indulging "his most valued organ," on which his Parisian reputation chiefly rests. In Paris he was thought to have "a great deal of eye." A figure of slender importance in other respects, Florimond does justice to the real virtues of his native scene:

> He made his way promptly into Beacon Street, and he greatly admired that vista. The long straight avenue lay airing its newness in the frosty day, and all its individual façades, with their neat, sharp ornaments, seemed to have been scoured, with a kind of friction, by the hard, salutary light. Their brilliant browns and drabs, their rosy surfaces of brick, made a variety of fresh, violent tones, such as Florimond liked to memorise, and the large, clear windows of their curved fronts faced each other, across the street, like candid, inevitable eyes. There was something almost terrible in the windows; Florimond had forgotten how vast and clean they were, and how, in their sculptured frames, the New England air seemed, like a zealous housewife, to polish and preserve them. . . .[44]

The "continuity of glass constituted a kind of exposure, within and without, and gave the street the appearance of an enormous corridor in which the public and the private were familiar and intermingled."

The sense of place is one of the poetic graces of James's novels, and of the American novel of manners as he conceived it. His devotees of European places, his "passionate pilgrims," belong to a type of American of which he never tired. Clement

[44] xxv. 78.

Searle himself, the original passionate pilgrim, and Theobald, the expatriate painter of "The Madonna of the Future," are well known. No less romantically forlorn than these is the young lady of "Four Meetings" (1877), who saves her money for a visit to Europe which ends, after a few hours, with the appropriation of her funds by an unspeakable cousin. Poor Miss Spencer's obsession with Europe wins from the much-travelled narrator an inflamed tribute, which could be applied to the rest of the inspired band, and which James, though with due sophistication, would have accepted as true of himself:

> "You've the great American disease, and you've got it 'bad'—the appetite, morbid and monstrous, for colour and form, for the picturesque and the romantic at any price. I don't know whether we come into the world with it—with the germs implanted and antecedent to experience. . . . We're like travellers in the desert—deprived of water and subject to the terrible mirage, the torment of illusion, of the thirst-fever. They hear the plash of fountains, they see green gardens and orchards that are hundreds of miles away. So we with *our* thirst—except that with us it's *more* wonderful: we have before us the beautiful old things we've never seen at all, and when we do at last see them—if we're lucky!—we simply recognize them. . . ."[45]

---

[45] XXI. 241-2.

IV

Sense of Type

JAMES's achievement in developing a fiction expressing the American character cannot be surveyed without a certain amount of sheer factual summarising, with large numbers of examples. His contribution was most impressive in quantitative terms: this needs to be emphasised. We may think of him as in the same category, in this respect, as Balzac, different though they are in other ways. James did not, like Balzac, deal with a wide range of trades, professions and social *milieux*. It was his task to do something more fundamental: to portray Americanness itself; and his abundance is in the variety of situations illustrating the national temper and outlook. Balzac could take the French character for granted, and concentrate on the special manifestations of it that were rampant in his own age. Other American novelists —Melville, Mark Twain, Frank Norris, Dreiser—found their subject-matter in special areas of the American world of action and enterprise, treating it with a profusion of local detail and, in some cases, with great imaginative power. In some respects they might seem more involved in the life of their country than James: but James was involved, more consciously and at more points, with the "complex fate" of being an American.

A justification for giving special emphasis to social content in James's works has already been suggested. Whatever else they may be about, here at least we are on firm ground. Limited though it may seem, this is as good a way into the novels and stories themselves as any that we are likely to find. The best and most crucial places in a story may be those in which the element of Americanness plays its most significant role. His turn of phrase is often happiest when his imagination is engaged with some expressive token of the national ethos. The examples that will be assembled here would serve equally well as general illustrations of James's skill in characterisation, description or dialogue, of his moral penetration or his humour; and indeed we would do well to look first at a large-scale passage that combines these different levels of interest.

The following paragraph has the advantage of being of the only kind that does not suffer by being transplanted from its context. It is the opening to *Roderick Hudson*:

Rowland Mallet had made his arrangements to sail for Europe on the 5th of September, and having in the interval a fortnight to spare, he determined to spend it with his cousin Cecilia, the widow of a nephew of his father. He was urged by the reflection that an affectionate farewell might help to exonerate him from the charge of neglect frequently preferred by this lady. It was not that the young man disliked her; he regarded her, on the contrary, with a tender admiration and had not forgotten how when his cousin brought her home on her marriage he seemed to feel the upward sweep of the empty bough from which the golden fruit had been plucked. He then and there, for himself, accepted the prospect of bachelorhood. The truth was that, as it will be part of the entertainment of this narrative to exhibit, Rowland Mallet had an uncomfortably sensitive conscience, and that, in spite of the seeming paradox, his visits to Cecilia were rare because she and her misfortunes were often uppermost in it. Her misfortunes were three in number; first, she had lost her husband; second, she had lost her money, or the greater part of it; and third, she lived at Northampton, Massachusetts. Mallet's compassion was really wasted, because Cecilia was a very clever woman and a skilful counter-plotter to adversity. She had made herself a charming home, her economies were not obtrusive, and there was always a cheerful flutter in the folds of her crape. It was the consciousness of all this that puzzled Mallet whenever he felt tempted to put in his oar. He had money and he had time, but he never could decide just how to place these gifts gracefully at Cecilia's service. He was no longer at all in the humour to marry her; that fancy had in these eight years died a very natural death. And yet her extreme cleverness seemed somehow to make charity difficult and patronage impossible. He would rather have chopped off his hand than offer her a cheque, a piece of useful furniture or a black silk dress; and yet there was pity for him in

seeing such a bright proud woman live in such a small dull
way. Cecilia had moreover a turn for sarcasm, and her smile,
which was her pretty feature, was never so pretty as when her
sprightly phrase had a lurking scratch in it. Rowland remembered that for him she was all smiles, and suspected
awkwardly that he ministered not a little to her sense of the
irony of things. . . .[1]

This is by no means his greatest opening. The first paragraphs
of *The Ambassadors* are in quite another class. Yet it would
compare favourably with most openings of English novels
of classic status. The ease and charm of the phrasing ("the
upward sweep of the empty bough," "a cheerful flutter in the
folds of her crape") are inseparable from the clarity and acuteness with which so much character and situation is stated in so
short a space. The reader already familiar with James's
works will recognise the distinguishing traits. Cecilia is the
shrewd, "bright" American woman. Like Mrs Tristram and,
in their different ways, Mrs Westgate and Maria Gostrey
(the type has its range of possibilities), she is adept at placing
the male, and we note a reference in the second sentence to
her somewhat demanding attitude to Rowland, another well-
known attribute of the American woman. As for Rowland,
the points of his type are recognisable enough: the exacting
New England conscience, characteristically sharpened by
aesthetic compunction; the suggestion of a basic ineffectiveness,
the failure to marry being the central symptom. Rowland
must be one of the first cases of this kind in American fiction.
As the novel develops he becomes indeed an extreme one. For
a full account of Rowland's character and background other
passages in the opening chapter would have served us better
than this—it is an exceedingly good expository chapter—
but this is a fair example of what James could do with the first
page of a novel.

There is no obvious point at which a survey of his character
types should begin, but we may conveniently start with an
example in his lightest style of portraiture, a neat study in the
obvious: Louis Leverett, who makes epistolary contributions
to "A Bundle of Letters" (1879) and its sequel, "The Point of

---

[1] *Roderick Hudson* [= *R.H.*], p. 1.

View" (1882). These pieces, together with "The Pension Beaurepas" (1879), which uses some of the same characters, would be useful five-finger exercises for anyone embarking upon a systematic study of American manners in fiction. The characters (whether American, English, French, German, Swiss) are all engagingly representative, and they are brought together, in *pensions* or in other circumstances, mainly to reveal their own national traits or to comment on those of the others.

Louis Leverett belongs to a type we have already encountered. He has something in common with Florimond Daintry, whose lively responses to the streets of Boston were the theme of a paragraph cited in the previous chapter. Florimond is a little coxcombical, but Louis is more so. Both give rein to artistic sensibility, but whereas Florimond, the more artistic, accepts the "hard salutary light" of his homeland, Louis on his return from Europe complains that "a terrible crude glare is over everything . . . the raw heavens seem to bleed with the quick hard light."[2] When Gaston Probert, in *The Reverberator* (1888), comes back to Paris from his first visit to America, he confesses to Mr Dosson that he didn't like the light, which he found "rather hard, too much like the scratching of a slate-pencil":[3] but it must be remembered that, if Florimond and Louis have become a little Frenchified, Gaston is virtually French. He is amiable, aesthetically given, but no coxcomb. "*Comme c'est bariolé, eh?*" Felix Young says gaily to his sister in a Boston street, after the snow ceases and the sky brightens, but she replies: "I don't like the colouring; it hurts my eyes."[4] An inability to come to terms with this aspect of the American environment would seem to be a symptom that places people. The hapless Theobald, of "The Madonna of the Future," included "our crude and garish climate," along with "our silent past" and "our deafening present," among the disadvantages of America for artists.[5]

Florimond Daintry, Louis Leverett, and Gaston Probert are members of a distinctive class of young Americans, to which Edward Rosier and Little Bilham also belong: expatriates all, and sorry exceptions to the famous rule that Americans must

[2] xix. 517.   [3] xviii. 175.
[4] *Eur.*, p. 12.   [5] xviii. 397

work. It is one of the jokes about this type that, in spite of
what they may take themselves or America to be, they are
nevertheless in their own fashion thoroughly American. We
read of Florimond that "his figure was much more in harmony
with the Boston landscape than he supposed."[6] "Oh he's all
right—he's one of *us*," Maria Gostrey says of Little Bilham,
after Strether's first meeting with the enigmatic young man;
and Strether, whose awareness is developing fast, understands
her: "He wouldn't have known even the day before what she
meant—that is if she meant what he assumed, that they were
intense Americans together." Bilham's "serenity," which
Strether had associated with European corruption, he interprets
now as "a special little form of the oldest thing they knew."[7]
One of the ways in which they all manifest this aspect of
Americanism is in the spirit with which they assimilate what
they take to be its opposite; and our liking for them, or otherwise, depends largely on the degree of success with which they
achieve a harmonious blend. In Felix Young, the best of the
type, the result is civilised and delightful: his Europeanism
qualifies him, as we have seen, to be a charming American.
Louis Leverett, the rawest of the renegades, shows his Americanness in the way he takes himself and his new-found aestheticism so seriously.   He has acquired the current Paterisms in
their undifferentiated form:

> ... The great thing is to *live*, you know—to feel, to be conscious
> of one's possibilities; not to pass through life mechanically
> and insensibly, even as a letter through a post-office. There are
> times, my dear Harvard, when I feel as if I were really capable
> of everything—*capable de tout*, as they say here—of the greatest
> excesses as well as the greatest heroism. Oh to be able to say
> that one has lived—*qu'on a vécu*. ... I want the knowledge that
> leaves a trace—that leaves strange scars and stains, ineffable
> reveries and aftertastes, behind it.[8]

The portrait is light, and a little absurd, but James does not
deny him a style. If he has nothing else, he has a feeling
for a phrase. "We are *thin*, my dear Harvard," Louis writes
to his compatriot. "We're pale, we're poor, we're flat,
there's something meagre about us; our line is wanting in

[6] xxv. 80.   [7] *Amb.*, I. 110-11.   [8] XIX. 440-1.

roundness, our composition in richness."[9]   And from America he writes: "There's no form here, dear Harvard; I had no idea how little form there is.   I don't know what I shall do; I feel so undraped, so uncurtained, so uncushioned. . . ."[10] With his exhibitionist preciosity, allied to what is detectable as a version of the American rueful, humorous loquacity, he presents a certain point of view in an eloquent if simplified form. The portrait is by no means negligible art.   It shows how easily James could have been the Peacock of his generation—the mimic, the parodist, the caricaturist of cultural fashions— if he had not had more exacting tasks to perform.

A limitation that recurs in these young expatriate aesthetes is an ineffectiveness in the actual handling of a brush, which they make up for in connoisseurship.   Florimond Daintry is typical:

> His power of rendering was questioned, his execution had been called pretentious and feeble; but a conviction had somehow been diffused that he saw things with extraordinary intensity. No one could tell better than he what to paint, and what not to paint. . . .[11]

Gaston Probert, also, "like many of his dawdling coevals," has given much attention to art:

> To make up for his want of talent he espoused the talent of others—and was as sensitive and conscientious about them as he might have been about himself.   He defended certain of Waterlow's purples and greens as he would have defended his own honour. . . .[12]

One sees no sign of serious frustration here, but Gaston has something in common with Rowland Mallet, that much more troubled figure, for whom it would have been a fulfilment if he could have painted pictures instead of merely buying them. Little Bilham is another painter *manqué*: "He had come out to Paris to paint . . . but study had been fatal to him so far as anything *could* be fatal, and his productive power faltered in proportion as his knowledge grew."[13]   There is an ominousness in these American case-histories.

[9] XIX. 444.   [10] XIX. 517.   [11] XXV. 76.
[12] XVIII. 37.   [13] *Amb.*, I. 111.

In various ways the interest of a story may be developed from the attitudes of some such specimen of the American temperament. "A New England Winter" is a series of studies of Boston life: but Boston seen from the viewpoint of Florimond Daintry takes on a singular freshness and piquancy. For him, as a returned expatriate with an eye, simply to see is an adventure, and his excursions into the streets are satisfying episodes for the reader. But Florimond's return is also an occasion for drama for his mother, whose New England consciousness has suffered various kinds of disturbance at the prospect. We see her, in the first chapter, exercised by a problem of Boston domestic manners. She has been trying for some time to improve the deportment of her servant girl— Florimond has been living in a country where servants observe more forms—and at the moment when the story opens the girl has just failed to show deference, by not holding the door long enough to allow her mistress to reach the sidewalk, from which otherwise she could have been dismissed, "with a benevolent and almost maternal smile." But Mrs Daintry cannot satisfy herself that this is "an act of homage that one human being has the right to exact of another."[14] It is an effective little scene, based on a close inspection of the detail of New England relationships. Florimond's response to home and kinsfolk has the effect for her of heightening aspects of ordinary life which she had taken for granted. For example, his gallicised nervous system is acutely sensitive to the relentless pressure of children in American domestic life. Mrs Daintry is quite surprised when he speaks of his sister Joanna as "completely submerged"; she spends so much of her own time "under the waves." "You ought to remember that they exist for you, and not you for them," he remarks, adding the further point of doctrine that "the perpetual presence of children was a great injury to conversation . . . it kept it down so much."[15] For the reader there is a heightening all round. Through Florimond we feel the densely-thronged, almost unbreathable atmosphere of the home; through Mrs Daintry, who knows the world, we are aware of the sharpness of the contrast between the two worlds.

[14] xxv. 50.   [15] xxv. 73.

F

The American child appears frequently as one of the portents confronting the European visitor or the returned expatriate in those stories which owe their main interest to such impressions. The "high firm note" of a child in the hotel dining room is one among the sensations that make Louis Leverett suffer. In the corridor "a pale little girl on parlour skates" shrieks to him to get out of her way. In the same piece ("The Point of View"), the sensible, middle-aged Miss Sturdy, who has returned to Newport, writes to her friend that life in the United States is entirely arranged for the young people, and everyone defers to them. They are well looked after physically, and go to the dentist every week. "But the little boys kick your shins and the little girls offer to slap your face. There's an immense literature entirely addressed to them in which the kicking of shins and the slapping of faces carries the day." She too finds that millions of little feet are "actively engaged in stamping out conversation." She adds that by children she means anyone under twenty. Miss Sturdy is witty and perceptive on the subject of their speech and pronunciation. Her niece is the opposite of many English girls, "who know how to speak but don't know how to talk. My niece knows how to talk but doesn't know how to speak."[16] James himself, in his sketch of Saratoga, comments on the children of that place. They usually open the "hops"; they are "beautifully unembarrassed"; their elders must borrow confidence from their "unfaltering paces." And, of course, they stay up late:

> You meet them far into the evening, roaming over the piazzas and corridors of the hotels—the little girls especially—lean, pale, formidable. Occasionally childhood confesses itself, even when maternity resists, and you see at eleven o'clock at night some poor little bedizened precocity collapsed in slumber in a lonely wayside chair.[17]

Late-rising children "seated in fastidious solitude" in the breakfast room at Newport are among the phenomena noted by the two English aristocrats in "An International Episode." Little Randolph, Daisy Miller's brother, is the most fully

---

[16] XIX. 501.   [17] *Portraits of Places* [= *P.P.*], pp. 333-4.

portrayed American child in James's documentary fiction (we may exclude for the present the remarkable Morgan Moreen, quite a national type in his rather special fashion, in "The Pupil"). He sums up the species. When Winterbourne first encounters him he notes his "aged expression of countenance." The boy speaks with a "sharp, hard little voice—a voice immature, and yet, somehow, not young." The following passage, where he is the subject of talk between Daisy and her mother, together with Winterbourne, has the virtuoso touch:

> "Did you get Randolph to go to bed?" Daisy asked.
> "No, I couldn't induce him"—and Mrs. Miller seemed to confess to the same mild fatalism as her daughter. "He wants to talk to the waiter. He *likes* to talk to that waiter. . . ."
> Randolph's mamma was silent; she kept her attention on the lake. But at last a sigh broke from her. "Well, I don't see how he lives!"
> "Anyhow, it isn't so bad as it was at Dover," Daisy at last opined.
> "And what occurred at Dover?" Winterbourne desired to know.
> "He wouldn't go to bed at all. I guess he sat up all night—in the public parlour. He wasn't in bed at twelve o'clock; it seemed as if he couldn't budge."
> "It was half-past twelve when *I* gave up," Mrs. Miller recorded with passionless accuracy.
> It was of great interest to Winterbourne. "Does he sleep during the day?"
> "I guess he doesn't sleep *very* much," Daisy rejoined.
> "I wish he just *would*!" said her mother. "It seems as if he *must* make it up somehow."
> "Well, I guess it's we that make it up. I think he's real tiresome," Daisy pursued.
> After which, for some moments, there was silence. "Well, Daisy Miller," the elder lady then unexpectedly broke out, 'I shouldn't think you'd want to talk against your own brother."
> "Well, he *is* tiresome, mother," said the girl, but with no sharpness of insistence.
> "Well, he's only nine," Mrs. Miller lucidly urged. . . .[18]

---

[18] XXIII. 28-9.

It is full of American character in the lightest details. James's skill in rendering not only *nuances* of idiom but also expressive intonations enables him to convey the American note with great effect. Comparable with this passage is his treatment of the vague, tender Americanness of Francie Dosson in *The Reverberator*. He applies a similar technique later to some of his English characters, notably in *The Awkward Age*, where it gives a remarkable fulness and finish to the style of Mrs Brookenham and her friends.

It is worth while to turn back to his earliest work for evidence, however limited, of a developing ability to present national characteristics. And here our survey of his American women can best begin. The heroine of "The Story of a Year" (1865), published before he was twenty-two, need not occupy us long, though a reader accustomed to recognising differences between American and English fiction will note the intellectually ambitious quality of her conversation with her *fiancé* in the early pages. But she is not, as it turns out, a strong character. The exchanges between the painter narrator and the pious but witty and self-possessed Miriam Quarterman, in "A Landscape-Painter," of only a year later, are much more readable. James had not yet learnt how to give an American *nuance* to speech and attitude, but the characteristic smartness of response and ability to put the male in his place are fully developed in Miriam. The painter complains:

> ". . . Then, as for being friendless, there are not five people in the world who really care for me."
> "*Really* care? I am afraid you look too close. . . ."[19]

Adela Moore, in "A Day of Days" (1866), is the most manifestly American of the women characters of the stories before 1869. Moderately travelled, socially competent, serious in the pursuit of self-improvement, she has committed herself to a rather limiting existence as her brother's housekeeper. A young Unitarian minister, with whom she talks about her "difficulties," is among her few resources. The sole action of the story is the visit to the house of a young man, who has called in the hope of seeing her brother, and with whom she

[19] *C.T.*, I. 117.

has a conversation so personal and promising that his un-
avoidable departure—he has arranged to go immediately
to Europe—is uncomfortable for both of them. Though he has
given the impression of not wishing to cut the encounter short,
it is very largely due to Adela's initiative that his stay lasts as
long as three hours. The slightly humorous, unromantic
way in which her experience with men is referred to may remind
us of James's later portraits of American women: "The truth
is—we say it with all respect—Adela was an old hand. She
was modest, honest and wise; but, as we have said, she had a
past—a past of which importunate swains in the guise of
morning-callers had been no inconsiderable part; and a great
dexterity in what may be called outflanking these gentlemen
was one of her registered accomplishments."[20]   Gertrude
Whittaker in "Poor Richard" (1867), conforms to the national
type in less specific ways. Her independence and moral
ascendancy over the men who court her are relevant so far as
they go, but this is all that can be said. She strikes no American
note. The brilliant Henrietta Congreve of "Osborne's
Revenge" (1868) shows no further advance in this direction.
She has a range of accomplishments that includes competence
in theological discussion, a fact that recalls an earlier figure
in American literature: Poe's Morella, whose erudition is
"profound," and her powers of mind "gigantic," and who
introduces the narrator of the story to early German mystical
writers. But Henrietta's cultural equipment is not exploited
as a specifically American phenomenon. The perspective
changes with the first productions following upon James's
1869-70 visit to Europe. Charlotte Evans, in "Travelling
Companions," is recognised by the narrator as essentially
a compatriot. He notes her appearance: she has "that
physical delicacy and that personal elegance . . . which seldom
fail to betray my young countrywomen in Europe."[21] Her
voice is "high, thin and nervous."[22] He is delighted with her
freedom and frankness, and the ease with which companionship with her can develop. Here we have the first example
in James's work of an American girl viewed as such by a
discriminating observer.

[20] *C.T.*, I. 148.   [21] *C.T.*, II. 173.   [22] *C.T.*, II. 178.

The peculiar role of women in American civilisation is
the theme of much documentary writing in James's work.
His impressions of the women of Saratoga and Newport, in
the sketches first published (1870) in the *Nation* and later
revised and reprinted in *Portraits of Places* (1883), are a remarkable combination of lyrical charm and sociological pointedness.
The separate descriptions—separateness is inherent in the
situation—of the men lounging in the hotel porticoes, with
negro waiters, boot-blacks and newsvendors, and of the
women, all elegance, "but dressed beyond [their] life and
opportunities,"[23] give pictorial vividness to the old truth.
It is not that the suggestive visual images render abstract
comment unnecessary. On the contrary, we find a great
deal of abstract comment. The images provoke it, they give
scope for wit and analysis, so that we get perhaps more sociology
rather than less through this mode of presentation. For example, the sheer abundance of feminine display, accompanied
by so much good taste, in this society suggests to him that
here we are confronted with "an interesting, indeed a quite
momentous spectacle: the democratization of elegance."
The level of education, of social experience, may be slight,
but she "walks more or less of a queen . . . each uninitiated
nobody."[24] The sketch of Newport tells a slightly different
story. Here, by way of exception, there are a certain number
of men who can use leisure, and the women, though still in
the majority, are less bereft. Observing that it is "part of the
complacent American tradition" that women elsewhere
triumph by "clandestine and reprehensible arts," and that here
they are "both conspicuous and unsophisticated," he offers
an illustration too charming to be refuted:

> You feel this most gratefully as you receive a confident bow
> from a pretty girl in her basket-phaeton. She is very young
> and very pretty, but she has a certain habitual assurance which
> is only a grace the more. She combines, you reflect with
> respectful tenderness, all that is possible in the way of modesty
> with all that is delightful in the way of facility.[25]

---

[23] *P.P.*, p. 331.   [24] *P.P.*, p. 329.
                    [25] *P.P.*, p. 341.

This treatment has all the advantages, with none of the disadvantages, of being dependent on impressions. The analysis never goes beyond what can be seen, and its finest effect is to heighten the image, to make it more significant. James is, on the whole, pleased with what he sees; his interpretative skill is exercised mainly in the interest of the enjoyable. He would be a heavy-handed critic who complained of the limits of his survey.

In the Newport scenes of "An International Episode," the same visually agreeable, sociologically tell-tale spectacle is seen through the eyes of the two English aristocrats. As they approach the Westgate home, passing bright, attractive villas with their shrubs and flower-beds, along the road come "a hundred little basket-phaetons,"[26] each with two ladies inside, openly interested in the English appearance of the visitors. We then have a description of the charming, welcoming Mrs Westgate: she is thirty years old, but has the eyes and smile of a girl of seventeen, and her manner is frank and spontaneous. Pleasant smiles, spontaneous sympathy and interest: these are the dominant notes; and amid all the walks and pastimes of the ensuing days, the "innumerable pretty girls saying innumerable quaint and familiar things,"[27] are the distinguising feature. Men scarcely come into it. Mr Westgate, of course, remains at his office in New York.

A picture to place beside these Newport impressions—but the scene is Boston, and our observer is again Florimond—occupies some pages of "A New England Winter." They present a busy scene of horse-cars and shoppers, with disconcerting symptoms of modern American commercial publicity, but Florimond notices more particularly the women, the immense number of them, "and the impression that they produced of a deluge of petticoats." He notes their look; that is, of being "perfectly at home on the road," of "always meeting the gaze of crowds."[28] He feels that he is in a city of women—a country of women; as if there were a war, and all the men were away. "A New England Winter" is, of course, a story about a woman's world. Whom does Florimond meet but women—his mother and her sister-in-law, his sister

[26] XIX. 265.   [27] XIX. 284.   [28] XXV. 109.

Joanna, Rachel Torrence and Pauline Mesh? Joanna's husband, Pauline's husband are not in it; we do not meet them; they make no contribution to the events that are unfolded, such as they are. They attend to their business.

Most of the epistolary commentators in "The Point of View" (returned expatriates or visitors to America) have some impressions to convey on this subject. For M. Lejaune, a hostile critic, the women are pretty, but as he sees them everywhere at large in streets and trains, and notes their frank appraising looks, he is aware of only one implication: the search for the husband. Some never find one, but they feel no disgrace: they just go about unmarried. They have "no imagination, no sensibility, no desire for the convent."[29] M. Lejaune is absurd, but his point of view is a contribution of a kind, rather of the nature of caricature. We see how American female society looks to a person who entirely misses its point and its charm. Miss Sturdy, as a woman herself and no romantic, is more helpful. She says of the American system of bringing up girls, that when it succeeds it produces "the most charming creatures possible," but when it doesn't the failure is disastrous. If the girl isn't nice, this method will give her no bias towards propriety of manners. But on the whole she approves of a world in which girls are not shy because there is nothing to be afraid of, and where manners are "very gentle, very humane."[30]

That it is "a diurnal necessity of the conscientious American woman" to buy something is one of James's observations in the Newport essay, made with indulgence. "An American woman who respects herself . . . must buy something every day of her life,"[31] Mrs Westgate asserts. Sophy Ruck and her mother (in "The Pension Beaurepas") represent the seamy side of this tradition. The patient, sacrificial male, no longer segregated by business but on vacation, in enforced idleness through overwork, now appears openly, not only in his role as an exploited figure but also as an example of pathetic incapacity to enjoy. Mr Ruck is ill, and his interest in life has been so restricted to making money that the visit to Europe which, for his wife and daughter, affords an opportunity for orgiastic

[29] XIX. 522.   [30] XIX. 504.   [31] XIX. 282.

spending, gives him no pleasure.   The function of the American
male (Strether reflects on this point *apropos* of Jim Pocock)
is to "pay."   The following passage where the narrator and
Mr Ruck witness the return of the ladies glutted with spoils
from the Geneva shops, provides a further demonstration,
comparable with the "Daisy Miller" excerpt, of what can be
done stylistically with the rock-bottom idiom of American
family life:

> "He can't make a fuss about *that*," said Mrs. Ruck.
> "Well, you'll see!"—the girl had unshaken confidence.
> The subject of this serenity, however, went on in the same
> tone.   "Have you got it in your pocket? . . .why don't you hang
> it round you?"
> "I'll hang it round *you* if you don't look out!" cried Miss
> Ruck.
> "Don't you want to show it off to this gentleman?" he
> sociably continued.
> "Mercy, how you do carry on!" his wife sighed.
> "Well, I want to be lively.   There's every reason to be.
> We're going up to Chamouni."
> "You're real restless—that's what's the matter with you."
> And Mrs. Ruck roused herself from her own repose.
> "No, I ain't," said her husband.   "I never felt so quiet.   I
> feel as peaceful as a little child."
> Mrs. Ruck, who had no play of mind, looked at her daughter
> and at me.   "Well, I hope you'll improve," she stated with
> certain flatness.[32]

The idiom has great possibilities, for these people are at their
ease in the use of language.   Where wit is lacking, there is a
stylistic value in flatness itself, combined with such assurance.
Remarks without salt or savour, inadequacies beyond criticism
or analysis, become the material of a dreadfully expressive
dialogue.   In their rudeness and casualness to Mr Ruck,
the women testify to certain unchallengeable rights and
immunities, the truths by which they live, and this gives their
speech more than ordinary domestic callousness.   Women in
America are the custodians of the finer values, those that
concern artistic sensibility.   Sophy Ruck and her mother

[32] XIX. 394.

interpret this role in their own fashion by putting such things as foreign cathedrals in their place. ("I don't know what it may be for regular attendants, but it doesn't meet my idea of a really pleasant place of worship. Few of these old buildings do.")[33] They can dispense with mountains (they are in Switzerland), having seen plenty at home. They claim an intellectual life: Mrs Ruck likes to study things for herself; she is "death on comparing." One of the enhancing qualities of their speech is a special version of what we should call "quaintness," were it not so shocking. We meet it in Sophy's speeches about her father: "He used to be so bright and natural, but now he's quite subdued. It's about time he should improve, anyway. We went out last night to look at the jewellers' windows. We saw some lovely things, but it didn't seem to rouse father."[34]

Miss Violet Ray, one of the letter-writers of "A Bundle of Letters," and a more refined specimen of the American girl abroad than Sophy Ruck, is no less adamant on the question of the function of fathers. Her letter from Paris to her New York friend opens with a page of irritable comment on her father's having received a telegram summoning him home. He has only been prevented by the most stubborn resistance on the part of her mother and herself from bringing them back too. She expresses the loftiest indifference to his business problems, of which she has never pretended to know anything, and resents his fussiness over her Parisian spending projects. The heroine of a much later story, "Miss Gunton of Pough-keepsie" (1900), is exposed to no such irritations. She has only to cable to a grandfather on the subject of "drawing," and invariably the reply is "draw."

Where exploitation in the material sense does not arise there are other ways in which the American girl may be demanding. Daisy Miller has always been accustomed to attentiveness on the part of her many "gentlemen friends." The lack of such society makes Europe irksome to her, and it is her naive stubbornness in making what she can of such male company as Rome offers that proves her undoing. Daisy makes demands on Winterbourne in Vevey, and when he

[33] XIX. 393. [34] XIX. 364-5.

arrives in Rome in obedience to her request she shows little recognition of his having adapted his plans for her sake. "He remembered how a cynical compatriot had once told him that American women—the pretty ones . . . were at once the most exacting in the world and the least endowed with a sense of indebtedness."[35] Miranda Hope, the earnest young woman from Bangor, Maine, whose letters to her mother form the longest epistolary contribution to "A Bundle of Letters," is demanding, in general, on behalf of her sex: European women she finds "downtrodden," "snubbed," "bullied."[36] And she is demanding, in a more particular way, in her pertly confident references to one William Platt of her home town. She insists that her letters for general circulation are not to be shown to him: he must write himself if he wishes to see letters from her. In her final missive she records that William Platt has written: "I knew he'd have to write, and I was bound I'd make him."[37] She illustrates the less alluring aspects of the independence of the young American female. As Louis Leverett puts it: "She looks at everything, goes everywhere, passes on her way with her clear quiet eyes wide open; skirting the edge of obscene abysses without suspecting them . . . exciting, without knowing it, the most injurious suspicions; and always holding her course—without a stain, without a sense, without a fear, without a charm."[38]

A few of James's young women have these uncomely traits, but the predominating impression is of niceness, freedom, frankness, and an attitude to men which makes for easy, innocent friendship. Before continuing with examples, we may note at this point that W. D. Howells's novels of the eighteen-seventies and early eighteen-eighties also have a number of pleasant portraits of American girls. The slightness and restricted range of these works are apparent enough, but his artistic modesty forestalls damaging comparisons with James, and his delicacy of touch gives him a distinction of his own. In tracing the emergence of the American girl as a central figure in the American novel of manners, we must give the heroines of Howells their place. In *A Foregone Conclusion* (1875),

---

[35] XXIII. 44.   [36] XIX. 426.
[37] XIX. 472-3.   [38] XIX. 445.

Florida Vervain presents a slight variation upon a familiar theme. The young American consul, Ferris, finds it "charming to be with a beautiful girl who neither regarded him with distrust nor expected him to ask her in marriage because he sat alone with her": this is the common form. But Florida is different in being stricter in certain respects than her cheerful indiscreet mother. She is more serious in her churchgoing, even to the extent of favouring ritualism. (Ferris conjectures that the latter comes from "mere love of any form she could make sure of.") Florida's mother provides her with a succession of male teachers, all of whom fall in love with her; and when Don Ippolito, the forlorn Venetian priest, is appointed to that delicate office, he does the same. He misunderstands Florida's generous but somewhat extravagant interest in his problems. He has lost his faith, and wishes to free himself from the priesthood; and she, with her innocence and ignorance, and her American unawareness of boundaries and limits, encourages this project. His hope that she will return his love is destroyed in an embarrassing scene, and disappointment brings him to a premature decline. *The Lady of the Aroostook* (1878) is the story of a simple American girl of country breeding, who travels on board the *Aroostook* from Boston to Trieste, as the captain's guest and without a chaperone. The point of the situation is that the male passengers behave with chivalry. "They were Americans and they knew how to worship a woman." Minor misunderstandings occur, however. Lydia is so free from coquetry that her readiness to walk the deck with anyone who invites her gives anxiety to the jealous Staniford, though he recognises that "her fearlessness was like that of wild birds in those desert islands where man has never come." When Lydia eventually reaches Venice, she meets with a succession of exemplary situations illustrating the difference in outlook, especially with respect to female behaviour, between Europe and the world she knows. Her hostess is appalled to learn the circumstances in which she has made her journey, but her English husband says: "I rather like it, you know. It strikes me as a genuine bit of American civilisation." *A Fearful Responsibility* (1883) is another story of an American girl who comes to Venice. The American Mr and Mrs Elmore are confronted with the problem of how to advise their newly-arrived guest who, on her journey to Venice, has been the object of a young Austrian officer's attentions. Mr Elmore, the less liberal by American standards, wonders how far she encouraged him: but his wife protests that anyway "it was all in the simplicity and innocence of her heart," and she is inclined to view indulgently the impulsive behaviour of the officer. Mr Elmore condemns the latter for presuming on her being American: for taking a liberty he would not have dreamed of taking with Italian or German ladies. The young Austrian writes to her: this again is thought irregular. She sees him at a dance, refuses at first to dance with him (he hasn't been introduced); and then, on learning that it is permissible to dance with a person to whom one has not been intrdouced, finds a means of asking him. And this Mr Elmore likes: "That was very pretty in her; it was sovereignly gracious." The novel is largely composed of incidents of this kind, illustrating differences and problems in the sphere of manners. There are occasions for conversation on the general topic of the young person, between Mrs Elmore who champions Lily and Mr Elmore who has serious reservations about the American style of upbringing. He finds her unresponsive to Tintoretto. "She has come here," he says, "from a country where girls have always had the best time in the world . . . ." and he holds that American girls who travel should be kept "in total exile" from good times, parties, attentions and so forth, and forced, "through the hard discipline of social deprivation, to take some interest in the things that make for civilisation—in history, in art, in humanity." Mrs Elmore replies: "Now, there I differ from you, Owen. I think American girls are the nicest girls in the world, just as they are. . . . If you are getting so Europeanised, I think the sooner we go home the better."

The variety of James's heroines almost tempts one to suppose that he planned deliberately to cover a range of types. Mary Garland, the *fiancée* of Roderick Hudson, is quite different from the girls of the Newport world and from those, like Daisy Miller, whose manners are from further west. She belongs clearly to a more conservative New England tradition, but she

shows no sign of relinquishing the austerity of outlook which is
suffering modification among the younger members of the
Wentworth family in *The Europeans*. When Rowland invites
Mary to go for a walk with him she hesitates, looking to Mrs
Hudson as if for permission; and when he reminds her that
they may not have further opportunities of enjoying each
other's company, she asks "with homely logic," why they
should then attempt to be friends. When Rowland refers
apologetically to his having no occupation, and says that
Europe makes this less of a burden and a disgrace, Mary does
not help him out. She recommends him to find something to
do. There is some development in her when she comes to
Europe. Though remaining entirely herself, in her fine
integrity and seriousness, she opens her mind to the wonders
of Rome, and Rowland notes with pleasure her awakened
desire to see and learn.

> She was always eager, alert, responsive; she had always her
> large settled smile, which reminded him of some clear ample
> "spare-room," some expectant guest-chamber, as they said in
> New England, with its windows up for ventilation. She might
> be grave by nature, she might be sad by circumstance, she
> might have secret doubts and pangs, but she was essentially
> young and strong and fresh—able to respond to any vivid
> appeal. . . . It was not amusement and sensation she coveted,
> but knowledge—facts that she might noiselessly lay away,
> piece by piece, in the fragrant darkness of her serious mind,
> so that under this head she should not be a perfectly portion-
> less bride.[39]

The New England conscience shows itself in a special way
in her desire to be sure that what she appreciates is really the
best. She is remarkably selfless in her relationship with
Roderick, making no personal claims though capable of
being wounded and of showing resistance when her sacrificial
devotion goes unrecognised by Mrs Hudson.

With Bessie Alden, in "An International Episode," we are
back in sociable Newport, though as an example of New
England good faith she is no less earnest than Mary. She is
Mrs Westgate's sister, but more "in the Boston style—the

[39] *R.H.*, p. 300.

quiet Boston." She even seems a little "grave and backward";[40] she certainly does not talk incessantly like her sister. Her conversation with Lord Lambeth turns on novels depicting English life, by Thackeray and George Eliot, which she has read and he has not. According to her sister, she has studied Greek. But, after attributing to her "a fine Boston *gaucherie*," Mrs Westgate says what is most to the point concerning her character: "She's a dear good girl. . . . She is not in the least a flirt . . . she doesn't know the alphabet of any such vulgarity. She's very simple, very serious, very true."[41] Her simplicity and straightforward American curiosity are mistaken for something else by Percy Beaumont, when she questions him about the young Lord Lambeth's "position." Passages of dialogue like the following, surely the material of good light comedy, are among those which make one wonder at James's not making anything of such opportunities in his plays. The Anglo-American misunderstanding could surely have furnished something highly stageworthy:

"Mr. Beaumont," she had said, "please tell me something about Lord Lambeth's family. How would you say it in England?—his position."

"His position?" Percy's instinct was to speak as if he had never heard of such a matter.

"His rank—or whatever you call it. Unfortunately we haven't got a 'Peerage', like the people in Thackeray."

"That's a great pity," Percy pleaded. "You'd find the whole matter in black and white, and upon my honour I know very little about it.

The girl seemed to wonder at this innocence. "You know at least whether he's what they call a great noble."

"Oh yes, he's in that line."

"Is he a 'peer of the realm'?"

"Well, as yet—very nearly."

"And has he any other title than Lord Lambeth?"

"His title's the Marquis of Lambeth. . . . He's the son of the Duke of Bayswater."

"The eldest—?"

"The only one."

"And are his parents living?"

---

[40] XIX. 275-6.   [41] XIX. 282.

"Naturally—as to his father. If *he* weren't living Lambeth would be a duke."

"So that when 'the old Lord' dies"—and the girl smiled with more simplicity than might have been expected in one so "sharp"—"he'll become Duke of Bayswater?"

"Of course," said their common friend. "But his father's in excellent health."

"And his mother?"

Percy seemed amused. "The Duchess is built to last. . . ."[42]

As a result of Percy's intervention Lambeth is quickly summoned home.

When Bessie pays her visit to England—her English books have prepared her for the classic "passionate pilgrim's" response—Mrs Westgate appears in a changed and highly significant role. All her New England generosity and openness leave her: she proves to be shrewdly knowing about the pitfalls that await simple Americans, and by warning Bessie against English prejudice and exclusiveness she adds greatly to the harm that has already been done. "Remember," she says," that you're not in your innocent little Boston"; and she explains that there are two sorts of American girls in Europe: those who walk alone and those who don't. Bessie is to be one of those who don't.[43] There will be no getting into touch with Lord Lambeth, whom Bessie admits that she likes very much; and she is very hurt when she learns that otherwise she will be suspected of having followed him. Eventually, by accident, they meet him and his aristocratic friends. Mrs Westgate, who has a fund of stories about the wrong way to treat Americans, maintains a sardonic and formidable manner. The crucial question now is whether Lambeth's mother, the Duchess, will call on them. She does call, but after some delay, and Mrs Westgate makes it clear to Bessie that it was with the intention of snubbing them. Lambeth, in spite of family opposition, actually proposes to Bessie, but in the state of mind which has been induced in her she refuses him.

The strange behaviour of Mrs Westgate, who not only amuses herself at the expense of the English, but seems to find a malignant satisfaction in killing Bessie's happiness, affords

[42] xix. 285-6.　　　　　[43] xix. 299.

a transition in this survey from the innocent American maiden to certain aspects of the American married woman. The partial segregation of the sexes, due to the male compulsion to overwork and the female monopoly of all cultural and social activity, could have a variety of consequences. One of the possibilities, if we may judge from this example, is an un-sweetening of the pretty American girl, with a compensatory development of her wit and her mental curiosity, sometimes to the point of inhumanity. The change in Mrs Westgate between Newport and London is rather drastic—a piece of foreshortening, perhaps. In Newport she could still conform to the traditional role of the pretty young American woman, free in manners and generous to visitors: but she knows enough to be aware that in London this charming scheme of things breaks down. In London she is a middle-aged woman, impatient and perhaps a little jealous of American innocence, and thrown back on the pleasures of a ready tongue. So little married herself, she is not to be trusted in her attitude towards Bessie's prospects.

But before we turn to other examples of middle-aged women, more must be said of their younger sisters. A special category of young girls, peripheral perhaps to American life but highly relevant to the study of American manners, merits brief consideration. These are the daughters of expatriates, who manifest the national traits in their own fashion, in spite of complete unfamiliarity with the environment where they were developed. One of these cases is Euphemia Cleve, who marries a "shining sinful Frenchman" and becomes Mme de Mauves, in the story named after her. The second section of the story gives a most instructive account of her history. The daughter of a wealthy American widow addicted to Homburg and Nice, she has been educated in a Parisian con-vent where she has acquired an especially perilous form of the national romanticism: an obsession with rank and with what she supposes to be the inherited virtues of the aristocracy. She wishes to marry an aristocrat (her mental image is of a gentleman "rather ugly than handsome and rather poor than rich,"[44] but proud and fine), and her wish comes to fruition

[44] XVIII. 202.

G

through her friendship at the convent with a French girl who has a penniless, dissipated but plausible brother. The account of the courtship, and of her dealings with the de Mauves family, has some telling points. For Richard de Mauves her style of innocence is a new sensation:

> Sometimes a word, a gesture of Euphemia's gave him the oddest sense of being, or of seeming at least, almost bashful; for she had a way of not dropping her eyes according to the mysterious virginal mechanism, of not fluttering out of the room when she found him there alone, of treating him rather as a glorious than as a pernicious influence—a radiant frankness of demeanour in fine, despite an infinite natural reserve. . . .[45]

M. de Mauves proposes to her *à l'Americaine*, that is, without first consulting her mother. Paradoxically, Mrs Cleve concludes that only very questionable French gentlefolk would go about things in that way, but her intervention only postpones the disastrous arrangement, which Euphemia soon has reason to regret. As the story develops, the aspect of her character that becomes most evident is a moral inflexibility that not only precludes a love affair with the young American, Longmore, but finally drives her erring husband to suicide. Her friend Mrs Draper says, in her introductory account of her for Longmore's benefit: "The lightest of *us* [*i.e.*, Americans] have a ballast that they [*i.e.*, the French] can't imagine, and the poorest a moral imagination that they don't require."[46] And her history seems to imply that the New England qualities may develop powerfully in a young woman whose mother has repudiated them, and in an environment not obviously favourable. What Euphemia has acquired in her convent is nothing Catholic and nothing French, but simply the special form of absolutism that shapes her for a classic American fate.

Aurora Church, in "The Pension Beaurepas" and "The Point of View," is an American girl who has lived in Europe and openly revolts against her mother's European attitudes. The mother is merely an entertaining caricature, but some of Aurora's comments, especially on her return to the United States, have a serious point, and are worth having as the expression of an unusual point of view. She notes, for example,

on the Atlantic voyage that the young men who seek her company might easily be one's brothers or one's cousins. ("The
extent to which one isn't in danger from them—my dear, my
dear!")[47] But later she sees an element of anticlimax in so
many harmless attentions leading to nothing in particular:
"Society seems oddly to consist of a sort of innocent jilting."[48]
She has looked forward to walking alone, but when one has
done it for a week or two, and driven out with a gentleman in a
buggy, "that's about all there is to it"; so she is mildly disappointed. Christina Light, the object of Roderick Hudson's
infatuation, presents an even more special case in that she is not,
as it turns out, wholly of American parentage. This accounts
for certain discriminations on the part of Rowland, who notes
on her first appearance that, "her beauty had, in spite of her
youth, an air of longer history than consorts, in general, with
the rather extemporised look of American loveliness."[49] Later,
in conversation with Roderick, he remarks that her charm
differs from that of the " 'nice girl' or the 'dear girl' as we have
been accustomed to know those blest creatures. Our American
girls are accused of being more forward than any others, and
this wonderful damsel is nominally an American. But it has
taken twenty years of Europe to make her what she is."[50]
Nevertheless, *femme fatale* though she is, Christina certainly
has her share of "ballast" and "moral imagination," and even a
touch of transcendentalism. She answers men back, and with
her loquacity goes sometimes a humorous freedom, faintly
American though lacking in the true flavour. She is very
much a mixture, and her role in life involves one side of her in
continual disharmony with the other, a complication which she
works off in rather fatiguing talk. "It was Christina's constant
practice to remind you of the complexity of her character, of
the subtlety of her mind, of her troublous faculty of seeing
everything in a dozen different lights."[51] With more physical
charm than is good for her or for anyone else, she is in other
respects something of a bore. However, as an example of how
the American characteristics can be distorted and misplaced
she makes an interesting addition to the collection.

[47] xix. 484.   [48] xix. 538.   [49] *R.H.*, p. 134.
[50] *R.H.*, p. 165.   [51] *R.H.*, pp. 394-5.

I have discussed in another place some of the more engaging American heroines—Verena Tarrant, Francie Dosson and also Isabel Archer, the greatest of all except Millie Theale, who belongs to the later phase of James's art. Verena is distinguished from the other New England girls by having a larger share of the traditional ease and openness. Her social background has made, in a special degree, for freedom: her preference for "free unions" over marriage chills Olive Chancellor. It has not given her ballast, but she has picked up remarkably little harm in her father's world of disreputable eccentricities. Basil Ransom's mental comment, that she has "queer, bad lecture-blood in her veins"[52] is mere humorous pessimism. Though a Southern conservative, he likes the good-natured assurance with which she answers him back. Like several of James's American heroines of scanty training she triumphantly avoids striking a wrong note, and her easy jokes sometimes have a beautiful rightness. What her antecedents have done for her primarily is to make her untrammelled and unpretentious. Francie is in the same category as Daisy, but admirably differentiated: one can see that having Mr Dosson as a father would account for some of the difference. (Mr Miller, the absent father of Daisy and Randolph, invites the imagination to do its worst.) Isabel Archer is different not only in her depth of sensibility and range of imagination, which enable her to represent American aspiration as none of the other heroines can, but also in background and upbringing. Albany, not New England; a handsome, sensitive if rather unreliable father; irregular education, but with visits to Europe; freedom from the narrower forms of puritanism; the dubious privilege of being the intellectual superior of all the other members of her family: these factors contribute to the making of Isabel herself as an individual, yes, but also as a type or with some of the traits of a type. James plants her firmly in a specific social, cultural and domestic setting. But there will be occasion to return to Isabel later in this survey. In James's last three great novels the portrayal of American heroines is carried several stages further and these will occupy us fully in their turn.

[52] *The Bostonians* [= *B.*], II. 33.

Of the middle-aged American women Mrs Tristram, in
The American (1877), to whom Newman owes the crucial introduction to Claire de Cintré, is of particular interest. The brief
but very effective account of her background and development
in the third chapter may be placed along with the second section
of "Madame de Mauves," which has already been noted, and
the more ambitious first chapter of *Roderick Hudson* with its
masterly study of the evolution of Rowland Mallet, and the
third and sixth chapters of *The Portrait of a Lady*, where the
early outlook of Isabel Archer is closely studied. They are
the equivalent in James's art to the fifteenth chapter of *Middlemarch*, with its introductory treatment of Lydgate's early
circumstances and aspirations. George Eliot's ability to place
a character in an environment, tracing the influences that form
it and the factors that make for limitation or self-deception,
is rightly praised: but James's application of this art, in his
earlier work, to American characters and their environment
deserves especial respect, in view of the imaginative effort
demanded by the relatively new national themes. In his acute
study of Mrs Tristram he depicts the restless, unsatisfied
American woman. Hers is an extreme case: her husband
is not a hardworking business man, but an idle expatriate.
With her plain face she has lost the man she was in love with,
and for perverse reasons has married a fool. Even for an
American woman, she is peculiarly concerned with her own
development and aspirations, which life has given her peculiarly little opportunity to further. The portentousness of outlook engendered in her by her particular conjunction of character and circumstances finds definition in an idiom saturated
in Americanism:

> ... Her taste on many points differed from that of her husband;
> and though she made frequent concessions to the dull small
> fact that he had married her it must be confessed that her
> reserves were not always muffled in pink gauze. They were
> founded upon the vague project of her some day affirming her-
> self in her totality; to which end she was in advance getting
> herself together, building herself high, inquiring, in short,
> into her dimensions.[53]

---

[53] *The American* [= *Amer.*], pp. 31-2.

. . . Restless, discontented, visionary, without personal ambitions but with a certain avidity of imagination, she was interesting from this sense she gave of her looking for her ideals by a lamp of strange and fitful flame. She was full—both for good and for ill—of beginnings that came to nothing; but she had nevertheless, morally, a spark of the sacred fire.[54]

James knew how to make a character-type work for him towards the building up of a novel, and a talkative, middle-aged woman with time on her hands is a valuable resource in the early part of this book. Mrs Tristram serves to draw Newman out, just as Maria Gostrey later draws Strether out. The long conversation in Chapter Three is sustained mainly by her persistent curiosity and freedom of comment. She tells him that he is "deep," threatens to say ("with a certain air") that he is "as cold as a fish," promises herself that some day she will see him "in a magnificent rage."[55] By various tactical strokes she leads him on to speak of what he really wants in life, and this brings us to the main action of the novel. Mrs Tristram is a mixed character: genuinely intelligent and kind, but with no settled sphere for the exercise of her virtues, obliged to take her mental exercise where she can, and liable (like Mrs Westgate, but less so) to amuse herself in slightly inhuman ways. After the conclusion of the Bellegarde affair, which she has helped to promote, she tells Newman that it would not have "really done"; and musingly adds: "I should have been curious to see; it would have been very strange."[56] And she admits that curiosity was partly the motive for her participation, upon which she receives from Newman the one angry look he was ever to give her. Curiosity about how other people's lives will shape, on the part of those who are reduced to the role of spectator, is one of the common themes in James.

Mrs Luna, the sister of Olive Chancellor in *The Bostonians* (1886), has some of the qualities of Mrs Tristram's type: shrewdness, humour, talkativeness and a tendency to take the initiative with the male; and James uses her to give the novel a lively opening. It is she who entertains the young visitor, Basil Ransom, before Olive puts in an appearance, and her brisk comments on the latter are an effective introduction.

[54] *Amer.*, pp. 33-4.   [55] *Amer.*, pp. 38-9.   [56] *Amer.*, p. 449.

This freedom of reference before a complete stranger may be seen as a point of American manners, but it is also a compositional resource for a novelist. Mrs Luna likes attentions ("mind you come and see me in New York"),[57] and reproaches Ransom later for neglecting her. At Mrs Burrage's party, where she tries to monopolise him and prevent him from hearing Verena, she really proves herself to be the most intolerable of her class ("vain, egotistical, grasping, odious").[58]

It is characteristic that the difference between the married women and the spinsters in James's novels is often not great. The spinsters, like Maria Gostrey, take the initiative in conversations with men, and the married women are glad to have another man to talk to. An inveterately managing attitude towards the male; an ascendancy, achieved by wit and superior knowledge, but also forced upon them, and therefore accompanied sometimes by a straining or distortion of the feminine note: these are recurring features.

Some characters may be seen as clear representatives of a type, others as having distant connexions with it. For example, the Baroness in *The Europeans*, in her cosmopolitanised way, and with her greater physical charm, is not so very far removed from the category we have just noted. Other characters seem to stand by themselves. One of these is the admirable Dr Prance in *The Bostonians*. Ransom does, in fact, see her as a type: "a perfect example of the 'Yankee female'—the figure which, in the unregenerate imagination of the cotton-States, was produced by the New England school-system, the Puritan code, the ungenial climate, the absence of chivalry. Spare, dry, hard, without a curve, an inflection or a grace. . . ."[59] But he comes to appreciate her individuality. Her dry quaintness and candour do duty for a sense of humour. In a room full of supporters of the woman's movement, she expresses superb detachment: "Men and women are all the same to me. . . . I don't see any difference. There is room for improvement in both sexes . . . they ought to live better; that's what they ought to do."[60] When she leaves the assembly without hearing the lecture, she says to Ransom: "All I

[57] *B.*, I. 10.   [58] *B.*, II. 50.
[59] *B.*, I. 48.   [60] *B.*, I. 49.

know is I don't want anyone to tell *me* what a lady can do!"[61]

Mrs Headway, the much divorced and compromised American woman who wants to be accepted in European society and to marry an English aristocrat; the appalling George Flack, representative of American journalism and enemy to all delicacy and privacy; Isabel Archer's friend, Henrietta Stackpole, the robust exponent of American values; these are among the figures one would expect to find in novels illustrating the national character. James does full justice to them as individuals, but he does not develop elsewhere, to any great extent, the types to which they belong. Matthias Pardon is in the same occupational category as Flack, and has similar aims, but is quite different as a personality. In such characters as Sam Singleton, the artist, and the reformers in *The Bostonians*, general national traits are swallowed up in more specialised qualities derived from their way of life. Some of James's American characters—Dr Sloper, Olive Chancellor—may seem to be memorable chiefly for strong personal qualities that are not specifically national: but there is room for discussion here, and Dr Sloper will be considered in the next chapter.

[61] *B.*, I. 61.

V

American Themes

JAMES, Howells and their disciple Edith Wharton come quite close together in certain parts of their work. For example, in the three novels, *The Rise of Silas Lapham* (1884), *The Reverberator* (with a little support from "The Pension Beaurepas" and other works) and *The Custom of the Country* (1913), we have virtually a tradition in miniature, depicting points of American manners. The relationship between them is interesting as a sample of James's participation in developments that belong to literary history. There are similarities in subject-matter. In all three novels there is a successful business man, with a marriageable daughter or daughters, moving in a different social environment from that in which his money was made, and in contact with Americans who represent a more conservative and civilised way of life than his own. Silas Lapham, who has made a fortune in paint, has come to live in Boston, but in an unfashionable area, and now he commits himself to building a house on the Back Bay. The Laphams wish to do their best for their two daughters, but have little idea of how to set about it. On holiday in New England resorts they have no skill in making contact with fellow holiday visitors: "They lurked helplessly about in the hotel parlour, looking on and not knowing how to put themselves forward."[1] And at home, "they lived richly to themselves, not because they were selfish, but because they did not know how to do otherwise."[2] They have elementary notions of hospitality. Lapham would bring "a heavy-buying customer home to pot-luck; neither of them imagined dinners."[3] The details of "tea" at the Laphams are documentary: "creamed oysters, birds, hot biscuit, two kinds of cake, and dishes of stewed and canned fruit and honey."[4] Problems arise when they become socially involved with the Coreys, an old

---

[1] *The Rise of Silas Lapham* [= *S.L.*], (1948 edn., World's Classics), p. 26.
[2] *S.L.*, p. 26. [3] *S.L.*, p. 24. [4] *S.L.*, p. 36.

Boston family, Tom Corey having become interested in one of Lapham's daughters. In one of their harassed conversations on the terrifying question of entertaining them, Lapham appals his wife with the suggestion that he might invite Mr Corey "to a fish dinner at Tafts."[5] The Coreys on their side are fully aware of the Lapham's deficiencies. Tom is explicit: "I don't believe they have the habit of wine at table. I suspect that when they don't drink tea or coffee with their dinner, they drink ice-water."[6] And his father, a much travelled old dilettante, feels that these drawbacks can be decisive: "people who have never yet given a dinner, how is society to assimilate them?"[7] These troubles reach their climax when the Laphams are invited to dinner with the Coreys. Mrs Lapham torments herself over the phrasing of the letter of acceptance, and hesitates between her husband's given name and her own in the signature. Ought they to wear low necks? Her husband recommends that she should order a dinner dress, and then at a later stage panics over his own sartorial arrangements. Having at first decided to wear a frockcoat, he suddenly rushes to his tailor to be measured for a dresscoat, only to suffer further torments of doubt over the colour of his waistcoat and the question of gloves. At the dinner itself Mr Bellingham, an established Bostonian, tucks the corner of his napkin into his collar ("He confessed himself an uncertain shot with a spoon"),[8] and Lapham follows his example, but changes his mind when no-one else does. He is in trouble over his wine glasses (he has heard of a well-known politician who turned his down at a public dinner), but finally he drinks what he is given—and takes too much. The whole episode might have been designed as a cautionary illustration for a manual of social etiquette.

Such situations as this, turning upon what to wear, how to answer an invitation, and so forth, would be quite uncharacteristic of James: but it is only fair to Howells to say that this is a rather simple and elementary example of his treatment of manners. James deals frequently with situations in which one person's attitudes or rules collide with those of another or of a community: but the centre of interest is never the point

[5] *S.L.*, p. 153.   [6] *S.L.*, p. 145.
[7] *S.L.*, p. 145.   [8] *S.L.*, p. 201.

of behaviour for its own sake or for the stock problems it raises or for its relevance to a phase of society, though all these considerations may make their contribution. When Isabel Archer proposes to sit up with the gentlemen after her aunt has gone to bed, the latter forbids her to do so with the words: "You're not at your blest Albany, my dear."[9] But this significant little incident is valuable mainly for what it reflects of the characters of all concerned, especially Isabel herself. There is a neat stroke in *The Bostonians*, in the scene where Olive decides not to introduce Basil Ransom to Verena, and again the point of manners in itself is subordinate to the witty use of it:

> The three stood together in the middle of the long, character-istic room, and, for the first time in her life, Olive chose not to introduce two persons who met under her roof. She hated Europe, but she could be European if it were necessary. Neither of her companions had an idea that in leaving them simply planted face to face (the terror of the American heart) she had so high a warrant. . . .[10]

It will be convenient to postpone consideration of *The Reverberator* until Edith Wharton's novel has been briefly considered. *The Custom of the Country* also contains episodes which might have been composed especially for the sake of the information and guidance that they provide on differences of social usage. The Spraggs, newly rich like the Laphams, differ from them in the grim fact that they live in an hotel, in the New York of a later date than Howells's Boston. Undine Spragg's exploitation of her father recalls Sophy Ruck, except for differences of style ("She had two ways of getting things out of him . . . the tender wheedling way, and the harsh-lipped and cold . . .").[11] Her invitation to dine with Laura Fairford, sister of Ralph Marvell whom she has already met and is later to marry, recalls Lapham's invitation to dine with the Coreys. Undine cannot understand Laura's role until the masseuse tells them that "when a young man in society wants to meet a girl again, he gets his sister to ask her."[12] Laura's letter has been addressed to Mrs Spragg—another lesson: "Don't you know it's the

[9] *P.L.*, I. 80.
[10] *B.*, I. 105-6.
[11] *The Custom of the Country* [= *C.C.*], 1954 edn., p. 33.
[12] *C.C.*, p. 10.

thing in the best society to pretend that girls can't do anything without their mothers' permission?"[13] Undine answers the letter (in her mother's name!), an operation which raises problems for her. She has read in the *Boudoir Chat* of a Sunday paper that "the smartest women are using the new pigeon-blood notepaper with white ink."[14] It was disappointing that Mrs Fairford should have used old-fashioned white writing paper. The dinner itself surprises Undine with its simplicity.

The hotel life of the Spraggs is in the tradition of American helplessness. Mrs Spragg relies on her masseuse for some kind of human relationship; her husband is "compelled to seek a semblance of social life at the hotel bar."[15] The description of the hotel breakfast room where "other pallid families, richly dressed . . . [were] silently eating their way through a bill-of-fare which seemed to have ransacked the globe for gastronomic incompatibilities,"[16] while the waiters turned their backs on them with studied indifference, is a typical example of Edith Wharton's ruthlessness in social rapportage. She does not shrink from the details: bananas and cream, crab mayonnaise, fried livers. Howells had been equally specific, we recall, about the Laphams' high teas. Maria Gostrey's achievement in making Waymarsh breakfast correctly should not be forgotten, but on the whole these points of manners are not prominent in James.

When James wrote *The Reverberator* he had already produced Mr Ruck, upon whom Mr Spragg is so closely modelled. Mr Ruck is the more human of the two, Edith Wharton's harassed creation being a slightly mechanical vehicle for the making of points about American businessmen and American fathers. Mr Dosson deviates in some pleasing ways from the type, though it might be claimed that in this he is no less documentary than characters who conform closely: we find Americanness in the line of his deviation. James's treatment is primarily pictorial, atmospheric, poetic:

> The court was roofed with glass; the April air was mild; the cry of women selling violets came in from the street and,

---

13 *C.C.*, p. 11.   14 *C.C.*, p. 17.
15 *C.C.*, p. 12.   16 *C.C.*, pp. 31-2.

mingling with the rich hum of Paris, seemed to bring with it faintly the odour of the flowers. There were other odours in the place, warm succulent and Parisian, which ranged from fried fish to burnt sugar; and there were many things besides: little tables for the post-prandial coffee; piles of luggage inscribed (after the initials or frequently the name) R. P. Scudamore or D. Jackson Hodge, Philadelphia, Pa., or St. Louis Mo.; rattles of unregarded bells, flittings of tray-bearing waiters, conversations with the second-floor windows of admonitory landladies, arrivals of young women with coffin-like bandboxes covered with black oil-cloth and depending from a strap, sallyings-forth of persons staying and arrivals just afterwards of other persons to see them; together with vague prostrations on benches of tired heads of American families. It was to this last element that Mr. Dosson himself in some degree contributed, but it must be added that he had not the extremely bereft and exhausted appearance of certain of his fellows. There was an air of ruminant resignation, of habitual accommodation in him; but you would have guessed that he was enjoying a holiday rather than aching for a truce, and he was not so enfeebled but that he was able to get up from time to time and stroll through the *porte cochère* to have a look at the street.

Following him in his stroll we are given further description of him:

> ... He was fair and spare and had no figure; you would have seen in a moment that the question of how he should hold himself had never in his life occurred to him. He never held himself at all; providence held him rather—and very loosely— by an invisible string at the end of which he seemed to dangle and waver. ... He looked for the most part as if he were thinking over, without exactly understanding it, something rather droll that had just occurred.[17]

But we learn that his clothes were made in Paris, and that he is not without some sartorial awareness. Tired American business men in the foyers of hotels we have encountered before: the two Englishmen in "An International Episode" see large numbers of them with their legs stretched out and with "a

[17] XVIII. 17-8.

dejected, exhausted look," their garments "not fresh, as if telling of some rush, or some fight, for life."[18] In this passage from *The Reverberator* what comes first is Paris, with its sights and sounds and stirrings of life. We have in fact the old story, the old charm of Europe, of which James and other like-minded Americans can never tire. Paris is here for Americans to respond to, if they can and will. When Mr Dosson is brought into the picture, it is with such graceful and pleasant turns of phrase that his kinship with his worn-out compatriots is softened: he has Parisian possibilities. If he has, in his facial expression, some signs of the national fate, the references to them are light. The story, as it develops, will not offer any serious occasions for "resignation." His deportment is, of course, in the American male tradition. Littlemore, in "The Siege of London," has "a good figure and a bad carriage,"[19] and even Christopher Newman, who could straighten himself like a grenadier if he chose, has an attitude and carriage of a "liberal looseness."[20] But Mr Dosson's variation of this tendency, combined with the element of fineness in his physical appearance and his Parisian clothes, cause him to harmonise quite successfully with his surroundings. The impression is conveyed that, poised somewhere between Americans who are perfectly at home with Paris (such as the novelist himself, who composes the scene) and those to whom it means weary exile and imposition (such as Mr Ruck), Mr Dosson is happy, and we can be at ease about him. The lightness of the note here, and the combination of the light and the quaint in Mr Dosson himself, have an entirely American charm.

If we turn to the more conservative families with whom the Laphams, the Dossons, and the Spraggs achieve acquaintance, we find that certain features and attitudes recur, though with variations, in some cases due to differences of region or period, in others more individual. In the Corey family, for example, the father, Bromfield, renounced work for a life of travel and dilettante painting; and we know how thoroughly in the tradition he is when we are told that he "said so much better things than he painted."[21] His son Tom reacts against this

---

[18] XIX. 249.   [19] XIX. 146.
[20] *Amer.*, p. 3.   [21] *S.L.*, p. 99.

way of life. He wants to work; he has met Silas Lapham and finds him attractive and convincing. Bromfield Corey is whimsical about Tom's desire to do something: "I am afraid Tom is selfish."[22] With a little sacrifice and economy he could have done nothing! Mr Probert, Gaston's father, in *The Reverberator*, has much in common with Bromfield Corey, including his dilettante way of life. Neither of them has any capacity for serious intolerance. When their sons confront them with uncomfortable new departures, they indulge in a few amiably fastidious comments, but make no difficulties. Old Mr Dagonet ("small, frail and softly sardonic," with a "reedy staccato voice, that gave polish and relief to every syllable")[23] plays a similar role in *The Custom of the Country*. In all these families the principle of accommodation prevails. Snobbery, so formidable a barrier in certain English novels, hardly asserts itself here; and the result is a softening of edges, a less bristling quality in the action than English readers would expect.

Ralph Marvell has much in common with some young men in James and Howells:

> Harvard first—then Oxford; then a year of wandering and rich initiation. Returning to New York, he had read law, and now had his desk in the office of the respectable firm in whose charge the Dagonet estate had mouldered for several generations. But his profession was the least real thing in his life. The realities lay about him now: the books jamming his old college bookcase and overflowing on chairs and tables; sketches too—he could do charming things, if only he had known how to finish them! . . . Nothing in the Dagonet and Marvell tradition was opposed to this desultory dabbling with life. For four or five generations it had been the rule of both houses that a young fellow should go to Columbia or Harvard, read law, and then lapse into more or less cultivated inaction.[24]

This does not at all points reproduce Bromfield Corey's way of life, in which "cultivated inaction" is quite unaccompanied by any pretence to practise law; and the Proberts, being expatriates, are far away from the environment in which Americans try to appear to work. But Bernard Longueville, whom we meet in the first chapter of *Confidence* (1879) making

[22] *S.L.*, p. 99.   [23] *C.C.*, pp. 63, 65.   [24] *C.C.*, pp. 53-4.

sketches in the neighbourhood of Siena, had studied law at College, and had not subsequently made much of it. The well-to-do Mr Burrage, in *The Bostonians*, admits that at Harvard he is not really studying law at all: "he had only come to Cambridge for the form. . . ."[25]

When Tom Corey begins to call on the Laphams, Mrs Lapham cannot understand "why he should be as attentive to her as to Irene"; a situation that is reproduced in *The Custom of the Country* when Undine is totally at a loss to know why Ralph Marvell has called on her mother and sat with her for a whole hour. In *The Reverberator* Gaston Probert surprises Mr Dosson by asking his permission to approach Francie. The old man subscribes to the American view that, in all matters relating to meetings between the sexes and courting, the young are independent of their parents. This doctrine is accepted even by the relatively conservative Coreys in Howells's novel:

> "If we were Europeans, even English, we should take some cognisance of our children's love affairs, and in some measure teach their young affections how to shoot. But it is our custom to ignore them until they have shot, and then they ignore us".[26]

And later, when the Coreys are curious to know where Tom stands in relation to Irene Lapham, and Mrs Corey says that she had better ask him outright, her husband explains that Tom won't tell them "if he is making love on the American plan":

> "He will tell us after he has told *her*. That was the way I did. Don't ignore our own youth, Anna."[27]

The Reverberator opens with a description of George Flack's visit to Francie Dosson in the Parisian hotel. The complete unimportance to which Mr Dosson is relegated as he humbly escorts him to her apartment is made evident in a description full of suggestiveness. Here James shows the tradition in operation; he catches it in the fact, before the reader has any knowledge of the characters who are enacting the scene, perhaps before he has any knowledge of these American assumptions. It is simply in the contrasted bearing of the two men that the significant relation between them appears. If one is not prepared for a documentary element one may not notice it quite so quickly as in reading Howells and Edith Wharton: but James may nevertheless be regarded as more documentary, in that his examples have more organic life and therefore more truth.

So brief and limited a comparison as this does not demonstrate very much. "The Pension Beaurepas" and *The Reverberator* are minor works, though useful here for the obvious parallels they invite. Many more works by the same novelists and by others would need to be inspected if James's place in the development of the American novel of manners were to be surveyed in detail. And, of course, no attempt has been made here to do justice to the aspects of Howells and Edith Wharton which have no parallel in James; notably, their interest in the economic forces of the world they depict, and in the careers of their characters as exemplary phenomena—this is especially relevant to *The Custom of the Country*—in a moneyed society. Edith Wharton's grasp of this side of life brings her nearer to Balzac than to James.

James's portrayal of American traits and types is, in general, far more deliberate than any English writer's portrayal of the corresponding points of English life. But it is worth while to ask whether some elements of American behaviour occur in his characters without his having intended to make this kind of point. The suggestion may seem hazardous, for not many authors have known so supremely what they were doing: but, as an American himself, James may conceivably have written sometimes in the national vein, just as English authors continually write in an English vein, without seeing all that an outsider would see.

In a celebrated passage of his book on Hawthorne he enumerates the features of European life which are absent from the American scene and therefore non-existent as resources for American novelists: "No sovereign, no court, no personal loyalty, no aristocracy, no church, no clergy . . . no country gentlemen . . . no great universities nor public schools . . ." and so forth. What this meant to American novelists

H

could have been developed more fully than it is here. No aristocracy, for example, meant no fire-eating Lord Chilterns, and therefore fewer duels. The absence of ingrained family prides and prejudices, obstinacies based on notions of class and property but also specially fostered by English individualism, meant an absence of family feuds such as tear human beings from each other in books like *The Mill on the Floss*. Tom Tulliver is a disconcertingly English figure; he has no American counterpart. Snobbery, as we have noted, takes less strident forms in novels about Americans than in novels about English characters. There is, after all, no serious barrier between the Laphams and the Coreys, in spite of the panic over the dinner; and, the newspaper scandal apart, the Proberts were ready to accept the Dossons, even though they refer to the French capital as "Parus." In novel after novel E. M. Forster preaches the very necessary moral of "only connect": coldness, separateness, if not actual hostility are seen as the inveterate characteristics of English people, where differences of race or class arise. Such a moral would be much less necessary in novels about American society; and, what is more to the point in a literary survey, a particular kind of drama of animosities and reversals of feeling such as Forster exploits so brilliantly could hardly occur in such works. How mild, by comparison, are the tensions in *The Europeans*!

There are some odd tolerances among James's characters; for example, in the following small episode from an early stage of Rowland's friendship with Roderick:

> They flung themselves on the grass and tossed stones into the river; they talked, they fell into intimacy, like old friends. Rowland lit a cigar and Roderick refused one with a grimace of extravagant disgust. He thought them vile things; he didn't see how decent people could tolerate them. Rowland was amused—he wondered what it was that made this ill-mannered speech so inoffensive on his companion's lips. He belonged to the race of mortals, to be pitied or envied according as we view the matter, who are not held to a strict account for their aggressions.[28]

---

[28] *R.H.*, p. 28.

Some readers may indeed wonder why the speech could be inoffensive: surely the kind of speech that in some societies causes people to be written off. We have a comparable moment in *The Custom of the Country*. Undine Spragg, in the company of the Marvells and the Dagonets, has said some unfortunate things about divorce, and everyone is pained except Ralph, who laughs. He is captivated by Undine's beauty, and so has no wish to be critical, but this is not all. His laughter expresses the note of accommodation and good-humoured acceptance of others' attitudes that recurs in the characters of all the three novelists that have been compared here. We may recall Strether's beguilement on his first meeting with Chad: his realisation that Chad is a pagan, and his reflexion that Woollett could do with a pagan. *The Bostonians* depicts such intense antagonisms that it might appear, at first sight, not to furnish examples of American flexibility and acceptance of differences. But there is much softening of edges in this book, though some readers have found it harsh. Extreme though Olive Chancellor's dislike is of men—in this respect she is a sick woman—she reacts generously in her loyalty to the New England code concerning "the friendship of a young man and a young woman,"[29] as it applies to Verena. She sees, justly, that Verena is "not in the smallest degree a flirt," but merely "enchantingly and universally genial,"[30] and accepts the inevitability of her friendships with men as a "little phase" to be gone through. Ransom on his side detests the woman's movement and the whole Bostonian atmosphere, but he becomes fond of Miss Birdseye and humours her delusions about his conversion, and he likes Miss Prance. The fact that Ransom falls in love with Verena, in spite of the nonsense —by his standards—that she utters fully typifies the American proneness to come to terms with opposites. As for Verena, before she is aware of him as a lover she enjoys the stimulus of his opposition and the pleasure of trying to convert him. It would be absurd to try to draw the line between what is American in all this and what might be found elsewhere, but taken together these examples are significant.

Curiosity, whimsicality, a proneness to experiment, often

[29] *B.*, I. 203.   [30] *B.*, I. 144.

in an atmosphere of the socially amorphous, operate in novels
by James to bring about relationships that would be less likely
to occur in a French or English novel. Some of Christopher
Newman's adventures are of this kind. How very characteristic
of his type that he should pick up Noémie Nioche, not for the
purposes for which she proves to be so eminently eligible,
but as a random experiment in art patronage! He is rich,
at a loose end, and in the mood to make some kind of gesture
of response to his immediate environment (the Louvre, Europe,
culture). Having made his gesture, he follows it through.
American whimsicality is oddly supported by American solidity,
so that he has the Nioches on his hands, daughter and father,
for the remainder of the novel. But how did James see this?
Newman is off-centre, in what seems to be a characteristically
American way, in taking up with the Nioches; in not seeing,
to put it crudely, that he could "do better." But perhaps James
himself is a little off-centre in giving us too much of the Nioches,
in conscientiously following up what might have been rounded
off earlier, in overdoing the consequences of what could appro-
priately have been treated as a random and unimportant
move on the part of the ingenuous newcomer. When Newman
leaves Paris for an extended tour of Europe he falls in with a
young New England minister who is on vacation, as different as
possible from himself in outlook, and they journey together.
Newman is amused by everything, Babcock is full of scruples.
Finally the young minister breaks away and ends the relationship with a rather agonised letter which produces in Newman's
mind "a singular mixture of exhilaration and awe."[31] Perhaps
we need not stress relationships contracted on holiday: there is
nothing specifically American in travelling with an incon-
gruous companion. But the absence of any suggestion that
the incongruity needs a reason or an excuse, the solemnity
with which Newman conducts a situation which at another
level he finds amusing: this is a piece of behaviour in the
national vein. One could argue that his relationship with
Claire, though so much more momentous, develops as the
outcome of an immense whim, which Mrs Tristram, also
thirsting for experiment, encourages. And in causing Newman

[31] *Amer.*, p. 86.

and Valentin to become close friends James may perhaps be showing his own Americanness a little. The way in which characters of unlike background are brought together in some of the other novels (American or otherwise in setting and theme) may be due to the unconscious operation of this national trait. Almost anyone, for example, may be found, sooner or later, in the room of the bed-ridden Rose Muniment in *The Princess Casamassima* (1886): first, Lady Aurora; then Captain Sholto; finally the Princess. Not that these tableaux are inadequately motivated, given the range of Muniment's activities and his attitude to his sister: but stylistically the effect is very Jamesian. Did he recognise these character-groupings as the expression of his own American feeling for facility in human contacts? The Princess's curious procedure with Hyacinth could be an expression of her American blindness to incongruity and addiction to whim: but if we agree that the situation is not wholly convincing, might this not be due to some kindred weakness in James himself as artist?

One of the outstanding differences between American and English fiction in James's period is the frequency with which, in the former, we come across cases of mysterious psychological and moral deformity. Some of Dickens's characters are queer enough, but the melodramatic convention tends to cover them. In Hawthorne the disturbing characters are not so much the product of Gothic distortion as of a New England mind, with an insight into evil, that recognised phenomena such as the English Victorian mind was less capable of dwelling upon directly. Among the besetting sins that recur in the characters of both Hawthorne and James is a malignant curiosity that preys upon the lives of others. A peculiarly appalling example is the case treated by Hawthorne in his short story "Wakefield": that of the man who whimsically absents himself from his wife, taking lodgings in a nearby street, with the intention of returning after he has enjoyed the fun of inflicting a few days' anxiety upon her. He stays away for twenty years. It is a story of great power, an extraordinary study of behaviour which, in all its inexplicable craziness, has the terrible, authentic ring of the humanly possible. Ethan Brand, with his unforgivable sin, is another case of the evil, preying mind. With James's Dr Sloper, in *Washington Square* (1880), we descend from the fantastic to what seems at first to be the embodiment of rationality and normal clear-headedness, though an element of inhumanity is discernible from the beginning. He proves to be a very strange person, stranger than we should expect to find in any English novel of that period.

Dr Sloper gives the situation in *Washington Square* most of its interest, through the curious kind of interest it has for him. Otherwise it has a rather limited theme. Morris Townsend is obviously shallow and worthless from the outset; neither he nor our knowledge of him undergoes any development. Catherine does develop; in a restricted way she is interesting, but her feeling for Townsend we must simply accept as given and fixed. Aunt Penniman, whose fostering of the whole business is tedious for Townsend and painful for Catherine, becomes irritating to the reader too. The best passages in the book are those in which the Doctor, in conversations with Catherine and the other characters, stamps his own intelligence upon the situation and seeks with his cool strength of character to control it. This exchange with Mrs Almond is typical:

> "And shall you not relent?"
> "Shall a geometrical proposition relent? I am not so superficial."
> "Doesn't geometry treat of surfaces?" asked Mrs. Almond, who, as we know, was clever, smiling.
> "Yes, but it treats of them profoundly. Catherine and her young man are my surfaces; I have taken their measure."
> "You speak as if it amused you."
> "It is immense; there will be a good deal to observe."
> "You are shockingly cold-blooded!" said Mrs. Almond.
> "I need to be with all this hot blood about me. Young Townsend indeed is cool; I must allow him that merit."[32]

The pointed quality in the dialogue, which expresses the Doctor's intention to make the most of the matter, enables us to do the same. In his scenes with Catherine fatherly tenderness is brought to bear ("You are a dear, faithful child," he says after one of her speeches), but this only makes his words

[32] *W.S.*, p. 135.

of reproach more painful, and when he has sounded the note of disappointed parenthood to the limits of his virtuosity and she has departed in misery, "By Jove," he says, "I believe she will stick!"[33] The idea promises entertainment! It is essential to the effect of such a speech that it comes as a shock to the reader. The fatherly tenderness is real so far as it goes, the ghastly humour an afterthought. If the Doctor cannot satisfy himself in one way he will do so in another. He is perfectly serious in his provision for Catherine's welfare, and the visit to Europe may be praised as a wise and handsome arrangement. He takes a pride in doing things handsomely, and he wishes to do his duty as a father: but he is not to be trusted when his wishes are frustrated. Her simplicity makes her infinitely vulnerable, and therefore tempting; and her resistance provokes him to atrocity. During the scene in the Alps he lets her know that essentially he is not a very good man, and even the unimaginative Catherine has an uncanny feeling that he has brought her to this lonely spot to frighten her. The most shocking moment in his relationship with her occurs when, obeying some freakish impulse of cruelty, at the moment of all moments when it will hurt her most, he lifts his hat to her "with an air of exaggerated courtesy":[34] a piece of grotesqueness that fills her with horror. In one of his speeches to Mrs Almond, before his problem has been solved (as it were) by Townsend's desertion, he states the case in his most malignantly whimsical style: "At first I had a good deal of a certain genial curiosity about it; I wanted to see if she really would stick. But, good Lord, one's curiosity is satisfied! I see she is capable of it, and now she can let go."[35]

Curiosity, whimsicality, a tendency to experiment: these qualities appear sometimes in James's good Americans, such as Ralph Touchett, and in relatively well-intentioned ones, such as Mrs Tristram. They occur in some of the narrators of his novels and tales, not all explicitly Americans: *The Sacred Fount* provides the most conspicuous example. It seems evident that James often projects something of himself into them, but the portrait of Dr Sloper makes it clear enough that he recognises the horrific possibilities of these qualities. Such

[33] *W.S.*, p. 122.   [34] *W.S.*, p. 194.   [35] *W.S.*, p. 175.

characters are, of course, an important technical resource wherever they appear. They cause things to happen and their viewpoint heightens situations.

The queer tale "Georgina's Reasons" (dealing with a woman who commits bigamy, thus coolly victimising her first husband, who neither exposes her nor profits by his "freedom") is another example of moral abnormality such as we should hardly expect to find in English fiction of the same period: but it could also, more specifically, be regarded as the final and most startling development of the independence of the American girl and her exploitation of the male, though this point does not emerge as James's intention and is almost certainly not so.

Another aspect of his treatment of American characters remains for consideration; and this has the highest importance.

James is interested in seeing how far and in what direction his American types will go, and what they are capable of. He sees them not merely in terms of national traits and habits that lend themselves—statically, as it were—to observation and description. He sees them prophetically. In his later novels, especially, he devises circumstances in which their capacities are given rare and prodigious opportunity for expression. These too are novels of manners, full of direct documentation of the kind shown in this survey, but they are also boldly imagined dramas of the American spirit, braving the extreme possibilities of their themes.

His exploration of the potentialities of the American character is developed further in *The Portrait of a Lady* (1881) than in the other early works. There is a hair-raising little passage in which Mr Touchett is said to be reminded by Isabel of his wife when the latter was in her teens: "It was because she was fresh and natural and quick to understand, to speak— so many characteristics of her niece—that he had fallen in love with Mrs Touchett."[36] Not that the resemblance will trouble the reader unduly; yet one can see in the peculiar way of living of Ralph's mother one of the possible outcomes of a youth given up to individualistic aspiration in the American style. As for her dryness, the epithets "cold and dry" are

[36] *P.L.*, I. 65.

applied to Isabel herself in one passage,[37] and in another we read that she bestows upon the rejected Caspar Goodwood, "the bright dry gaze with which she rather withheld than offered a greeting."[38] The desire to please is not the most obvious note of her conversation; she can be sharp, sometimes offhand, especially with her suitors. "You only care to amuse yourself,"[39] is one of Lord Warburton's remarks to her. A tendency to undervalue others—she fails at first to appreciate Ralph—accompanies her early wish to be independent and uncommitted. All these represent ominous possibilities in an American girl. If she had not been enriched and so rendered an eligible prey for an Osmond, she would still not have been exempt from all dangers. Basically noble and generous though she is, and much loved, Isabel carries rather more than a heroine's usual load of faults, and they are American faults. *The Portrait of a Lady* is very much a novel about what happens to Americans if they are not careful. Mr Touchett *has* been careful:

> Americans, rightly or wrongly, are commended for the ease with which they adapt themselves to foreign conditions; but Mr. Touchett had made of the very limits of his pliancy half the ground of his general success. He had retained in their freshness most of his marks of primary pressure; his tone, as his son always noted with pleasure, was that of the more luxuriant parts of New England.[40]

His American physiognomy has been "kept in the best order." He could have taken it back to the United States without misgivings.

Osmond is an extreme case of what can happen to Americans. In one of his speeches of courtship to Isabel he provides the clue to his type: it is a type of which examples have already been noted here. He describes himself as "not a man of genius," with not even talent but (referring to his earlier days), "simply the most fastidious young gentleman living."[41] This does not mean that in his twenties he was as acceptable as Little Bilham or Edward Rosier, or that at forty

[37] *P.L.*, I. 63.   [38] *P.L.*, II. 37-8.   [39] *P.L.*, I. 99.
[40] *P.L.*, I. 44.   [41] *P.L.*, I. 336.

they will have become as poisoned as he is: Osmond deviates from the type in his extreme unpleasantness. The combination of fastidiousness with lack of creative ability has bred in him a peculiarly vicious habit of refined indolence and pretence. When Edward Rosier delights in Pansy as an American *jeune fille* (the passage is a *locus classicus* on the type in question)[42] we have no immediate fear that his connoisseur's taste will triumph over his gentleness and affection; though, of course, where such connoisseurship enters into relationships with people there is always peril. Isabel is impressed by Osmond's view of Pansy. His claim that to have brought up a daughter "in the old way" is a mark of not having altogether failed in life strikes her as "one of his fine, quiet sincere notes."[43] We note a difference between this and the cruel sham of his speech of some years later on the occasion of Pansy's return to the convent. Osmond on the principle of the convent ("it's a school of good manners, it's a school of repose")[44] is consummate. But it would be difficult to draw the line firmly between the relatively harmless and the pernicious versions of this attitude. The father and his *jeune fille* of a daughter are central to the composition that captivates Isabel:

> . . . She had carried away an image from her visit to his hill-top which her subsequent knowledge of him did nothing to efface and which put on for her a particular harmony with other supposed and divined things, histories within histories: the image of a quiet, clever, sensitive, distinguished man, strolling on a moss-grown terrace above the sweet Val d'Arno and holding by the hand a little girl whose bell-like clearness gave a new grace to childhood. The picture had no flourishes, but she liked its lowness of tone and the atmosphere of summer twilight that pervaded it. It spoke of the kind of personal issue that touched her most nearly; of the choice between objects, subjects, contacts—which might she call them?—of a thin and those of a rich association; of a lonely, studious life in a lovely land; of an old sorrow that sometimes ached today; of a feeling of pride that was perhaps exaggerated, but that had an element of nobleness; of a care for beauty and perfection so natural and so cultivated together that the

---

[42] *P.L.*, II. 94-5.   [43] *P.L.*, II. 73.   [44] *P.L.*, II. 305.

career appeared to stretch beneath it in the disposed vistas
and with the ranges of steps and terraces and fountains of a
formal Italian garden—allowing only for arid places freshened
by the natural dews of a quaint half-anxious, half-helpless
fatherhood.[45]

Here is the quintessence of the expatriate way of life, an
excellent specimen of the American's gift for appropriating
values not his own. Osmond combines the carefully-studied
with the "natural." His indolence is natural: he "strolls,"
not being openly American enough to "dawdle." Something
of the "fine rage" of the American has gone into the effect.
Osmond is dangerous to such as Isabel because, with all his
falsities, he cares supremely about certain effects, certain
nuances. We may not wish to call them human values, but
human values are involved: those that Pansy embodies operate
poignantly and decisively upon Isabel, and Osmond knows
how to use her. For this vision Isabel surrenders her freedom
and narrows her life. She does not quite know what awaits
her when she marries Osmond, but even the things she consciously marries him for are smaller than the things she dreamt
of in her earlier, more aspiring days.

In this novel the characters are all Americans together.
At the risk of labouring the obvious, it must be said that it is
not at all a book about innocent America and corrupt Europe,
a stereotype that has been one of the curses of Jamesian
criticism. In so far as it deals with things inimical to moral
health and happiness, these things are seen as part of the
national character, operating through good and bad alike.
Osmond plays "theoretical tricks on the delicate organism
of his daughter,[46] but Ralph has also experimented with
Isabel, and it is his eagerness to know the whole outcome of
his experiment (he whimsically claims) that keeps him alive.
Isabel's view of her marriage has much in common with
Osmond's. He speaks of "living decently together, in spite
of such drawbacks,"[47] and she says: "I can't publish my
mistake. I don't think that's decent."[48] Both serve an
aesthetic ideal.

[45] *P.L.*, I. 352-3.   [46] *P.L.*, II. 305.
[47] *P.L.*, II. 312.   [48] *P.L.*, II. 249.

The primary theme of *The Portrait of a Lady* is the question of what Isabel will do with her life. Beginning with the account of her hopes and desires in youth, James puts her through a very full and exacting cycle of experience that tests and reveals her, but at the end we are still left with questions unanswered. This is one of the more abrupt of James's endings, but many of his works raise issues that can only remain unsettled so long as the characters are capable of change and growth; and it was not his method to mask this fact by contrived solutions. Another novelist might have furnished a drowning accident to dispose of Osmond and shorten Isabel's wretchedness, or might have made Caspar Goodwood more eligible as a husband, but James did not see his way to do either. Perhaps it is inherent in her fate that Isabel does not meet the "right" man. The fact of being critical and independent, and a little cold and dry at times, rather lay her open to that possibility. Caspar, in spite of his final challenge, is quite irrelevant: the unlucky emblem of the inadequacy of the American businessman as a partner for the brilliant American girl. Isabel has a craving for the especially distinguished, and we see how it leads her astray. But she suffers for her mistake, and the question at the end is what phase of the struggle awaits her next.

A memorable passage occurs in one of the later chapters, where Isabel's reflexions, as she makes the journey to Ralph's deathbed, turn from an optimistic to a pessimistic vision of the future:

> . . . Deep in her soul—deeper than any appetite for renunciation —was the sense that life would be her business for a long time to come. And at moments there was something inspiring, almost enlivening, in the conviction. It was a proof of strength—it was a proof she should some day be happy again. It couldn't be she was to live only to suffer; she was still young, after all, and a great many things might happen to her yet. To live only to suffer—only to feel the injury of life repeated and enlarged—it seemed to her she was too valuable, too capable, for that. Then she wondered if it were vain and stupid to think so well of herself. When had it ever been a guarantee to be valuable? Wasn't all history full of the destruction of

precious things? Wasn't it much more probable that if one were fine one would suffer? It involved then perhaps an admission that one had a certain grossness; but Isabel recognised, as it passed before her eyes, the quick vague shadow of a long future. She should never escape; she should last to the end. Then the middle years wrapped her about again and the grey curtain of her indifference closed her in.[49]

There is no inevitability in this direction of her thought, no certainty either of happiness or of unhappiness for her. As we turn back from the sadness of the later part of the passage to the words "inspiring, almost enlivening," we can take pleasure in the note of resilience in adversity, one of the most engaging traits in the national character as James sees it.

The question of what to do with one's life is universal: to claim it as a specifically American theme would be obviously wrong. But it has more poetical possibilities in representatives of a young society with an ethos still in process of formation. The American combination of individualistic aspiration with a tendency to seek new ways of living in new places makes for excursions into the unknown such as the imagination of the English novelist of that period was unlikely to be confronted with. The story of Isabel Archer has a scope beyond that of any English heroine of the nineteenth century. It was not James's province to produce an "epic" of the American world of action like *Moby Dick*, but the emergent American spirit called for something like an heroic treatment, and in this novel and one or two others he achieved it.

[49] *P.L.*, ii. 343.

VI

English Types

JAMES's treatment of English ways is heightened and simplified by a sense of sheer contrast with those of America.
He dwelt with delight on the ripest manifestations of the
former; ripeness, the work of time, being what one might expect
to find in the products of so well established a society. But
Laura Wing, the young American girl in *A London Life* (1888),
marvels at the element of waste in institutions like the English
landed gentry: it takes so much to produce so little!

> The sweet old wainscoted parlour, the view of the garden that
> reminded her of scenes in Shakespeare's comedies, all that was
> exquisite in the home of his forefathers—what visible reference
> was there to these fine things in poor Lionel's stable-stamped
> composition?[1]

But one sees a kind of cherishing even here, in this delicate
sense of the inadequate, and in his small way Lionel is a
finished type.

In the documentary scene in *The Tragic Muse* (1889-90)
where Lady Agnes Dormer orders a meal in a Parisian res-
taurant James abandons himself to rhetoric:

> "*Poulet chasseur, filets mignons sauce béarnaise,*" the man sug-
> gested.
> "You'll give us what I tell you." said Lady Agnes; and she
> mentioned with distinctness and authority the dishes of which
> she desired that the meal should be composed. He interjected
> three or four more suggestions, but as they produced absolutely
> no impression on her he became silent and submissive, doing
> justice apparently to her ideas. For Lady Agnes had ideas,
> and, though it had suited her humour ten minutes before to
> profess herself helpless in such a case, the manner in which she

---

[1] xv. 257.

imposed them on the waiter as original, practical, and eco-
nomical, showed the high executive woman, the mother of
children, the daughter of earls, the consort of an official, the
dispenser of hospitality, looking back upon a lifetime of
luncheons.[2]

It may be contrasted with passages in *The Reverberator*, where
the helpless, charming Dossons have their Parisian meals
ordered for them by the knowing Flack, and with the reference
in *The Ambassadors* to the expensive dishes which it is Jim
Pocock's function and privilege to place before Sarah and
which they scarcely touch.

In descriptions of handsome specimens of the English
leisured class the word "perfect" frequently occurs:

> Lord Lambeth repaid contemplation; tall straight and strong,
> he was handsome as certain young Englishmen, and certain
> young Englishmen alone, are handsome; with a perfect finish
> of feature and a visible repose of mind, an inaccessibility to
> questions. . . . It was not that he looked stupid; it was only,
> we assume, that his perceptions didn't show in his face for
> restless or his imagination for irritable.[3]

We often see them exposed, as here, to the contemplation of
Americans. In the crucial scene where Jackson Lemon, as
Barbarina's suitor, converses with the latter's father, the
combination of a splendid presence with a sort of aristocratic
simplicity and homeliness of manner is fully appreciated
by the young man:

> No man, as I have intimated [there is a fine, full-length
> portrait of Lord Canterville earlier in the story] bore better
> being looked at than this noble personage; he seemed to bloom
> in the envious warmth of human contemplation and never
> appeared so faultless as when most exposed. "My dear fellow,
> my dear fellow," he murmured . . .
> "Are you surprised, sir?" Jackson asked.
> "Why I suppose a fellow's surprised at any one's wanting one
> of his children. . . . He wonders what on earth another man
> can make of them. . . ."[4]

---

[2] *The Tragic Muse* [= *T.M.*], I. 33.   [3] XIX. 277.
[4] XIX. 47-8.

Jackson views Barbarina as much from the connoisseur's as from the lover's angle, perhaps rather more so, and perhaps part of his subsequent unhappiness is traceable to this fact, though James does not invite us to make this point: "She was so blooming, so complete, of a type so rarely encountered in that degree of perfection."[5]   Her limitations, which Jackson discovers after their marriage, are precisely the opposite to those we should expect in one of James's American heroines: lack of curiosity, complete unwillingness to interest herself in new places and pastimes, a general dislike of conversation. There is no better illustration than in James's little gallery of English aristocrats of Matthew Arnold's analysis of the "Barbarians," with their physical beauty and disinclination for the things of the mind.   The fact that the descriptions are so glowing, so frankly appreciative of all that merits admiration, makes them all the more effective as social criticism. A Bostonian heroine would be a reader of George Eliot (if not a student of Greek); Americans in Europe visit galleries and museums, even Henrietta Stackpole having her favourite Correggio; and Christopher Newman is first introduced to us in the Louvre, where his response to the arts is princely if uninitiated.   But in the opening chapter of *The Tragic Muse*, also set in the Louvre, Lady Agnes Dormer utters her repeated protests against the statuary and all that the place represents; and in the same novel Julia Dallow, in some respects an impressive person with a fine, inherited sense of social duty, admits openly her hatred of art.   The richly theatrical scene where Julia finds Nick painting Miriam's portrait and drives off in a high temper is a portentous piece of English upper-class behaviour.   Julia's social manner is the subject of a humorous aesthetic appraisal on the part of Gabriel Nash, not ostensibly an American but with some characteristics pointing in that direction, notably his whimsical connoisseurship:

> The lady with whom you were so good as to make me acquainted is a beautiful specimen of the English garden-flower, the product of high cultivation and much tending; a tall, delicate stem with the head set upon it in a manner which, as a

thing seen and remembered, should doubtless count for us as a
gift of the gods. She's the perfect type of the object *raised* or
bred, and everything about her hangs together and conduces
to the effect, from the angle of her elbow to the way she drops
that vague, conventional, dry little 'Oh!' which dispenses
with all further performance. That degree of completeness
is always satisfying.[6]

It would be unfair to James to give the impression that he is
concerned only with these rich, obvious, exotic appearances.
The scenes with Julia and Nick reveal subtler points of behaviour.
Julia's restlessness during the evening in Paris[7]—she is disturbed about Nick's hesitancies—and her indifference to the
phenomena all about her, are very interesting manifestations
of a certain kind of English breeding and temperament. But
James does not, of course, enter into an English character's
experience of being English; there is no approach to the
imaginative intimacy of his American portraiture, no exploration, no discovery.

The relatively tolerant manner in which American characters deal with certain types of situation provides a contrast
to the complete failure of sympathy, sometimes amounting to
violence, that similar situations give rise to in the English
stories. There is an utter finality in Mr Carteret's withdrawal
of support from Nick when he fails to fulfil his expectations.
We can be sure that in the world of Lady Agnes Dormer and
Julia Dallow there will never be any room for Gabriel Nash;
there will be no quaint laying aside of prejudice, no whimsical,
humorous recognition of differences. For James such oppo-
sitions were a technical opportunity for staging a truly English
brush-off, or something sharper. The absoluteness with which
Owen Wingrave's family, which has bred soldiers from time
immemorial, abhors the young man's decision to throw up his
military career is given a knife-edge keenness. How powerfully
in two sentences the grandfather is presented!

... Sir Philip Wingrave, a relic rather than a celebrity, was a
small brown erect octogenarian, with smouldering eyes and a
studied courtesy. He liked to do the diminished honours of

his house, but even when with a shaky hand he lighted a bed-room candle for a deprecating guest it was impossible not to feel him, beneath the surface, a merciless old man of blood.[8]

James's susceptibility to the expressive notation of English social life gives a characteristic colouring to many of the stories. The events tend to take place very explicitly within the framework of the fashionable round. In "The Chaperon" (1891) there is an evocation of an evening at Covent Garden when the air, "through banging doors, entered in damp, warm gusts, heavy with the stale, slightly sweet taste of the London season when the London season is overripe and spoiling."[9] When Oliver Lyon, in "The Liar," broaches the question of painting the portrait of Colonel Capadose it is noted that, "it was now very late in the season—there would be little time before the common dispersal. He said they must make the most of it; the great thing was to begin; then in the autumn, with the resumption of their London life, they could go forward."[10] Mark Ambient, in conversation with the narrator of "The Author of Beltraffio," "had a deal to say about London as London appears to the observer who has the courage of some of his conclusions during the high-pressure time—from April to July—of its gregarious life."[11] In one of his London sketches, reprinted in *English Hours*, James writes:

> . . . I might claim that you don't really know the charms of London until on one of the dog-days you have imprinted your boot-sole in the slumbering dust of Belgravia, or, gazing along the empty vista of the Drive, in Hyde Park, have beheld, for almost the first time in England, a landscape without figures.[12]

In "The Chaperon" Mrs Charles Tramore, Rose's compromised parent, cherishes one craving—the desire to "go out," a "passion for lighted candles, for squeezing up staircases and hooking herself to the male elbow."[13] "The Marriages" opens rather elaborately with a dinner party from which the main body of the guests are departing. Laura Chart is "conscious of the queerness, the shyness, in London, of the gregarious flight of guests, after a dinner, the general *sauve qui peut* and panic

[8] XXII. 247.	[9] XV. 409.	[10] XVII. 322.
[11] XXI. 24.	[12] *E.H.*, pp. 152-3.	[13] XV. 414.

fear of being left with the host and hostess."[14]   Laura and her
father are in mourning, which explains why they are not
"going on" to some other party (references to "going on" are
frequent in James): but the point is noted that the difference
in principle between going on, and coming in the first place
to a dinner of twenty people, is perhaps a little difficult to
catch.   These people ride in Hyde Park and Rotten Row;
in this setting Lord Canterville and Lady Barbarina are first
introduced.   We are told of Mrs Churchley, the lady in "The
Marriages" (1891) who finally does not marry Laura's father,
that she was habitually to be seen in the Row, "perched on a
mighty hunter."   It is in the Row that Maurice Glenvil, in
"The Wheel of Time" (1892), makes up to Fanny Knocker,
with whom he subsequently has a canter "most days in the
week."

He portrays a world of furious, competitive match-making,
in which the mother may play a very active, even ruthless
part: another obvious contrast with American society.   In
"The Chaperon" Rose Tramore senses that Guy Mangler
is on the point of saying: "By the way, mamma told me to
propose to you"; and further that, unless she accepts Guy,
the latter's mother and sister will do nothing to help Rose to
"launch" her mother socially ("If you'll accept me they'll
call, but they won't call without something 'down' "—words,
of course, left unsaid).[15]   The theme of "marrying one's
daughters" is prominent in "Lord Beaupré," where a terrifying, gate-crashing mother forces her daughter upon a country
house party.   A more thoughtful mother, who ought to have
known better, precipitates her daughter into a fictitious
engagement with Lord Beaupré, ostensibly to protect him from
the importunity of others, but actually with a view to its
becoming a real engagement, which it doesn't.

James's attitude to this way of life is not a matter for simple
generalisation.   In "The Chaperon," where Rose Tramore
dedicates herself to the task of rehabilitating her mother, the
mark of success being invitations to country houses, the desire
of the mother to achieve this may seem a weakness, but there
is no suggestion that the loyal daughter has sacrificed her

[14] XXIII. 229.   [15] XV. 421-2.

energies for a valueless project. The fashionable round is somehow accepted as inevitable by James's characters. There is a curious example of this in "The Death of the Lion" (1894). After his undesired newspaper publicity the exquisite novelist Neil Paraday comes to town, to find himself the lion of the season—another undesired success. But why does he come at all? Why does he not stay unfashionably in the country and write his next masterpiece? The narrator says of him: "He was far from unsociable, but he had the finest conception of being let alone that I've ever met,"[16] to which the reader might reply that, for a man who likes to be let alone, Paraday makes himself remarkably accessible. Explanations for this are offered, but the narrator's use of the word "sophistries" is tell-tale:

> For the time, none the less, he took his profit where it seemed most to crowd on him, having in his pocket the portable sophistries about the nature of the artist's task. Observation too was a kind of work and experience a kind of success; London dinners were all material and London ladies were fruitful toil. "No one has the faintest conception of what I'm trying for," he said to me, "and not many have read three pages that I have written; but I must dine with them first—they'll find out why when they've time." It was rather rude justice perhaps; but the fatigue had the merit of being a new sort, while the phantasmagoric town was probably after all less of a battlefield than the haunted study.[17]

One might well wonder what Paraday can reasonably expect in the way of appreciation if he keeps such company. One of the weaknesses of this story is that his fate is not clearly enough attributed to his wanting it both ways. In "The Next Time" (1895) Ray Limbert, another exquisite novelist, withdraws altogether from fashionable life, as a desperate economy, and his mother-in-law protests, using the Paraday argument, that "he would be deprived of that contact with the great world which was indispensable to the painter of manners."[18] But Limbert thrives, artistically if not in the worldly sense, on the deprivation. James himself had no settled attitude on this question. No doubt, the social round for him could be, at

[16] xx. 108.　　　　[17] xx. 108-9.　　　　[18] xx. 185.

different times, a nuisance, an insidious temptation, a preventer of work, a stimulus to work. On the whole, since he was the greatest imaginative interpreter of this particular society, we may conclude that he was right in immersing himself in the destructive element. He accepted the world of wealth and fashion; accepted it, that is, with an artist's negative capability. Its moral implications are all the more fully evident for his being able often to withhold moral comment while responding fully with his imagination to its heavy, expressive rituals. The late Victorian and Edwardian period in English society has a peculiarly florid style which James captures to perfection.

The sense of type was for James the basis of successful portrayal of character. In those cases where his people do not convince, it is usually because his sense of type has failed him, and the individual has been developed without sufficient regard to the question of what kind of society could have produced such a person and what general characteristics he shares with its other products. This seems to be true of his sensitive literary men: Neil Paraday, Ralph Limbert, Hugh Vereker and the rest of the "supersubtle fry." James was accused, he tells us, of being unable to give "chapter and verse" for them. Dedicated artists of this quality, it was maintained, were not to be found. His reply was: "If the life about us for the last thirty years refuses warrant for these examples, then so much the worse for that life." They embodied for him the protest against vulgarity and "the rule of the cheap and the easy," in the name of a "tradition of high aesthetic temper."[19] But does the history of the English Novel quite support James's reference to such a tradition? At what period in the past were artistic values pursued with the severity and remoteness from popular prejudice of James's heroes? Fielding, Sterne, Smollett, Scott, Jane Austen, Dickens, Thackeray, George Eliot: these writers, with all their great merits, and in spite of the strenuousness and subtlety of some of their works, hardly represent the attitude that he invokes. A tendency to be of the world, with the tone of the world, has been generally characteristic of the English novel. None of these novelists cultivated the aesthetic austerity that he appears to demand.

[19] *A.N.*, pp. 222-3.

James himself, Conrad and Joyce, did something to make the art of the novel more exacting; and none of them were Englishmen. (But part of the purpose of this study is to show that, so far as James is concerned, this aspect of him represents only a portion of the truth.)

The fact is that these artists, and the stories in which they appear, reflect James's quarrel with his public. They misrepresent him—he is not at all like the Verekers and the Paradays—and also the literary situation. If we could take the stories as mere *jeux d'esprit*, the distortion of the facts would hardly matter, but they are intended more seriously. The literary world that James depicts is one in which writers like Hardy, Trollope, Kipling, Mark Rutherford, George Moore, Gissing, and Stevenson (representatives of the thirty years of which he speaks) do not exist. He recognises only the inscrutably refined and the insufferably crude. Since the supersubtle fry are untypical of the English literary tradition and of English society, it is difficult for the reader to believe in their works. Great works are nurtured by tradition; these writers compose in a void. The effect is unfortunate, for if they are regarded as mouthpieces of Jamesian teaching we must not be surprised if he too is associated with a thin-blooded aestheticism. The image, propagated by "The Author of Beltraffio" (1884), "The Death of the Lion," and "The Figure in the Carpet" (1896), of an artist supremely urbane and sensitive, but rootless and exclusive, has done much harm, and is responsible for some of the legends and *clichés* relating to James that need to be fought. He was driven by his own mortification to accentuate the divorce between artists and society, and to portray artists who are as unindebted to their environment as possible. James himself is intelligible only in terms of his relation to the young but nourishing tradition of American literature and of his American capacity to assimilate the virtues of other literatures. We forget this point if we associate him with these insufferable and unconvincing aesthetes.

Perhaps his most notable aberration in character portrayal is Gabriel Nash, the whimsical philosopher of *The Tragic Muse*; and here again what we miss is the element of type. Perhaps unconsciously, James has given him some of the traits of the coxcombical, aesthetic, American expatriate. But in portraying Florimond Daintry or Louis Leverett he knew to a nicety with what species he was dealing, and each component has just the right weight—or lightness. These young Americans are all, in their own fashion, "intense": it is an old joke, how intense they can be without ever doing anything. Nash has this trait: he refers to "the conscience that's within us—that charming, conversible, infinite thing, the intensest thing we know," and then proceeds to take the charm out of it by insisting on it excessively, with his images of "treating the oracle civilly," "not striding into the temple in muddy jack-boots" and other verbiage.[20] Nash can be humorous. When Peter Sherringham says that he has seen him often before, his reply is: "Ah, repetition—recurrence: we haven't yet, in the study of how to live, abolished that clumsiness, have we?" which is agreeable nonsense, but he follows it up with:

> "It's a poverty in the supernumeraries of our stage that we don't pass once for all, but come round and cross again, like a procession or an army at the theatre. It's a sordid economy that ought to have been managed better. The right thing would be just *one* appearance, and the procession, regardless of expense, for ever and for ever different."[21]

The levity has been killed and clumsiness wins, after all.

Had Nash been specifically intended as a New Englander, endowed with colloquial eloquence in the manner of an Oliver Wendell Holmes philosopher, but also an expatriate and aesthete influenced by Pater and Wilde, intense but something of a humorist after the American fashion, the portrait, in spite of the mixture, might have had outline. The materials he is actually composed of are not unlike these, but James has not placed them; he has failed to get their relations right. The American tone is not there, nor any other. The lighter and the more serious elements in Nash are at odds with each other.

If we consider him as a serious figure, how can we not ask certain awkward questions about him? For example, has he no sexual life, no commitments, no obligations? One does not

[20] *T.M.*, II. 22.   [21] *T.M.*, I. 44.

need to be a Marxist to ask where the money comes from for a
life so pure of all productiveness and social purpose. How can
one avoid the feeling that he is a very deficient human being,
and that the imperturbable ease is a disguise? He describes
himself as "a merman wandering free,"[22] an image that does
not greatly help matters. A merman is a monster. How is
one to take his claim that he will never grow old ("For me
there'll be no collapse, no transition, no clumsy readjustment
of attitude . . .")?[23] Nash contracts out of too much.

Nick says of Nash: "He helped me at a difficult time,"[24]
but it is difficult to see in what way. Nick has involvements;
he must wrestle with the claims of love, duty and art. How
could Nash's inhuman detachment from all commitment
have been relevant to him? But Nick also has doubts about
him. He asks him directly whether he is "the greatest humbug and charlatan on earth, or a genuine intelligence. . . ."[25]
In a conversation with Peter he speaks of Nash's merits in the
past tense: "He used to be so gay. . . . He was a wonderful
talker";[26] rather a disconcerting piece of evasion on James's
part. We are prevented from judging Nash entirely on his
present showing, but we are not told enough about what he was
at his best to enable us to accept or to challenge this tribute.
But Nick's doubts about him do not keep pace with the
reader's. It is clear enough from his first appearance that he
has the makings of a bore.

Nash is not explicitly an American, and it is difficult to
see how he could possibly be English. The fact of his not having
the style of any nationality or society does not make him more
satisfactory as an individual: there can be no such thing as a
completely individual style. James may have wished him to
appear as a civilised cosmopolitan, without a style based on
national or social type: but this would be unrealistic. A
style must have been formed somewhere.

The reader's difficulty with Nash is not so much that he is
altogether unlifelike. On the contrary, he reminds one uncomfortably of people one has met, whose serenity has been
irritating, whose bright intelligence has somehow not thrown

22 *T.M.*, I. 151.   23 *T.M.*, II. 358-9.   24 *T.M.*, II. 346.
25 *T.M.*, I. 151.   26 *T.M.*, I. 68.

light on anything, and who seem a little detached from the common run of human preoccupations. Such people are unsatisfactory partly because they are unplaceable, just as Nash is unplaceable. James goes wrong in allowing such a figure to impose himself to the extent that Nash does; here we have perhaps a piece of Americanness on James's part, an example of the national tolerance. Perhaps Nick's serious valuation of Nash is also a piece of Americanness, improbably projected into an English character.

Something similar has happened with Miriam Rooth, but the effect is by no means so unfortunate. She belongs explicitly to no society; she has lived in an unsettled manner in several places: but in her overflowing goodwill, her lack of coquetry in situations where she has power to attract, her genial ascendancy over the male, and her rather excessive loquacity, she has much in common with the American girl, without having the advantages of a specific American *nuance* in speech or manner. (An element of Jewishness must also be taken into account.) Miriam is a successful creation, as a vessel of artistic energy and conviction, but she has something of the anomalous, the unplaceable, that prevents her from being quite so charming to the reader as James's American girls or even some of his English ones. Paradoxically, it is only through the *nuances* of type that individuality can make itself intimately felt.

James was adventurous in his choice of characters, and often strayed far from the spheres with which he was most familiar. Creations like Millicent Henning and Mr Vetch are remarkable as evidence of his ability to beat very different novelists at their own game. It is admirable that he should have included such types in his great range of portraiture, yet he is less Jamesian, more like other writers, when he makes the attempt. If *The Princess Casamassima* reminds us usefully of how little James restricted himself to any favourite world or worlds of social manners, it does not quite reach the level of his finest work.

Part III
JAMES'S ART: THE CULMINATING PHASE

VII

Method and Style

THE conventional view of James as the impeccable master of form intimidates more than it endears. We shall be nearer the truth if we think of him as having to contend with a certain amount of natural clumsiness. His triumphs in his best work are so extraordinary that no harm will be done if this phase of the discussion of his art begins with a few examples of typical weaknesses. They occur mainly in works of the early and middle periods, but there are vestiges also in later books.

Uneconomical development of situations is one of his faults. It often takes the form of a multiplication of encounters between characters, beyond the needs of their relationship (or, at least, of an adequate treatment), and sometimes of a repetitiveness in their encounters. *The Tragic Muse* furnishes a large-scale example in the handling of the relationship between Miriam Rooth and Peter Sherringham. We may begin at the place [1] where Peter, travelling from Paris to London—that is, away from Miriam—realises that he is in love with her. Up to this point, in all that he has done to encourage her aspirations as an actress, he has imagined himself to be emotionally uninvolved, but now he sees that he has really loved her from the outset. When we return to Peter[2] (after a few episodes of Nick's story), we find him reflecting on the implications of this predicament. Resolved to succeed in his career as a diplomat, he realises that it would be wise to marry, but "the last thing he expected the future ambassadress to have been was a *fille de théâtre*."[3] Artist as she is to the core of her nature, can she be expected to relinquish her vocation, uncertain though her prospects are at this point, for the sake of such a life as he can offer her? Peter has steadfastly kept away from her during his holiday in England, and has even taken

[1] *T.M.*, I. 205.   [2] *T.M.*, I. 279.   [3] *T.M.*, I. 283.

advice about seeking a post in a distant country: but when
he returns to Paris he visits her[4] during one of her sessions with
Mme. Carré, and finds that her talent has taken a great stride
forward. The new accomplishment and confidence of the
girl, and the changed attitude of the hitherto sceptical Mme
Carré, are handled here with a fine sense of the adventure
of becoming an artist; and although much of Miriam's
technical prowess has to be taken on trust, James does describe
the effect of her performance very eloquently. The scene that
follows,[5] in which Peter and Miriam pay a visit together to
the Théâtre-Français and see Mlle Voisin in her dressing
room is also admirable: James's feeling for the type and the
milieu leaves nothing to be desired. At this point Peter makes
his first declaration: "Give it up and I'll marry you tomorrow,"
to which she mockingly replies: "This is a happy time to ask
it! . . . And this is a good place."[6] In fact, she confirms the
conclusion that Peter had arrived at earlier. She has gone
too far to turn back; she desires more than ever the success for
which, with his help, she has striven. Miriam puts an alternative to him: that, instead of her sharing his glory, he might
share hers; and this brings out the basic contradiction of
Peter's position as a devotee of the theatre: "The husband of an
actress? Yes, I see myself that!"[7] We recall an earlier passage
where he realises that, for him, "the beauty of a love of the
theatre was precisely in its being a passion exercised on the
easiest terms."[8] He had always kept it in its place.

Their position would now seem to be completely defined It
is a deadlock, and Peter tries to conquer his feeling for her. He
absents himself from London during the first months of her
success there, but finally comes over and seeks her again. There
is a charming reunion; she kisses him with affection and
gratitude, calling him her dear master,[9] and he goes to the
theatre every night, marvelling at the growth of her powers.
After a further lapse of chapters, we find him once again
resolved to control the situation and put his career first:
"It was a case for action—for vigorous, unmistakable action."[10]

[4] *T.M.*, I. 296 f.   [5] *T.M.*, I. 310 f.   [6] *T.M.*, I. 328.
[7] *T.M.*, I. 331.   [8] *T.M.*, I. 280.   [9] *T.M.*, II. 113.
                          [10] *T.M.*, II. 194-5.

Virtue and honour demand the quenching of a personal passion. Peter has a talk with one of his superiors, and is quickly appointed minister to a Central American republic. Miriam desires to see him, and in their conversation he again returns (but only "in passing") to his previous claim, that if she marries him she will be "the greatest of all possible ladies."[11] He confesses again to a consuming passion for her, but recognises again that they are both "tied fast" to their conflicting ambitions. Their scene ends with an embrace interrupted by Miriam's mother. When Peter, with Nick Dormer, attends the first performance of her new play[12] (after which he must depart to his post), Nick is surprised that he has no intention of speaking to her, but Peter replies that he has already said goodbye. He tries to preserve an attitude of detachment from what is clearly a great artistic triumph; he looks for Miriam's mistakes. But at the end of the performance he sends her a message requesting her to leave the first night celebrations and meet him once more in her St John's Wood residence; and, in a very long scene,[13] they have it all out again. He makes a last effort to persuade her. If she has more to give up than ever before, he has more than ever to offer:

> "Give it up! . . . I'll marry you tomorrow if you'll renounce; and in return for the sacrifice you make for me I'll do more for you than ever was done for a woman before."[14]

As Miriam tells him, these are indeed "old words and foolish ones." Again she brings up the alternative, at which he again cries: "The husband of an actress!"[15] At the end of this prolonged encounter their relationship has remained unchanged, except that certain things have been said more vehemently than before.

So brief a synopsis as this does an injustice to their conversations, in which many interesting things are said about the nature of the artist, the position of actresses in society, and so forth. The novel is very rich in discussion of such matters. But a fuller analysis would also have revealed that both speakers say too much. Miriam, in the last scene especially, is full of her success, and Peter in his desperation cannot

---

[11] *T.M.*, II. 223.   [12] *T.M.*, II. 282 f.   [13] *T.M.*, II. 290 f.
[14] *T.M.*, II. 294.   [15] *T.M.*, II. 299.

let go. Even from this summary it can be seen that James sins against economy. And the whole contrivance of the last conversation is a stroke of violence, on his part as well as on Peter's: impotent violence, because nothing new results from it. Tension is weakened, not increased by this repetition. It hardly seems now to matter how often Peter returns to the attack; the outcome will be the same. The reader loses count. Peter is actually ready to return again in the last chapter, but he learns that Miriam has married Dashwood, and we are spared.

There are some places in which repetitiveness, obsessive insistence on the same pattern of events, may be highly effective; for example, in the first volume of *Clarissa*, where the family pressure upon the heroine, renewed in similar terms in scene after scene, finally drives her to desperate measures. The repetitiveness of *The Tragic Muse* is artistically clumsy. Yet there is something engaging in all this concern for the great issues of art and life, and some readers may not be greatly offended by the over-treatment.

The pattern of "repeated pressure" occurs in earlier novels; notably, in the relations between Newman and the Belle-gardes in *The American*. If we begin by counting the stages by which he achieves the consent of the family to his marriage with Claire,[16] we find that there are no redundancies, but a pattern of applied pressure has been established which becomes tedious when repeated later, after the Bellegardes have with-drawn their consent[17] and Newman exposes himself to a series of encounters, first with Claire herself, then with the disdainful and sinister Urbain and his mother, who treat him in much the same style of aristocratic contempt, somewhat exaggerated, on each occasion. Not that Newman's meetings with them show no progression in content. He learns from Valentin and further from Mrs Bread of the evil secrets in the Bellegarde family, and this puts him in a position to threaten them. The story keeps moving: but in form and atmosphere these encounters are too much alike. Only by an effort does the reader distinguish one from another or remember how many there are.

[16] *Amer.*, p. 196.   [17] *Amer.*, p. 318.

The question of artistic clumsiness does not, however, arise with *Washington Square*, where repeated pressure is again the main structural feature. Dr Sloper has some four or five conversations with his daughter, all on the same issue, but varying in accordance with the growing strength of her convictions and his bitterness. His personality renders each occasion a new exercise of his virtuosity, and the total effect testifies to James's. That such a limited structure should yield so much interest is impressive, the result of each encounter being, crudely speaking, predictable.

The repeated appearances of Caspar Goodwood and Lord Warburton in the life of Isabel Archer raise similar artistic questions, though not blatantly. We learn that Isabel has already refused Caspar before she comes to Europe.[18] Their encounter in London,[19] a scene of considerable bitterness, also ends in his rejection; and when Isabel is on the point of marrying Osmond he comes to Italy in the vain hope again of moving her.[20] The two episodes do not differ sufficiently. The point has been made in the first that Caspar, with all his devotion, is too limited for her. Caspar visits Isabel and Osmond in Rome, to keep an eye on her, and in the last scene at Gardencourt, after Ralph's funeral, he makes his final and fiercest appeal, with no more success than before. This ending to the novel has been the subject of much discussion. Some readers have seen in it evidence for a shrinking on Isabel's part from any kind of intense sexual experience: but this can hardly be the point. Our real difficulty, surely, is to discover James's reason for allowing Caspar this further attempt, and at a point in the book where violent wastage of feeling is even more painful than elsewhere. Miss Dorothea Krook's comment may help in some degree to justify it: "In this I think we are meant to see a last proof of Isabel's ultimate integrity. Even in her misery and despair at the prospect of resuming her life with Osmond, her judgement in this vital connection remains unimpaired. she knows that she ought not to give herself to Caspar Goodwood now any more than she ought to have given herself to Gilbert Osmond then. . . ."[21]

---

[18] *P.L.*, I. 41.   [19] *P.L.*, I. 190 f.   [20] *P.L.*, II. 37 f.
[21] *The Ordeal of Consciousness in Henry James* (1962), p. 363.

K

But one may doubt whether this point really needed to be made, and with such violence.

Lord Warburton proposes to Isabel at Gardencourt,[22] and when he visits Rome[23] confesses to her that his feelings are unchanged. Isabel's response, of course, remains the same. There are no more attempts on his part, and when Lord Warburton turns up again in Rome it is with different prospects. His changed role, as a possible suitor for Pansy, is well conceived as a development in himself and as a subtly contrived complication for Isabel. As for their last encounter at Gardencourt, nothing could be more appropriate than her finding him there at Ralph's funeral; it involves no actual repetition, since his prospects have again changed. Yet his reappearances in her life, like those of Caspar and taken together with them, have the effect of a series of regularly timed, almost predictable confrontations. They do something to give the book its shape. As her fateful career proceeds through its stages, Isabel meets again and yet again one or another or both of these figures who were associated with her early decisions. The structural effect, if we compare it with the brilliantly varied composition of some of the later novels, may seem a little commonplace. But to say this is to judge *The Portrait of a Lady* by exceedingly high standards, in addition to ignoring its finer features.

The same pattern occurs again in *The Bostonians*, but Basil Ransom's successive meetings with Verena are beautifully placed and timed and there is great charm in the unfolding of their relationship. All is well, in fact, until the last episode, another of James's regrettable strokes of violence. Verena's resistance to Ransom has already been weakened. The novel does not need so traumatic an ending.

A further example of this technical habit occurs in *The Awkward Age*, which will be examined in a later chapter. James was well aware of a tendency to overtreat his material, but he did not discuss, and seems not to have been aware of this particular manifestation of it.

It is sometimes difficult, in discussions of James's technical preoccupations, to get the facts straight. One needs to realise,

[22] *P.L.*, I. 129 f.   [23] *P.L.*, I. 370 f.

for example, that in the Prefaces he sometimes exaggerates in retrospect the significance for him of the "point of view" method. In the Preface to *The Portrait of a Lady* he makes much of his decision to "place the centre of the subject in the young woman's own consciousness,"[24] treating the other characters' relation to her, and her effect upon them, as a lesser interest "contributive only to the greater one."[25] This is all very well: it suggests a nice distribution of weight: but was the novel really planned with so much care? Isabel's consciousness dominates less than it might, and the places where it does not operate may raise questions for us. Her impression of the Osmond she marries, one might complain, is not so circumstantially presented as Osmond himself is by the all-seeing novelist in the first episodes where he appears, and in these passages he strikes the reader as decidedly unpleasant. Not that Isabel's response to him is quite unaccounted for. The relevant passages describing her feelings have been noted earlier: but the reader needs to make an effort to believe in her charged consciousness during this period of her life.

What, after all, is meant by James's placing the subject in the central character's consciousness? The answer differs according to which work we are considering; and, in general, the main difference lies between early and late. With either case misconceptions are common. To continue with *The Portrait of a Lady*: even when Isabel is central, what we have, of course, is the novelist's view of her; and sometimes the novelist's omniscience resembles that of George Eliot, especially in those admirable early chapters, the third and the sixth, where he gives an account of her upbringing and mental development. In the great "backward glance" chapter (the forty-second), the subject is Isabel's marriage as she now sees it, but he does not present her view in terms that reflect closely her actual mental operations at this point in the story. The backward glance, in fact, must be regarded as a technical device. After the unpleasant scene with Osmond she sits for hours by the fireside, and we would suppose her thoughts to be a renewal of those that have occupied her for a long time: but the novelist uses this reflective vigil for his own purpose, freely

[24] *A.N.*, p. 51.   [25] *A.N.*, p. 51.

transcending its particular scope, and makes it an occasion
for a great revelation of her plight, a comprehensive imaginative and analytical statement.

There are a number of places in *The Portrait of a Lady* where
he uses the idiom of the omniscient or "historian" novelist.
We read in one place that "no report had remained"[26] of one
of Isabel's speeches.   Her most crucial scene with Lord
Warburton contains the words: "Our heroine's biographer
can scarcely tell why, but the question made her start. . . ."[27]
The chapter dealing with her exploration of Rome begins:
"I may not attempt to report in its fulness our young woman's
response to the deep appeal of Rome. . . ."[28] In a description
of Mme Merle, seen ostensibly from the viewpoint of Isabel,
it is said of her eyes that they are "small but full of light and
incapable of stupidity—incapable, according to some people,
even of tears. . . ."[29] These passages do not perhaps loom very
large in the novel but they are tell-tale. James, at this period,
had not abandoned the traditional flourishes of the old school of
narration.   In so far as they have the effect of establishing
the novelist's point of view and of placing a distance between
the novelist and the character in question, they are a useful
reminder of the limits of his "centre of consciousness" technique.

What of the later examples of this method?   Certainly
they are different.   In *What Maisie Knew* the subject-matter
may be defined in terms of what the little girl witnesses and
is in a position to interpret: but, as James shows in the Preface,
it is the narrator's business to take fuller advantage than she
can of her experience. The narrator certainly does not withdraw himself, though his overt appearances are perhaps less
frequent than in the earlier books. From time to time he calls
attention to his handling of his precious theme with sentences
beginning: "The statement may surprise . . ."[30] or "I am not
sure that Maisie . . ."[31] or "I so despair of counting her noiseless
mental footsteps here that I must crudely give you my word
. . ."[32] Taken in isolation they could be a little disconcerting,
but so beautifully is the balance struck between Maisie's vision

---

[26] *P.L.*, I. 34.   [27] *P.L.*, I. 136.   [28] *P.L.*, I. 365.
[29] *P.L.*, I. 219.   [30] *What Maisie Knew* [= *W.M K.*], p. 189.
[31] *W.M.K.*, p. 248.   [32] *W.M.K.*, p. 248.

and her interpreter's management of it that these few touches
of narrative notation, embedded in their context, do nothing
to break the spell. The novelist does not withdraw, but he is
marvellously tactful. The presentation of Maisie's experience
involves a process of conversion. Somehow her uncertain
glimpses of truth are translated into formulations of quite
elaborate literary charm without ceasing to be cherished as
the thoughts of a child. By controlling his perspectives the
narrator enables the composed effect to be both one thing and
the other, the child's picture and the adult's. Part of our
pleasure in the adult component is in its quietly taking the onus
of exposition and development, so that Maisie's immaturity
and tentativeness are preserved. The narrator's function is
to keep her secrets as well as to reveal her insights.

James's account of his method, in the Preface to *What
Maisie Knew*, tallies with his actual practice: but in the Preface
to *The Golden Bowl* he credits himself with a unity and tightness
of effect which are not there in the novel. He claims that
the Prince, in the first part, "virtually sees and knows and
makes out, virtually represents to himself everything that
concerns us," which seems hardly true. Later he states that
we see all the other characters, "but as they are visible
in the Prince's interest, so to speak—by which I mean of course
in the interest of his being himself handed over to us."[33] What
does this mean? That in those passages where the Prince
absents himself the omniscient author supplies a substitute
that does not conflict with his viewpoint? This is certainly
as much as can be said for the account of Adam Verver's
billiard room crisis and the retrospective survey of his career
that follows.[34] What of his trip to Brighton with Charlotte?[35]
These are not burning issues, so very generalised is the Prince's
viewpoint on most of the occasions when it actually functions.

His first scene with Fanny raises technical issues:

> The spectator of whom they would thus well have been worthy
> might have read meanings of his own into the intensity of their

---

[33] *A.N.*, p. 330. The sentence contains the words "at first." If this means
"at least on their first appearance" it accounts for much, but modifies the
earlier claim.   [34] *G.B.*, I. 111 f.   [35] *G.B.*, I. 187 f.

communion—or indeed, even without meanings, have found
his account, aesthetically, in some gratified play of our modern
sense of type, so scantly to be distinguished from our modern
sense of beauty. Type was there, at the worst, in Mrs. Assingham's dark, neat head. . . .[36]

Why the supposititious observer? Evidently the Prince's point
of view, operative until this moment, is no longer good enough
for James. The imaginary observer postulated here is in fact
doing duty for the novelist himself; standing in for him until
he assumes the omniscient role in the passage that follows
dealing with Mrs Assingham's early life and marriage. But
this shifting of the narrative viewpoint does not strike the reader
very forcibly. The tone of the narrative, in fact, changes very
little. Whether the Prince's perceptions are being exploited
or not, the narrator's style—James's style—is the factor that
counts. Transitions from one point of view to another are
easily negotiated within this medium.

In all these later works in which centres of consciousness
are used, it could be claimed that the point of view is really
the novelist's, and that he appropriates and interprets the
experience of the characters more than in the earlier works.
Far from having withdrawn, he manifests himself more than
ever. The interpretative equipment has been adapted to the
sensibility of a Milly or a Strether; and their sensibility has
been heightened by his powers of interpretation. The result
is difficult to describe, but impersonality is certainly not the
word for it. We are confronted with a paradox. The later
works are distinguished by a closer cherishing of the subject,
and this at once gives an intenser life to the consciousness that
is being cherished and a further opportunity for the interpreting
narrator to be in possession.

To return to *The Golden Bowl*, it would be easy to formulate
a charge of unwieldiness against the first book. As we have seen,
it is by no means held together by the Prince's point of view.
How can anyone, on a first reading, not be somewhat incom-
moded by the successive blocks of episodes, separated by lapses
of time and representing stage after stage of what is still only
preparation for the significant grouping of the characters that

[36] *G.B.*, I 30-1.

is to constitute the main subject? Some readers may recognise even from the outset that these episodes are of exceptionally rich quality, and when this is appreciated the slow, clumsy development and lack of shape matter little. The individual episodes or sequences are finely constructed and well contrasted with each other. James's sense of form can be active in the parts of a work even when his spirit of excess rules the larger whole.

These comments on James's use of the point of view are, of course, very selective and simplified. Their object is to challenge briefly certain ideas that are still very much abroad. That his favourite method involves the elimination of the author, and that he became more impersonal in his later work, are part of the critical legend.

It seems strange that in discussions of James's achievement critics so seldom recognise that he is a supremely great prose writer, and that one of the chief reasons for reading him is the incomparable pleasure that his language gives. No other novelist in English has anything approaching his range of idiom. It may be doubted whether any other novelist has reached the height of his best passages, but if Emily Brontë, Melville and George Eliot may be said to have done so, theirs is a more infrequent best than his. Writing specifically of the late style Miss Dorothea Krook gives the measure of James's quality when she describes it as "an artistic achievement comparable in originality and power with the blank verse of Shakespeare's mature plays."[37] Only with continual reference to the actual writing can one attempt to touch on the nature of his success in the novels and stories. Of the great variety of his skills only a slight indication will be given here. His ability to set a scene and place a character effectively in it is worth mentioning first (it has, of course, been noted in an earlier chapter) because it is by this means that he gives brilliant openings to so many stories. There are early examples of it in "The Madonna of the Future" and "Madame de Mauves"; and the first pages of "An International Episode," *The Portrait of a Lady*, "Lady Barbarina" and *The Tragic Muse* also illustrate this gift. If anything, it improved with the years.

[37] *The Ordeal of Consciousness in Henry James* (1962), p. 390.

In the opening of a very late short story, "Crapy Cornelia,"
he achieves this effect with an intimacy of touch that comes of a
lifetime of fine strokes.   The story, as it develops, is not one of
his best: the theme of the sensitive, middle-aged gentleman
waking up to the fact that the woman he intends to propose to
is showy and superficial has irritating implications.   But the
introductory scene, with White-Mason sitting in the Park
(it is New York) on an April afternoon, waiting for the hour
of his visit and of his destiny, is a little masterpiece of luxurious
composition.

His feeling for places has greater intensity in the later works;
the scenes are more powerfully evoked.   Especially impressive
is the account, in *The Sense of the Past*, of Ralph Pendrel's
spellbound exposure to London in the first days of his so long
delayed visit.   Such an effect of saturation, of almost agonised
awareness, is only achieved by language that combines a
precise and suggestive notation with great imaginative pressure
and excitement.   The description of Ralph looking out of the
old house into the London square has this quality:

> . . . The cold rain was on his window-pane, and it damped the
> great London hum.   These squares of old glass were small and
> many and the frames that enclosed them thick; the appropriate
> recess, of which no window failed, was deep, and Ralph could
> as he looked out rest a knee on the flat cushion, all flowered
> and faded, that covered the solid bench.   He looked out only
> to look in again under the charm of isolation and enclosure,
> of being separated from the splashed Square and its blurred
> and distant life much more by time than by space; under
> the charm above all of the queer incomparable London light—
> unless one frankly loved it rather as London shade—which
> he had repeatedly noted as so strange as to be at its finest
> sinister, and which just now scattered as never before its air
> over what surrounded him.   However else this air might
> have been described it was signally not the light of freshness
> and suggested as little as possible the element in which the first
> children of nature might have begun to take notice.   Ages,
> generations, inventions, corruptions had produced it, and it
> seemed, wherever it rested, to have filtered through the bed
> of history.   It made the objects about show for the time as in
> something "turned on"—something highly successful that he

might have seen at the theatre. What was one to call the confounding impression but that of some stamp, some deposit again laid bare, of a conscious past, recognising no less than recognised?[38]

But an even longer quotation would be needed to do justice to Ralph's haunted and possessed condition, which lasts for days upon days. ("He gasped on reminding himself as his tenth day dawned that the glimpse accompanied for him with so much ado was yet but a small millionth of the whole.")[39]

One of James's most heartrending stories, "The Bench of Desolation," also very late (1910), owes much to the same gift. The setting in itself does not matter much, though a seaside resort in the "long autumn blankness" after the holiday season is appropriate enough as a background for the loneliness of Herbert Dodd. The story shocks one's sense of the humanly possible, while imposing itself with its deeply troubling power. The woman who has ruined Herbert Dodd by a cruel breach of promise action, causing the poverty which has killed his wife, comes back with the money she has saved for him. A scene of anguish between them is followed in the next chapter (written from the standpoint of a later stage in their relationship) by an account of his immediate agitation:

> ... After leaving her at the hotel that last Sunday he had gone forth in his reaggravated trouble and walked straight before him, in the teeth of the west wind, close to the iron rails of the stretched Marina and with his tell-tale face turned from persons occasionally met and toward the surging sea. At the land's end, even in the confirmed darkness and the perhaps imminent big blow, his immemorial nook, small shelter as it yielded, had again received him; and it was in the course of this needless session, no doubt, where the agitated air had nothing to add to the commotion within him, that he began to look his extraordinary fortune a bit straighter in the face. . . .[40]

In passages like this language is given its fullest rhetorical licence: "On that Sunday night he had wandered wild, incoherently ranging and throbbing. . . ." His "swollen

[38] *The Sense of the Past* (1917), pp. 63-4.
[39] *Op. cit.*, p. 59.   [40] XXVIII. 459.

consciousness . . . fairly split in twain the raw shell of his sordid
little boarding-place. The arch of the sky and the spread of
sea and shore alone gave him space. . . ."[41] Less lurid, nearer
to the common human lot, is the otherwise comparable episode
in *The Wings of the Dove* (1902) where Milly rushes away after
her visit to the doctor, losing herself in the streets of London
and finally resting in Regent's Park. It would be wasteful
to quote lengthily from so well-known an episode. A sentence
or two will illustrate the strength of the bond between the
component elements of situation and scene:

> She passed along unknown streets, over dusty littery ways,
> between long rows of fronts not enhanced by the August light;
> she felt good for miles and only wanted to get lost; there were
> moments at corners, when she stopped and chose her direction,
> in which she quite lived up to his [the doctor's] injunction
> to rejoice that she was active.[42]

James's style, especially in the later works, expresses an
ever-varying narrative mood. One element, throughout all
the changes, is maintained: his pleasure in narration itself.
Here the question of imagery can most conveniently be introduced. James's imagery is very much a vehicle of his narrative
(or descriptive) mood, and one of his ways of manifesting
pleasure in narration. A prodigious image often serves to
give an unexpected heightening to a turn of events: but sometimes at a painful moment a comic image may occur. For
example, in *The Spoils of Poynton* (1897): "It was as if everything
at Ricks had been poured into a common receptacle, a public
ferment of emotion and zeal, out of which it was to be ladled
up, with a splash, to be tasted and talked about."[43] But this
image immediately follows one of a completely different kind,
expressing the painful aspect of Fleda's problem: "Pressed
upon her, goodness knew, the crisis had been, but it now put
forth big encircling arms—arms that squeezed till they hurt
and she must cry out."[44] Since the metaphysical poets came
into vogue earlier in this century imagery everywhere has
tended to be subjected to criteria which are not appropriate

---

[41] XXVIII. 460.   [42] *The Wings of the Dove* [= *W.D.*], I. 219-20.
[43] *The Spoils of Poynton* [= *S.P.*], p. 115.   [44] *S.P.*, p. 115.

to all writers. Some of James's imagery, examined by quasi-metaphysical standards, would emerge with high credit: but in general the approach is mistaken, and many of his finest flourishes would fare no better at the hands of certain critics than the great similes of *Paradise Lost*. The element of gesture, the open pleasure, sometimes almost irresponsible, of the *raconteur* in the game he is playing, must be taken into account.

Going to extremes at a chosen moment is one of James's favourite forms of virtuosity. We enjoy the following passage for the rhetorical sweep of the image rather than for its exact fitness as a vehicle for expressing Mrs Gereth's response:

> ". . . I'm thinking of his general undertaking—to give her the house as she originally saw it."
>
> "To give her the house!"—
>
> Mrs. Gereth brought up the words from the depth of the unspeakable. The effect was like the moan of an autumn wind, and she turned as pale as if she had heard of the landing, there on the coast, of a foreign army.[45]

In another place Fleda sees Mrs Gereth as a wounded bird, making her way "with wings of anguish"[46] to her nest, and as "a lioness deprived of her cubs."[47] These are not tragic images. Mrs Gereth is not tragic, but she has tragic airs, she provokes the imagination to the portentous, and the portentous is a welcome source of rhetoric in a narrative otherwise subdued to the tone of Fleda's inwardness. James is not too proud to indulge in an occasional flippant image. The description of Mrs Brigstock in the same novel may perhaps be condemned as beneath the level of the master: but, whether bad or good, it allows levity to have its way at a trying moment in the story:

> She had a face of which it was impossible to say anything but that it was pink, and a mind it would be possible to describe only had one been able to mark it in a similar fashion. As nature had made this organ neither green nor blue nor yellow there was nothing to know it by; it strayed and bleated like an unbranded sheep.[48]

---

[45] *S.P.*, p. 102. [46] *S.P.*, p. 217.
[47] *S.P.*, p. 217. [48] *S.P.*, p. 151.

A droll image in a serious crisis may, of course, express the sufferer's resilience or wry stoicism, especially if he or she is an American. A fabulous image is often used to express the narrator's or central character's play of fancy as it hovers about the extreme implications of a stage of affairs. James's pleasure in such gestures, and in all the more extreme joys of narration, especially in the later works, gives a buoyant and familiar quality even to passages which are a little difficult to construe.

The recognition of an element of gesture, whether humorous or portentous, in James's imagery may be a helpful background to appreciation of those passages where the demands upon his virtuosity are greatest and his poetic powers at their fullest stretch. There is one such passage near to the conclusion of *The Wings of the Dove* where, in a succession of images of almost unbearable poignancy, he seems not only to be giving a final statement of Densher's plight but to be carrying his own performance as narrator to a culmination. The passage expresses Densher's yearning to feel all that can be felt on the subject of what is lost to him: Milly's love and, more specifically, her unread letter, relinquished to Kate and thrown into the fire by her. His need to feel and be hurt, to lose what has hitherto been most desired, in order to possess a thing of great price that can be possessed only in thought, and even so only partially, is a rare thing for an artist to undertake to express. Throughout the novel James has presented most convincingly the force of attraction between Kate and Densher; and here he is to convey the force of the spell that holds Densher and renders Kate powerless:

> He watched her, when she went her way, with the vision of what she thus a little stiffly carried. It was confused and obscure, but how, with her head high, it made her hold herself! He really in his own person might at these moments have been swaying a little aloft as one of the objects in her poised basket. It was doubtless thanks to some such consciousness as this that he felt the lapse of the weeks, before the day of Kate's mounting of his stair, almost swingingly rapid. They contained for him the contradiction that, whereas periods of waiting are supposed in general to keep the time slow, it was the wait, actually,

that made the pace trouble him.   The secret of that anomaly, to be plain, was that he was aware of how, while the days melted, something rare went with them.   This something was only a thought, but a thought precisely of such freshness and such delicacy as made the precious, of whatever sort, most subject to the hunger of time.   The thought was all his own, and his intimate companion was the last person he might have shared it with.   He kept it back like a favourite pang; left it behind him, so to say, when he went out, but came home again the sooner for the certainty of finding it there.   Then he took it out of its sacred corner and its soft wrappings; he undid them one by one, handling them, handling *it*, as a father, baffled and tender, might handle a maimed child.   But so it was before him—in his dread of who else might see it.   Then he took to himself at such hours, in other words, that he should never, never know what had been in Milly's letter.   The intention announced in it he should but too probably know; only that would have been, but for the depths of his spirit, the least part of it.   The part of it missed for ever was the turn she would have given her act.   This turn had possibilities that, somehow, by wondering about them, his imagination had extraordinarily filled out and refined.   It had made of them a revelation the loss of which was like the sight of a priceless pearl cast before his eyes—his pledge given not to save it—into the fathomless sea, or rather even it was like the sacrifice of something sentient and throbbing, something that, for the spiritual ear, might have been audible as a faint far wail. This was the sound he cherished when alone in the stillness of his rooms.   He sought and guarded the stillness, so that it might prevail there until the inevitable sounds of life, once more, comparatively coarse and harsh, should smother and deaden it—doubtless by the same process with which they would officiously heal the ache in his soul that was somehow one with it.[49]

The narrator's idioms—"doubtless," "to be plain," "in other words"—prosaic though they are, enhance the effect by involving him personally in the effort to formulate the momentous fact of Milly's power.   The combination of the rhetorical with the colloquial and personal gives extraordinary potency and appeal to many passages in James's late works.

[49] *W.D.*, II. 350-1.

VIII

Short Stories

SUCH virtues as economy, severity of form and consistency of method have not so far been the main emphasis in this study. In the last chapter examples were given of James's clumsiness in certain places, and of departures from his professed practice of adhering to a chosen point of view. But let us make no mistake here. There are plenty of works in which artistic logic and economy prevail, and where the result is inordinate success. Consistent use of a character's point of view (often a first person narrator, a device found in no long work except *The Sacred Fount*) is very effective in a considerable number of the short stories. The four stories chosen for rather full treatment here all have these virtues.

In a summary of a short story one can attempt to convey certain aspects. The means of narration, the narrator's relation to the events, can be identified. Some impression of the shape or point of a story may be given, and also of the quality of the detail, though very selectively. But other aspects are too elusive. For instance, much of the art of a story lies in the timing of the events. James had a fine sense of the kind and degree of preparation that most enhance the introduction of a new development. The notation he uses to indicate changes in situations may vary from the light to the ominous; and only in the full context can all this be appreciated. In the stories selected here the timing is of the most piquant.

The Pupil (1891) is the story of a young expatriate American who accepts a post as tutor to a boy in a genteel but impecunious family, also expatriate American, who fail to pay him regularly, relying on the bond of affection that makes it difficult for him to desert his pupil. The boy has a weak heart, and the story is brought to an end by his collapse and death at a moment of extreme tension for the family—they are being turned ignominiously out of their rooms—and for his tutor, who is threatened with the prospect of permanent responsibility for him.

It is very much the tutor's story. Pemberton's decency, forbearance, endurance make the situation possible and keep it going. There is something painful in this: he has a touch of Rowland Mallett, with his New England moral compulsions. But he has also the national gift of appreciation, so that through his eyes the Moreens are seen in all their charm—so long as it is possible to view them in this light. They are, of course, suspect from the beginning, but they are interesting. Pemberton indeed "felt a glow of joy" on his realisation that "living with them would really be to see life."

> Their sociable strangeness was an intimation of that—their chatter of tongues, their gaiety and good humour, their infinite dawdling (they were always getting themselves up, but it took for ever, and Pemberton once found Mr. Moreen shaving in the drawing-room), their French, their Italian and, cropping up in the foreign fluencies, their cold tough slices of American. They lived on maccaroni and coffee—they had these articles prepared in perfection—but they knew recipes for a hundred other dishes. They overflowed with music and song, were always humming and catching each other up, and had a sort of professional acquaintance with Continental cities. They talked of "good places" as if they had been pickpockets or strolling players. They had at Nice a villa, a carriage, a piano and a banjo, and they went to official parties. They were a perfect calendar of the "days" of their friends, which Pemberton knew them, when they were indisposed, to get out of bed to go to. . . . Mrs. Moreen had translated something at some former period—an author, whom it made Pemberton feel *borné* never to have heard of. . . .[1]

He notes their genuine affection and admiration for his pupil Morgan, though from an early stage he sees also how they contrive to "reconcile the appearance, and indeed the essential fact, of adoring the child with their eagerness to wash their hands of him."[2] There is a stage in the story, not very early, when he realises in simple terms that he has made a mistake: "He had simply given himself away to a band of adventurers."[3] With his American's curiosity and capacity for coming to terms with ways of life foreign to his own, combined with his

[1] XVI. 460-1.   [2] XVI. 462.   [3] XVI. 473.

basic innocence and uprightness, he has been slow to pass
sentence on the Moreens.   The co-existence of these qualities
in Pemberton provides an ideal narrative resource.   His
personal drama and moral dilemma are balanced in interest
by observations of expatriate manners of the most acute and
entertaining quality.   The amount of pointed detail achieved
in the compass of so short a piece is impressive.   With James's
characteristic economy a whole phase of their disastrous history
may be summed up in one charged and ominous paragraph,
such as that which describes the flight from Florence termina-
ting in the dismal four months' sojourn in Paris.[4]

But the picture of the Moreens as seen by Pemberton is
intensified by Morgan's own view of his disastrous family.
At first the boy strikes the reader simply as a special variation
of the classic American type, with his mocking "Oh la-la!"
at his mother's mention of remuneration to his tutor,[5] and his
"small satiric face,"[6] sometimes infantile but at other times
precocious.   But gradually Pemberton finds him more interesting
than this.   Somehow the upbringing to which he has been
condemned by his parents' way of life and his own poor health
have given him a sensitive individuality:

> He had the general quality of a child for whom life had not
> been simplified by school, a kind of home-bred sensibility which
> might have been bad for himself but was charming for others,
> and a whole range of refinement and perception—little musical
> vibrations as taking as picked-up airs—begotten by wandering
> about Europe at the tail of his migratory tribe.   This might
> not have been an education to recommend in advance, but its
> results with so special a subject were as appreciable as the marks
> on a piece of fine porcelain.[7]

Morgan's sense that there is something wrong in his parents'
treatment of Pemberton—that they are, in fact, no good—
gives the story its most touching theme.   He begins by teasing
Pemberton affectionately for the unfailing correctness of his
references to the parental motives: "You're a jolly old humbug."[8]   On a later occasion he is more explicit: "You ought to

---

[4] XVI. 468.   [5] XVI. 455.   [6] XVI. 456.
[7] XVI. 463.   [8] XVI. 466.

filer. . . . You know they don't pay you up."[9] Pemberton
handles him lightly, and their lesson proceeds pleasantly,
but at the end of the morning Morgan buries his head in his
arms and bursts into tears. He tells of a former nurse, Zénobie,
who had finally left because she had not been paid. When the
Moreens realised that she liked Morgan they stopped giving
her anything; and this is, in fact, the basis on which Pemberton is now living.

Pemberton becomes increasingly aware of the qualities
that mark the boy out from the rest of his family: "a temper,
a sensibility, even a private ideal, which made him as privately
disown the stuff his people were made of. Morgan had in
secret a small loftiness which made him acute about betrayed
meanness. . . ."[10] After an outburst on the subject of their
dishonesty, their snobbery, their regard only for worldly
appearances, and the contempt in which they are held by really
nice people, Morgan concludes with: "You're the only really
nice person we know."[11] He has a "romantic imagination, fed
by poetry and history [all this is beautifully in the national
vein], and he would have liked those who 'bore his name' . . .
to carry themselves with an air. But their one idea was to get
in with people who didn't want them and to take snubs as if
they were honourable scars."[12]

Pemberton's point of view encompasses the whole story,
but Morgan's point of view is part of what he has to deal with,
part of the value of what he has to tell. The play between the
two awarenesses, the mixture of reserves and confidences
and evasive pleasantries (in the American evasive humorous
manner) give great charm to a relationship in an environment in which "the surface of one's delicacy got rather
smudged."[13]

The crises in the Moreen history are occasions for James's
skill in staging a piquant scene. There is a fine one with a
Venetian *décor*:

> One sad November day, while the wind roared round the old
> palace and the rain lashed the lagoon, Pemberton, for exercise

---

[9] XVI. 475.   [10] XVI. 484.   [11] XVI. 487.
[12] XVI. 489-90.   [13] XVI. 471.

L

and even somewhat for warmth—the Moreens were horribly frugal about fires; it was a cause of suffering to their inmate—walked up and down the big bare sala with his pupil. The scagliola floor was cold, the high battered casements shook in the storm, and the stately decay of the place was unrelieved by a particle of furniture. Pemberton's spirits were low, and it came over him that the fortune of the Moreens was now even lower. A blast of desolation, a portent of disgrace and disaster, seemed to draw through the comfortless hall. Mr. Moreen and Ulick were in the Piazza, looking out for something, strolling drearily, in mackintoshes, under the arcades; but still, in spite of mackintoshes, unmistakable men of the world.[14]

Rivalling this is the culminating spectacle of disorder that confronts Pemberton as he returns with Morgan from the Bois de Boulogne, and finds the family, after "a scene of the last proprietary firmness,"[15] virtually in a state of dissolution.

One of the structural features of the story consists of a duel between two extremes: the Moreens' technique of exploitation and Pemberton's capacity for sacrifice. Mrs Moreen has a gift for sounding, in all her exorbitance, the very chord that corresponds to his own feelings: "it was useless for him to pretend he didn't know in all his bones that his place at such a time was with Morgan."[16] There is no end to the Moreens' effrontery and hypocrisy, and Pemberton is momentarily shaken by the boy's joyous response to their final proposal that he should take Morgan permanently off their hands. He has no opportunity to deal with the proposal, for at this moment the boy has his fatal attack.

"The Coxon Fund" (1894) may perhaps not be James's best story; in human content it has less weight than "The Pupil": but it is unsurpassed among works of this scale as a *tour de force* of technique, especially as a case of what can be done with a first person narrator. The story is peculiarly dependent for its existence on the narrator's special connexion with the other participants, beginning at a point when their connexion with each other is still undeveloped and no sign appears of a story

---

[14] XVI. 492-3.　　　　[15] XVI. 508.　　　　[16] XVI. 500-1.

taking shape. We must wait until the pattern gradually tightens—the emergence of the relevant and ominous details is skilfully managed—and we see the characters' fates converging in a situation the outcome of which emerges as the narrator's own doing.

Everything depends on what he, and certain other characters, think of the central figure of the story, Frank Saltram, a kind of unsystematic philosopher (based on Coleridge, but with much less to show for himself), whose chief medium is conversation, and who is adopted by a generously admiring couple, the Kent Mulvilles, who take him into their home and try to make his wisdom available to their friends through drawing room conversation or lecture schemes. They suffer a number of betrayals and disappointments, partly owing to his alcoholic aberrations; and there are other aspects of him— his dubious past, his bad manners, his unprepossessing appearance (the fine eyes apart)—that stand in the way of all but the most fanatical of his supporters. The question of Mr Saltram's merits takes a particular form: is he worthy of the emoluments of a certain Fund, intended for the advancement of Moral Truth? The young woman, Ruth Anvoy, upon whom the disposal of the money will devolve after her aunt's death, makes her first appearance in the story at an earlier point, as a member of a lecture audience that Mr Saltram disappoints by absenting himself; and it is the narrator himself, one of the promoters of the fiasco, who nevertheless gives her the first hint of the sage's genius, thus causing her later, when the Fund comes into being, to view him as a likely candidate. The narrator, who has mixed feelings about Mr Saltram, is at first shocked at his being seriously considered in such a light, though somewhat amused by Ruth's earnest interest—she is an intense young American—and he has no great aversion to her disappointing her *fiancé*, the young M.P., George Gravener, who badly needs her money for himself. The situation is one in which chance plays a large part. Saltram can, on occasion, be very impressive, and he chooses his occasions happily. The narrator has had an inspiring evening with him immediately before a certain incriminating letter about his past conduct comes into his hands. If the letter were handed over and read it might make all the difference, but he invites Ruth not to read it; and Mr Saltram gets the money.

The narrator is a wit and a gossip, in addition to being keenly susceptible to the things of the mind. He appreciates Mr Saltram, but he also savours the gross situations he gives rise to. He is, in fact, the ideal interpreter of the whole sequence of events. The opening sentences of the story, which recall his first encounter with Saltram at the Mulvilles, sets the tone:

> "They've got him for life!" I said to myself that evening on my way back to the station; but later on, alone in the compartment (from Wimbledon to Waterloo, before the glory of the District Railway) I amended this declaration in the light of the sense that my friends would probably after all not enjoy a monopoly of Mr. Saltram. I won't pretend to have taken his vast measure on that first occasion, but I think I had achieved a glimpse of what the privilege of his acquaintance might mean for many persons in the way of charges accepted. He had been a great experience, and it was this perhaps that had put me into the frame of foreseeing how we should all, sooner or later, have the honour of dealing with him as a whole. Whatever impression I then received of the amount of this total, I had a full enough vision of the patience of the Mulvilles. He was to stay all the winter. . . . I remember that at dinner that evening he wore slippers, new and predominantly purple, of some queer carpet-stuff; but the Mulvilles were still in the stage of supposing that he might be snatched from them by higher bidders. At a later time they grew, poor dears, to fear no snatching. . . .[17]

He enjoys balancing an issue where there are little base suspicions to be resisted. He resists, but the point of wit remains unscathed. He notes, for example, Saltram's awareness that the Mulvilles' dinners are "*soignés*": but adds that he has no calculation in his nature: "no man who was so much of an absorbent can have ever been less of a parasite."[18] When he hears of Ruth's having handed thirty pounds to Mrs Mulville to give to Mr Saltram (who, of course, was not looking at that moment), he cannot help connecting this with the fact that the sage was on especially good form during that visit:

> ... After a moment I added: "Had he peradventure caught a glimpse of the money in the table-drawer?"
> At this my companion honestly flushed. "How can you be so cruel when you know how little he calculates?"
> "Forgive me, I do know it. But you tell me things that act on my nerves. I'm sure he hadn't caught a glimpse of anything but some splendid idea."[19]

His first conversation with Ruth is a good example of his sprightly play with the different facets of the philosopher:

> I held my tongue about the natural children engendered, to the number of three, in the wantonness of his youth. I only remarked that he did make efforts—often tremendous ones. "But the efforts never come to much: the only things that come to much are the abandonments, the surrenders."
> "And how much do they come to?"
> "You're right to put it as if we had a big bill to pay, but, as I've told you before, your questions are rather terrible. They come, these mere exercises of genius, to a great sum of poetry, of philosophy, a mighty mass of speculation, notation, quotation. . . ."[20]

On the subject of his mind, he gives her a phrase: "The sight of a great suspended swinging crystal—huge lucid lustrous, a block of light—flashing back every impression of life and every possibility of thought,"[21] and is startled several episodes later when it is quoted back at him by Mrs Mulville as Ruth's own eloquent summing up. His special idiosyncrasy is the habit of registering amusement. As narrator he makes this fact subsidiary to some other statement, the cause of his mirth being left to the reader's recognition and often beyond the ken of his interlocutor:

> ". . . What particular importance do you attach to the idea of her being impressed?"
> Adelaide turned her mild pale eyes on me as for rebuke of my levity. "Why the importance of her being as happy as *we* are!"
> I'm afraid that at this my levity grew. . . .[22]

---

[19] xx. 293.   [20] xx. 269.
[21] xx. 270.   [22] xx. 305.

"... You mustn't suppose he's good-looking," I added.
"Why, his wife says he's lovely!"
My hilarity must have struck her as excessive. . . .[23]

The narrator's sense of the comedy, and also of the awfulness of the whole affair, makes his exchanges with the other characters (all simpler than himself) extremely amusing. In another passage on the subject of Saltram's talk with Ruth he asks Mrs Mulville:

"... And what was it all about?"
"His talk? It was apropos of her engagement, which I had told him about: the idea of marriage, the philosophy, the poetry, the sublimity of it." It was impossible wholly to restrain one's mirth at this, and some rude ripple that I emitted again caused my companion to admonish me. "It sounds a little stale, but you know his freshness."
"Of illustration? Indeed I do!"
"And how he has always been right on that great question."
"On what great question, dear lady, hasn't he been right?"
"Of what other great men can you equally say it?—and that he has never, but *never* had a deflexion?" Mrs. Mulville exultantly demanded. I tried to think of some other great man, but I had to give it up.[24]

As for the central character in this situation, Saltram hardly makes a direct appearance, and of his wonderful eloquence we are given not a single sample. The attitudes that he begets in others are all we know him by. Were it a more serious work and not just a brilliant *jeu d'esprit*, this might possibly be a fault. Technically, it is very effective that in the penultimate section of the story, and not until then, he should at last come so far into the foreground as to be shown to the reader, seated on a bench, "with sad far-wandering eyes and plump white hands folded on the head of a stick,"[25] and addressed directly by the narrator. For this of all encounters leads to their fatal evening together and settles the matter of the Fund.

It is a very dense piece of narration. The events cover a number of years and, in addition to the significant conversations

in which the narrator participates, there is a wealth of little
reported episodes—Gravener's election campaign at Clock-
borough, Saltram's misbehaviour during the period of his stay
with the Pudney's, innumerable visits paid by the narrator to
the other persons of the drama, and his conversations with the
unspeakable Mrs Saltram—which are neatly handled. (Mrs
Saltram, we are told, has washed her hands of her husband
but she has "carefully preserved the water of this ablution, which
she handed about for analysis.")[26]   One of the threads in
the story is the narrator's interest in Ruth Anvoy, and in the
stages of her engagement with Gravener.   He is never very
direct about this; he has no serious project to become a rival
suitor: but his attitude helps to sharpen certain points in the
narrative.

The story is "English" in its *décor* and its pictorial effects.
The following little sketch provides a happy opening for a new
section after Mr Saltram's return to the fold following upon the
disgraceful Pudney phase:

> One of the consequences, for the Mulvilles, of the sacrifices they
> made for Frank Saltram was that they had to give up their
> carriage.   Adelaide drove gently into London in a one-horse
> greenish thing, an early Victorian landau, hired, near at hand
> . . . a vehicle that made people turn round all the more when
> her pensioner sat beside her in a soft white hat and a shawl,
> one of the dear woman's own. . . .[27]

"Europe" (1899) has an American theme, the central characters being an immensely aged Bostonian mother and her
three ageing daughters, of a family representing New England
culture at its most rarefied.   The absorbing issue for them and
their friends is whether the daughters will ever make the
journey to Europe that their mother has designed for them—
that is, whether her state of health (she is ailing, but indestruct-
ible) will not always intervene as an obstacle at the last moment.
She has made a tour of Europe herself, at a remote period of the
past, and maintains that they have a "duty" to perform by
going: "if it be only that of laying-up for the years to come
the same store of remarkable impressions, the same wealth

[26] xx. 271   [27] xx. 289.

of knowledge and food for conversation as, since my return,
I've found myself so happy to possess."[28] She had once had the
idea of going again herself "for her health," and taking them
with her: but it was her health that prevented it.   "She
hadn't gone, and Becky, Maria and Jane hadn't gone, and this
was long ago."[29]

The narrator, a native of "loud longitudinal New York,"[30]
has the sensibility to appreciate the "almost pastoral sweetness"[31] of the Boston suburb where the Rimmles live, and the
moral atmosphere of their exemplary household.   In this world
of "puritanism refined and reclaimed" the question of whether,
after their mother has had an unusually good winter, two
members of the family could be spared, has been "threshed as
fine" as "any case of conscience has ever been threshed";[32]
but if that were settled favourably, there would still be
the exquisite need for each daughter to offer herself for the
sacrifice of staying.   The story, as it develops, exemplifies
some of the extreme possibilities of this way of life; and it is
in the increasing dreadfulness of the situation that the drama
consists.   The narrator's sense of the macabre flavours his sense
of the impeccable tone of the Rimmles.

His sense of time gives the story its shape.   The opening
sentences place the whole sequence of events engagingly within
a framework of memory:

> "Our feeling is, you know, that Becky *should* go."   That
> earnest little remark comes back to me, even after long years,
> as the first note of something that began, for my observation,
> the day I went with my sister-in-law to take leave of her good
> friends.   It's a memory of the American time, which revives
> so at present—under some touch that doesn't signify—that it
> rounds itself off as an anecdote.   That walk to say goodbye
> was the beginning; and the end, so far as I enjoyed a view of
> it, was not till long after; yet even the end also appears to me
> now as of the old days.[33]

Mrs Rimmle's sense of time has become deranged.   She thinks
of her return from Europe as very recent, while "the future

[28] XXI. 305.   [29] XXI. 303.
[30] XXI. 301.   [31] XXI. 301.
[32] XXI. 304.   [33] XXI. 301.

of her daughters was somehow, by a different law, to be on
the scale of great vistas, of endless aftertastes."[34] Or is she not
secretly enjoying her position, perching over them "like a
vulture," waiting for them to die before her? The subject of
age is haunting, a theme for rhetoric. On his first acquaintance
with them, the narrator thinks of the mother as having reached
her limit: "She was old, and her daughters were old, but I
was destined to know them all as older."[35] "What the deuce
is her age," he asks his sister-in-law on a later occasion:

> "I can't tell you to a year—but she's immensely old."
> "That of course I saw," I replied—"unless you literally mean so
> old that the records have been lost."
> "My sister-in-law thought. "Well, I believe she wasn't
> positively young when she married. She lost three or four
> children before these women were born."
> We surveyed together a little, on this, the "dark backward."[36]

On one of his visits near to the story's culmination he is
greeted by a figure that he takes at first to be Mrs Rimmle,
but immediately recognises as Becky:

> . . . I knew no one but her mother of that extreme age. Becky's
> age was quite startling; it had made a great stride. . . .[37]

As for Mrs Rimmle herself, Becky believes now that she is no
longer alive, but as "Maria isn't so clear," she invites him to
judge for himself. But even this stage of her decay (her face
is like that of "some immemorial sovereign, of indistinguishable
sex, brought forth to be shown to the people in disproof of the
rumour of extinction")[38] is not final. She lives on and Becky
dies. Reluctantly, for the story of the Rimmles tells upon his
nerves, he pays another visit, and finds that nothing has changed
with the mother, but that Maria is different: "if Becky, on
my last seeing her, had looked as old as her mother, Maria—
save that she moved about—looked older."[39]

The point of view of the narrator acquires edge through

[34] XXI. 305.
[35] XXI. 302.
[36] XXI. 309.
[37] XXI. 319.
[38] XXI. 322.
[39] XXI. 325.

contact with more conventional attitudes. His sister-in-law provokes him to extremes:

> ". . . It's a pity they're so infernally good," I mused.
> "No—don't say that. It's what keeps them up."
> "Yes, but isn't it what keeps *her* up too?"
> My visitor looked grave. "Would you like them to kill her?"
> I don't know that I was then prepared to say I should—though I believe I came very near it. . . .[40]

But with all their goodness they have inscrutable possibilities. When Jane actually "goes" we learn what she is capable of in the way of development under favouring influences. Europe "brings her out"; she "tastes blood." She is reported to have become flirtatious; she refuses to come back. And Becky supports her financially.

As the monstrosity piles up, the behaviour of the Rimmles, mother and daughters alike, takes on more and more of the character of a performance. To the charged imagination of the narrator their appearances are theatrical; and the story becomes a kind of quiet little Greek drama of the New England psyche, depicting the horrors of an ancient house before its extinction. Placed as it is in a period of the past ("the American time"), it has from the outset a legendary flavour.

"Fordham Castle" (1904), one of the less well known of the stories, is nevertheless a formidable piece, and, like "The Pupil" and "Europe," has a theme of considerable enormity. Abel Taker's banishment to the Swiss *pension* under an assumed name wished on him by his wife, now in England seeking the social triumph impossible for her in his company, is the *terminus ad quem* of that ruthlessness in the Middle West girl making good, of which Edith Wharton's Undine Spragg is a bracing but less fantastic example.

James's technique, used also in *The Sacred Fount* and elsewhere, of placing two queer situations, comparable in pattern, side by side, gives the effect of sinister laws in operation. We learn on the first page—that is, before we have grasped Abel's plight—that an American lady has recently arrived at the *pension*. The proprietress, "Sharp little Madame Massin,"

[40] XXI. 309-10.

recommends her to his friendly attention: "I shall put you next the American lady—the one who arrived yesterday. I know you'll be kind to her. . . ."[41] And in the curious atmosphere achieved by Abel's reflexions on his position, and by Mme Massin's apparent recognition of it as she hands him a letter addressed to him under his new name, it comes naturally to him—too naturally for real life, but with a baleful appropriateness in this sinister tale—that the lady must be in the same boat: she too has been exiled and, like himself, has "learned to butter her bread with a certain acceptance of fate."[42] And he is right, even to his surmise that the name on her letter also is not her own. Mrs Vanderplank is really Mrs Magaw, and her relegation the work of a daughter moving in English society with the aim of catching a titled husband.

The art of the story lies largely in the felicitous adjustment of viewpoint whereby the monstrous theme unfolds itself in the course of Abel's reflexions as merely the culmination of the habitual, the last of many marital humiliations. His acceptance of it is tinged with recognitions and appreciations which have the effect of giving an edge to understatement. The arrangement of the prose is such that the awful truth about Abel's situation comes to us not as the main substance of his reflexions at that point, but as something associated with it and belonging to the familiar and the inevitable. Cover is thus provided for revelations offered, as it were, casually, but which give us a quiet shock. The episode of the letter addressed to C. P. Addard, exhibits this technique at the outset of the story. The tone of the passage is set by Abel's smaller embarrassments rather than by the shame of his position at large:

> . . . Moreover, since Madame Massin's establishment counted, to his still somewhat bewildered mind, so little for an hotel, as hotels were mainly known to him, he had avoided the act of "registering", and the missive with which his hostess was practically testing him represented the very first piece of postal matter taken in since his arrival that hadn't been destined to some one else. He had privately blushed for the meagreness of his mail, which made him look unimportant. That however

---

[41] XXI. 349.   [42] XXI. 352.

was a detail, an appearance he was used to; indeed the reasons
making for such an appearance might never have been so
pleasant to him as on this vision of his identity formally and
legibly denied. It was denied there in his wife's large straight
hand; his eyes, attached to the envelope, took in the failure
of any symptom of weakness in her stroke; she at least had
the courage of his passing for somebody he wasn't, of his passing
rather for nobody at all, and he felt the force of her character
more irresistibly than ever as he thus submitted to what she was
doing with him. . . .[43]

The theme of this story—if we insist on saying it, thus turning
James's treatment inside out—is the pathos of the ineffective
and unwanted; and, by the same token, the horrifying inhumanity of those who condemn them to their limbo. Here
we have a simple moral for a moralising reader to extract, but
James's story does not come to us in these terms. The fact is
that Abel and his companion are both characteristic Americans,
and they do not seriously rebel against that side of the American
way of life which has brought them to their present pass. Abel,
who is nothing if not tolerant in the manner of his countrymen—the touch of irony with the mildness being also typical—
accepts the view that his wife had been "nothing worse . . .
than a very pretty girl of eighteen out in Peoria, who had seen
at that time no one else she wanted more to marry. . . ."[44]
It is Abel's habit of mind to see her problem as she sees it,
in her terms: "She hadn't known herself originally any more
than she had known him—hadn't forseen how much better
she was going to come out, nor how, for her individually, as
distinguished from him, there might be the possibility of a big
future."[45]   And he sees Mrs Magaw as Sue would have seen
her, as "neither fair nor slim nor 'bright' nor truly, not even
falsely, elegant, nor anything that Sue had taught him, in
her wonderful way, to associate with the American woman at
the American woman's best—that best than which there was
nothing better, as he had so often heard her say, on God's
great earth."[46]   Sue would have "banished her to the wildest
waste of the unknowable."[47]   But in conversation with Mrs

[43] XXI. 350-1.   [44] XXI. 356.   [45] XXI. 356.
[46] XXI. 362.   [47] XXI. 362

Magaw he cannot help playing a little with the implications of their common plight. Mrs Magaw's simplicity stimulates him. When Mrs Magaw refers to her daughter's "liking" the *pension*—that is, as the "right *sort* of place" for her exiled mother —Abel replies:

> "The right sort to pass for dead in?"
> "Oh she doesn't want me to pass for *dead*."
> "Then what does she want you to pass for?"
> The poor lady cast about. "Well, only for Mrs. Vanderplank."
> "And who or what is Mrs. Vanderplank?"
> Mrs. Magaw considered this personage, but didn't get far.
> "She isn't any one in particular, I guess."
> "That means," Abel returned, "that she isn't alive."
> "She isn't more than *half* alive," Mrs. Magaw conceded.[48]

She says, with touching complacency, "We shall feel we've helped. And it isn't so *very* much to do."[49] To which Abel replies: "You think it isn't so very much to do—to lie down and die for them?"[50] One of the most pleasing moments in the relationship is that in which Mrs Magaw, all humility with regard to herself, expresses surprise at Abel's not being wanted. It strikes him "as the prettiest word ever spoken to him," unaccustomed as he has been to "tributes to his adequacy."[51]

Abel receives further evidence of his wife's powers of contrivance. In accordance with the symmetry of the story, Mattie Magaw and Sue Taker meet—at Fordham Castle, which is as much the inevitable theatre for their ambitions as the Swiss *pension* is the appointed place for the unwanted. But Sue has changed her name, thus placing herself at two removes from him. This inspires Abel to sallies of wit. Mrs Taker has died and gone to Fordham Castle: "She had to die to go—as it would be for her like going to heaven. Marriages, sometimes, they say, are made up there. . . ."[52] "Her baser part, her vulgar part, has ceased to be, and she lives only as an angel."[53] She may marry: why not, since Abel is now dead?

When Mrs Magaw receives the telegram announcing her daughter's engagement to Lord Dunderton, with the additional words "Sue thinks you can come," Abel continues in the same

[48] XXI. 366. [49] XXI. 367. [50] XXI. 367.
[51] XXI. 368. [52] XXI. 372. [53] XXI. 373.

vein in his farewells. He urges her to tell Sue that she "has
seen the last of him," and when she asks if he would come to
Fordham Castle at her invitation, he replies: "I'll come as a
ghost. Don't old castles always have one?"[54] But when she
has gone, and he is left "in his solitude, to the sense of his
extinction," it is in a different tone that he utters, as his final
word: "Why certainly I'm dead."

Looking back over the four stories and their narrators
or "centres of consciousness", one notices that the three
Americans really are American: their Americanness counts as a
value, and contributes to the effect of the point of view. The
narrator of "The Coxon Fund," on the other hand, though
presumably English, is not very markedly so in outlook. His
attitude to Mr Saltram, who seems to be a sort of trans-
cendentalist, could easily be that of an American. His combination of intellectual conscience and sense of humour, though
not exactly American in flavour, is the kind of combination
that would suit the American character. The story as a whole
has been helped out by a certain amount of unconscious
Americanisation.

One might well ask how often James really uses an un-
equivocally and typically English point of view. Fleda Vetch
is not an American girl, but her moral refinement accords with
what a New England atmosphere might have produced. She
sees the Gereths—*they* are English enough—almost as exotics.
It is noteworthy that the events in the story of "Owen
Wingrave" (1892), with its drastically English materials, are
seen through the eyes of Spencer Coyle, the military crammer,
presumably English himself also but with too much of the
artist in him (he resembles a "concert-giving pianist") and
too much moral flexibility to be very typically so. This is
another example of what a well chosen point of view can
contribute to a story. Coyle's horrified response to Owen's
decision to give up his army career ("Upon my honour, you
must be off your head . . . I'm unspeakably disgusted . . .")
provides a true military opening. It is Owen's baptism of
fire, as it were: he will have a good deal of bitter hostility to
face and the first page rings with the sound of it. But after

[54] XXI. 375.

this first explosion Coyle is gradually revealed as a man of fine sensibility; his fierce loyalty to his profession makes his love for Owen all the more impressive. The excellence of Coyle vouches for Owen, on the score of courage and character, and in more general respects. The difficulty, he finds, in his dealings with the Wingrave family, is that "the boy's the best of them."[55] In consequence, the somewhat idealistic conception of the young pacifist, which might have been difficult to uphold successfully, comes over with considerable grace. "Owen Wingrave" may not be one of James's most substantial stories, but it is a very delicate piece of art.

A feeling for the "tall tale," a delight in "building high," is, of course, one of the great assets of an American narrator. And James can be thoroughly American in this respect. There is no reason why extravagant situations should not occur in non-American settings and be recorded by non-American narrators; but when the narrator of such a story happens to be American he acts in character, he draws upon a national tradition. The tall tale with an English setting and point (for example, "The Beldonald Holbein") is liable to be a mixed product: the events are developed in a more American way than James realised. We are conscious of a straining of English possibilities, a slightly false heightening of the drama. But a certain amount of Americanisation in his treatment of English material—that is, attribution of American attitudes to English people—was inevitable.

[55] XXII. 252.

IX

Two English Novels

THE *Awkward Age* (1898-9) confronts us with two quite different aspects of James which many readers cannot easily accept. On the one hand there is his desire to come to terms with the contemporary theatre. He was affronted, of course, by its standards, but he wished very much to be of it. He needed the money; and he could make concessions. Sometimes indeed we may ask whether he is making a concession or is himself infected by some inferior element. This should be distinguished from his wish, entirely laudable if somewhat quixotic at times, to make the fashionable talk of the contemporary drawing-room (the material upon which the contemporary theatre's comedy of manners depends) serve him as a medium for purposes that go far beyond the comedy of manners. The charm of such an attempt for him would lie in its difficulty. Using only a limited area of his characters' lives, material that includes much of the trivial, he was committed to the utmost that art and ingenuity could do to make it express important issues. James adheres to certain unspoken conventions whereby the characters are seldom exposed below the social level. Situations that could lead to such an exposure are in the air, but Nanda's outburst of weeping in the final episode is the rare, chosen occasion when all defences are down.

The two aspects are not easy to keep apart, and indeed the distinction between them may sometimes break down. If one side of him is drawn towards vulgar material, the desire to improve it is always present. The other side may seek to use vulgar material for higher ends.

It is relevant to our understanding of *The Awkward Age* that it was originally intended as a shorter piece. In his Notebook account of it he refers to the subject as "a real little situation for a short tale";[1] and in the Preface he writes of the story as "planned, in perfect good faith, for brevity, for levity, for simplicity, for jocosity, in fine, and for an accommodating irony. I invoked, for my protection, the spirit of the lightest comedy. . . ."[2] If he had handled it more briefly it might well have become one of those works (like *The Other House* and *The Outcry*) which exist as stories and also in stage versions. Much of it seems to have been written with this thought (however platonically) in mind.

We do well to know that a novel otherwise so remote from popular appeal was planned for "levity." The parts that have this character are the most obvious successes and weaknesses of the book, and for this reason it is useful to consider them first. Prominence needs to be given to any part of James's work in which entertainment is offered on relatively easy terms.

Harold Brookenham, the heroine's brother, a borrower and even purloiner of fivers, belongs to a level of vulgarity with which he should have had no dealings. But with the theatre even remotely in view he could depart very far from the standards of his fiction. *The Reprobate* is a chastening example of this, and the stage version of "Daisy Miller" even more so. The nonchalant ease with which Harold lays Mr Cashmore under contribution, in a scene that opens a section, is depicted with great verbal suavity.[3] James might almost be giving a demonstration of how such a moment can be managed by a literary master, but it is painful to see it done at all. One of the obvious successes—but by the standards applicable to the comedy of manners aspect of James's medium—is the Duchess. To get her true measure we must compare her with the conventional aristocratic (or *nouveau riche*) matron of English comic fiction or drama; and in this company she holds her head high. She is a monster, but a credible monster. Even at her most unctuous, the Duchess represents a tenable

---

[1] *The Notebooks of Henry James*, ed. F. O. Matthiessen and Kenneth Murdock (1947), p. 192.
[2] *A.N.*, p. 98.
[3] *The Awkward Age* [= *A.A.*], pp. 139 f.

M

social philosophy. She believes in the *jeune fille* with all the fervour of one not to the manner born:

> "*I* see but one consistent way, which is our fine old foreign way and which makes—in the upper classes, mind you, for it's with them only I'm concerned—*des femmes bien gracieuses.* I allude to the immemorial custom of my husband's race, which was good enough for his mother and his mother's mother, for Aggie's own, for his other sisters, for *toutes ces dames.* . . . She would have been brought up there under an anxious eye— that's the great point; privately, carefully, tenderly, with what she was *not* to learn—till the proper time—looked after quite as much as the rest.[4]

The speech in which she tells Mr Longdon of her pious gratitude for her success in marrying off Aggie has a quintessential grossness, but without caricature:

> ". . . Things have turned out so much as *I* desire them that I should really feel wicked not to have a humble heart. There's a quarter indeed . . . to which I don't fear to say for myself that no day and no night pass without my showing it. However, you English, I know, don't like one to speak of one's religion. I'm just as simply thankful for mine—I mean with as little sense of indecency or agony about it—as I am for my health or my carriage. . . ."[5]

James achieves rich farce in her succession of embarrassed moments at Mrs Brook's when, with little Aggie, she is taken aback by the announced arrival of all the wrong people.

The neatest and most charming piece of absurdity in the book is the encounter between little Aggie and Mr Longdon at Mertle. Mr Longdon belongs to a former generation, for whom the "ceremony of innocence" had meaning, but even to him Aggie is a new species. She is a lamb, with her neck in a pink ribbon, with "no consciousness but that of being fed from the hand with the small sweet biscuit of unobjectionable knowledge."[6] In her conversation with Mr Longdon she testifies to the fineness and completeness of her incomprehension:

> "Oh, Nanda, she's my best friend after three or four others."
> "After so many?" Mr Longdon laughed. "Don't you think that's rather a back seat, as they say, for one's best?"

---

[4] *A.A.*, p. 49.   [5] *A.A.*, p. 353.   [6] *A.A.*, p. 211.

"A back seat?"—she wondered with a purity!

"If you don't understand," said her companion, "it serves me right, as your aunt didn't leave me with you to teach you the slang of the day."

"The 'slang'?"—she again spotlessly speculated.

"You've never even heard the expression? I think that a great compliment to our time if it weren't that I fear it may have been only the name that has been kept from you."

The light of ignorance in the child's smile was positively golden. "The name?" she again echoed.

She understood too little—he gave it up. . . .[7]

Mrs Brookenham, so far as her style and manner are concerned (her role in the action raises other issues) shines as an easily recognised success. James's notation for her nuances of speech and facial expression is extensive. Harold's behaviour makes her "beautifully desperate."[8] An "innocence dimly tragic," in certain circumstances, is noted as giving "an immense effect to her other resources."[9] An "artless wail,"[10] a "sweet world-weariness,"[11] a "muffled exaltation,"[12] a "dolorous drop":[13] these are a selection from the repertory; and, of course, they need a context. Her manner varies in response to the speaker and the occasion. She reacts thus when the Duchess, aggressive in her policy for Aggie, asks Mrs Brook what she is doing for her own daughter, Nanda:

"If you mean socially"—Mrs. Brookenham looked as if there might be in some distant sphere, for which she almost yearned, a maternal opportunity very different from that—"if you mean socially, I don't do anything at all." . . . Jane's hostess now spoke as simply as an earnest, anxious child. She gave a vague, patient sigh.

"I suppose I must begin!"[14]

A considerable number of lines in the novel strike one as intended to be played for obvious laughs. The Duchess says of Edward Brookenham that he "figures in [his wife's] drawing-room only as one of those queer extinguishers of fires in the corridors of hotels. He's just a bucket on a peg."[15] Compared with the dialogue of *The Ambassadors*, or of any of the other

[7] *A.A.*, pp. 211-12. [8] *A.A.*, p. 38. [9] *A.A.*, p. 38.
[10] *A.A.*, p. 56. [11] *A.A.*, p. 74. [12] *A.A.*, p. 247.
[13] *A.A.*, p. 254. [14] *A.A.*, p. 47. [15] *A.A.*, pp. 224-5.

mature works with American characters, this kind of wit is
thin: one misses the humanity and subtlety of the national
ethos. James is content to outshine in cleverness the contemporary writers for the English theatre. In general, his
witty English characters sound a more metallic note than his
Americans; and when he has an eye to the stage, even as a
merely imaginary possibility, there is no place for certain *nuances*.

His nostalgia for the theatre reveals itself in an idiosyn-
cratic use of the equivalent of stage business. Characters
are introduced on to the "set " by footmen or "discovered" in
postures or actions that make an opening scene; conversations
are interrupted by the bringing in or clearing of tea, and such
details as the ringing of a bell or a quiet word to the butler are
part of the precisely selected subject-matter—a subject-
matter from which so much that we normally expect in novels
has been excluded. There is much use of producer's directions.
Nervous passes with a billiard cue are Mr Longdon's way of
manifesting tension at the beginning of his important conversation with Vanderbank at Mertle. In a conversation with
Mitchy, Vanderbank moves about aimlessly; stands with
his back to the chimney; smokes and looks at the tip
of his cigarette, instead of at Mitchy; resumes his seat again,
"as a sign of being at his friend's service"; and then stretches
himself out in it—all within about a page of carefully pointed
dialogue.[16]

His feeling for stage routines is reinforced by his feeling
for the routines of the social class with which fashionable
plays tend to deal. *The Awkward Age* and the other experiments in this style are another way of doing justice to the
phenomena of English civilisation. The technique enables
him to play with its surfaces. Delight in surfaces is indeed the
first note struck in the opening pages. The four-wheeler that
"under the glazed radiance, waited and trickled and blackly
glittered," as the guests depart from Mrs Brookenham's, is of a
piece with Vanderbank's smooth amiability towards Mr
Longdon, who shares his vehicle, and with the room, "all
convenience and character," into which, "with a touch to the
quick light," he ushers him; and also with the neatness and

[16] *A.A.*, pp. 326-7.

distinction of his older companion's appearance: "the perfection of his evening dress" and "the special smartness of his
sleeveless overcoat."[17] Vanderbank's kind of charm has novelty
for Mr Longdon, while the latter embodies for Vanderbank
an old order of manners in a beautiful state of preservation.
The whole of the first book is occupied with their soundings
of each other and explorations of the associations they have in
common. It has all the fine detail of a first encounter in a
society where the amenities are cultivated. It is full of light-
nesses and courtesies. But James now uses his medium for
something of subtle importance. One of the functions of this
encounter is to establish Vanderbank for us. Mr Longdon's
true nature is apparent from the beginning, but Vanderbank
will be a problem character. The older man's relations with
him are therefore crucial. They add weight to our impression
that, in situations of this kind, he can be quite acceptable.
But Vanderbank's manner calls for some detailed comment.
Amiability is the aspect that first shows itself. In one passage
his look of "indulgence" is mentioned;[18] in another we read
that he "considered him with a benevolence, a geniality of
approval, that he literally had to hold in check for fear of
seeming to patronise . . .":[19] expressions that may be construed,
if the reader insists, as evidence of speciousness, but Mr
Longdon takes to him, and he has excellent taste. Another
recurring note is one of amusement. Though Mr Longdon
is not young "he came near—strikingly and amusingly—
looking new."[20] Vanderbank laughs frequently. He is gay
when he brings up, for Mr Longdon's mystification, the young
girl question, later to be the main theme of the novel. Mr
Longdon, still uncomprehending, plies him further on the
subject of the alleged "strain" of a daughter's presence with her
elders in the drawing room, and the section ends with his
interrogation; so that the next section opens with the spotlight
rather strikingly on Vanderbank:

> Vanderbank at this left his corner of the sofa and, with his
> hands in his pockets and a manner so amused that it might

---

[17] *A.A* , p. 5.   [18] *A.A.*, p. 7.
[19] *A.A.*, p. 30.   [20] *A.A.*, p. 5.

have passed for excited, took several paces about the room while
his interlocutor, watching him, waited for his response. . . .
Vanderbank stopped before him with a face in which something
had been still more brightly kindled. . . .[21]

This, in isolation, might seem a little ominous: but Vanderbank's private amusement gives way immediately to good-
natured, hospitable talk, and Mr Longdon is easily pressed to
stay a little longer. Whatever can be read into Vanderbank's speeches and expressions, Mr Longdon, always a
critical observer, continues to enjoy his companionship. The
play between them is beautifully managed. When Vanderbank makes a flippant ironical reference to Edward Brookenham Mr Longdon "fixed on him a gravity that failed to prevent
his discovering in the eyes behind them a shy reflexion of his
irony."[22] Mr Longdon's "curtailed murmur"[23] as he refrains
from pursuing a certain topic; his "soft smothered sigh,"[24]
occasioned by the photographs; his "droll conscious leap"[25]
when he conjectures that, Vanderbank's name being Gustavus,
Mrs Brookenham perhaps calls him Gussy; the " slow, droll
headshake"[26] with which he responds to Vanderbank's laughing
suggestion that he may now have all the young girls' photographs he wishes for: all this notation, together with the
sweetness and seriousness of his words, has the effect of placing
Vanderbank. Mr Longdon sees serious faults in him and his
circle, but he accepts him; and this is the beginning of the trust
that expresses itself later in the offer of the money to enable
him to marry Nanda. The fact that Mr Longdon accepts
him thus gives some measure of how the reader is invited to
accept him; unless we think that we are invited to be so very
much more critical than Mr Longdon, which seems to me
against the spirit of James's treatment.

The presentation of Vanderbank is continued in the third
book, where Mr Longdon meets Nanda and is overcome by
her resemblance to her grandmother, Lady Julia, whom he
had once loved. When Mr Longdon retires to the next room
Vanderbank shows his sensibility: "[His] handsome face had a

[21] *A.A.*, p. 24.   [22] *A.A.*, p. 8.
[23] *A.A.*, p. 10.   [24] *A.A.*, p. 20.
[25] *A.A.*, p. 12.   [26] *A.A.*, p. 15.

fine thought in it."[27]   Mr Longdon's feeling is "one of
the most beautiful things" he has ever seen.[28]   When
he joins him, he shows that easy considerateness ever at
his command when a matter of sentiment arises.   But his
sensibility is of a rather indolent, facile kind, and his manner
enables a little of it to go a long way.   The word "kind," sometimes coupled with "amused," occurs frequently in descriptions of his manner when Nanda and her dubious friends are
present.   He genuinely likes to be nice, but he admits to Mrs
Brook that, so far as relations with Mr Longdon go, he is in
danger of boredom.[29]   In the last, most catastrophic of his
appearances, when we see him trying and failing to cover
up his bad treatment of Nanda, we read that he "had not
been in the room ten seconds before he showed ever so markedly
that he had arrived to be kind."[30]   His kindness "filled the
place to the exclusion of everything else, with a familiar
friendly voice," though there are references also to a "constant
. . . perhaps misapplied laugh," and an element of "inatten-
tion."   These expressions help us to interpret afresh all that has
passed for pleasant in his earlier behaviour.   We realise the
extent to which he can be insensitive and hypocritical, and
even socially inept.   He is revealed as no good in a situation
where anything important is required of him.   His indolent
nature has caused him to let things drift, and they have
drifted to a point where, on Nanda's summons, he can only
give the lamest account of himself, ineffectively disguising
his confusion with empty patronising fussiness—rather similar
to the fussiness with which he apologetically welcomes his
guests in the earlier scene that brings Nanda and Mr Longdon
together: a point that would be relevant in a stage production.

But this final scene may raise some doubts.   Is it not slightly
overdone?   Vanderbank's blunders are so many and so gross.
Did James sacrifice his elegant creation to theatrical effect—
to the requirements of an imagined stage version?   If Vanderbank had behaved with a little more poise, more intelligence,
the effect could still have been one of moral exposure, but it
would have been less theatrical.   This suggestion is not put

[27] *A.A.*, p. 123.
[28] *Ibid.*
[29] *A.A.*, p. 160.
[30] *A.A.*, p. 436.

forward as a firm opinion. James may have intended, quite deliberately, to show how very bad such a person could be when caught at a sufficiently unfortunate moment.

On the whole the portrayal of Vanderbank is a great success, a fine example of what the notation employed in this novel can do. It is, of course, understood that we must accept him within the terms of the convention. As for what goes on beneath such an exterior, or in the non-social areas of such a life, the technique implies that they are neither the novelist's business nor ours. These conditions impose themselves, for the most part, without opposition. There is a sense in which we know Vanderbank very well, in spite of the unanswered questions. As a piece of specifically English portraiture he is subtler than the products of James's early and middle periods. Failure on the emotional side, together with good looks, good humour and pleasant manners; an air of amateurism combined with a life of actual hard work: the type has been well observed. Were it not for certain aspects of his role in the plot, we should be entirely content to know him in this way. But the intimate question of what his relation has been with Mrs Brookenham all these years cannot be altogether suppressed. Without knowing this we remain rather unclear about what Mrs Brook hoped to achieve by her "exposure" of Nanda at Tishy Grendon's. (It is a relief to learn that other writers on James have been in difficulties over this scene!) Similarly, Mrs Brook succeeds totally as a piece of elaborate portraiture, and we should be content to leave it at that, were it not for her relation with Vanderbank and its effect on her treatment of Nanda. But these are so crucial that any obscurity about them—if they are obscure, and the fault does not lie with readers like myself—must be regarded as a flaw in the book. What is our knowledge on these matters?

The Duchess has assured Mr Longdon that Vanderbank is not in love with Mrs Brook, and also that they have not "done, as it is called, anything wrong."[31] Mrs Brook, in one place, goes so far as to say to Van: "How can any one love you . . . without wanting to show it in some way? You know all the ways, dear Van . . . in which *I* want to show it."[32]

³¹ *A.A.*, p. 355.   ³² *A. A.*, p. 159.

Does this mean simply that she would like to take him as a lover, but that he is unwilling? And what does she mean, in a later scene, by the statement that at one time they "rather enjoyed each other's dim depths"?[33] All the evidence points to there being no consummated relationship between them, and no likelihood of one. There is no reference to any other woman in Vanderbank's life. Mrs Brook knows her Van well enough to know that he will not propose to Nanda. "For he may 'like' Nanda as much as you please: he'll never, never . . . he'll never come to the scratch,"[34] she announces on first learning of the state of Nanda's affections. And in a later scene: "Dear Van will think conscientiously a lot about it, but he won't do it. . . ."[35] This comes before the party at Tishy's. We do not know the exact basis of Mrs Brook's knowledge—how far, for example, she recognises in him a dislike of Nanda's initiated state: but we know that Vanderbank has already manifested this dislike, *apropos* of her association with Mr Cashmore.[36] Whatever knowledge Mrs Brook has of him, her exposure of Nanda seems intended to reinforce a reluctance already well established. Since Mrs Brook's relations with Vanderbank deteriorate as a result of this occasion, her intentions and James's in such a conspicuous *scène à faire* remain difficult to penetrate. Does the point lie simply in her having blundered?

What with Vanderbank's abortive attempts to speak to Nanda and his repeated temporising, added to Mrs Brook's prophecies that he will remain inactive to the end and her efforts to ensure this, the whole situation looks like another case of the old Jamesian habit, discussed earlier, of prolonging the obvious. It is perfectly in keeping with Vanderbank's character to be dilatory, but it seems to be a defect of construction that this elementary, unchanging theme should crop up again and again, especially in a novel which, with its atmosphere of rarity and elaboration, leads us to expect something different. *The Awkward Age* is, in fact, a curious mixture of the obvious and the obscure, and the reader may sometimes be at a loss to know with which of these qualities he is dealing.

[33] *A.A.*, p. 395. [34] *A.A.*, p. 81.
[35] *A.A.*, p. 265. [36] *A.A.*, p. 171.

Some of the problems raised by the novel may be the result of James's lengthening of what was originally intended for "brevity." Certain parts of the plot may have suffered mere elongation. The main subject of the novel—that is, the "talk" to which young girls are exposed on promotion to adult company—taken as it is in isolation and in its simple generality, could have been more happily treated in a shorter work. It has affinities with those hard, clear-cut, very limited problems used by Dumas *fils* in plays like *Le Demi-Monde*. The lengthier treatment causes one to expect more of the theme. James does not invite the reader to differentiate between the various kinds of initiated talk that Nanda might be involved in, or the various kinds of boldness (from *avant-garde* to mere lubricity) that might be encountered in a French novel of the period; and here he is quite right. We do not really expect or desire this sort of documentation from James; nor would it have been possible in England in 1899. But the continual references to the "talk," with so little development of what is implied, in a novel of such length, expose James to the charge of disproportion.

How good *is* the talk? This remains uncertain. In his Preface James refers to "'real' talk," "play of mind," "explicit interest in life," in a passage that suggests a certain quality of civilisation.[37] There is nothing to indicate here that the "play of mind" might, in some cases, be specious and irresponsible. How far does the description in the Preface fit Mrs Brookenham's little circle? Nanda clearly expects that her coming into the drawing-room will be an important experience. Mitchy has advised her to come: it "helps to form the young mind."[38] In a conversation with Mr Longdon, Mitchy admits to an abject admiration for Vanderbank, their leading spirit, describing him as "formed for a distinctly higher sphere."[39] How are we to take Mitchy's admirations and recommendations? Since he is genuinely good, and James vouches for his "subtlety,"[40] this might seem to indicate that the talk *is* good, but one suspects that, as a man without "background" and essentially humble, Mitchy may be too

[37] *A.N.*, p. 102.   [38] *A.A.*, p. 131.
[39] *A.A.*, p. 110.   [40] *A.N.*, p. 117.

easily dazzled by mere cleverness. Or again: being without humbug himself, and recognising a freedom from humbug in Nanda, he may be also a little without standards. The drawing room is a place of intellectual entertainment: why shouldn't Nanda join in? But in some of the poorest pages of the novel Mrs Brook and her friends have nothing better to talk of than the possible elopement of Lady Fanny Cashmore with her hovering paramour. In what spirit does James handle this frivolous material? These are not easy questions.

Some critics of *The Awkward Age* have expressed themselves more confidently about the moral significance of the book, and about James's attitude to the Brookenham circle.[41] It *is* a deeply serious book, in spite of so much lack of definition of issues. The inadequacy of the world into which Nanda makes her *début* becomes evident enough: the death of her happiness is genuine tragedy. The later scenes between Vanderbank Mitchy and Mrs Brook may be obscure in places, but the weariness, bitterness and ironical resignation that pervade them are authentic.

It is very much a novel of anomalous relationships. The Brookenham family, unlike James's English aristocrats (the Warburtons, the Cantervilles, the Dormers), is untidy. Its members and associates are a hopeless mixture, reflecting no readily identifiable pattern in English social life. An amorphous world such as this would present greater technical difficulties than the English material of earlier works. As an American, James had no fear of the anomalous, and up to a point this is a merit. Mitchy, Vanderbank and Mrs Brook make a very life-like group of disparate figures, such as an English writer would hardly have brought together into an intimate circle. Mitchy himself, anomaly incarnate, is an admirable and most original creation. (The originality of the characters is at least as striking a feature of this book as any point of artistic form. A nice girl who reads an improper French book, admits the fact, and remains entirely nice, is surely an advance in Anglo-Saxon fiction in 1899!) But some anomalies are hard to bear. How are we to take Mr Cash-

---

[41] John Holloway, Ian Gregor, and Dorothea Krook have made interesting comments on these issues. See Bibliography, p. 235.

more's visits to Nanda? Not that the situation is impossible, but for an Aristotle or a James this is not the relevant plea. A battered vulgarian like Cashmore, in a society so lacking in forms, might perhaps impose upon the bouncing immaturity of a good-natured girl like Nanda, with vaguely sentimental and prurient motives: surely a situation either to avoid or to treat with a special sense of the malodorous or the freakish.

On the first reading or readings of *The Sacred Fount* (1901), the desperate need to solve the riddle is liable to inhibit other kinds of interest. When the riddle has been abandoned as insoluble, the novel can be enjoyed as other novels are enjoyed. The artistic effect of the queer theme is to give a prodigiously heightened quality to elements that belong to life as we know it. The tortuosities, when they cease to torment, can be cherished for what they add to relationships between characters, dramatic effects and so forth. The success of the work can be seen quite simply as one of style, the prodigy of the heightening being in the language.

Here is a special kind of English novel. The tone is very adequately set on the first page, where the narrator conveys the mood of expectancy of a weekend guest about to leave London by train for a country house:

> It was an occasion, I felt—the prospect of a large party—
> to look out at the station for others, possible friends and even
> possible enemies, who might be going. Such premonitions,
> it was true, bred fears when they failed to breed hopes, though
> it was to be added that there were sometimes, in the case,
> rather happy ambiguities. One was glowered at, in the
> compartment, by people who on the morrow, after breakfast,
> were to prove charming; one was spoken to first by people
> whose sociability was subsequently to show as bleak; and one
> built with confidence on others who were never to reappear
> at all—who were only going to Birmingham. . . .[42]

The deceptiveness of appearances announces itself from the beginning, but more perplexing ambiguities than those instanced here are soon to occupy us. What is perhaps more to the point in this passage is the peculiar absorption—a longer excerpt would do fuller justice to it—of the narrator in the

[42] *The Sacred Fount* [= *S.F.*]. p. 1.

business of country-house visiting, and the exclusion from his mind of everything that does not relate to this elaborate game— and, of course, of people who are only going to Birmingham. He is fascinated by the rules of the game; for example, by the "wondrous new fashion" whereby Mrs Froome and Lord Lutley, "and their servants too, like a single household," were "starting, travelling, arriving together."[43] The byplay in this opening chapter, with porters, servants, newspaper boys briefly interrupting the conversation of the fellow-passengers, helps to stress a closed-in opulence that can take for granted a world of minor human agents who exist to keep it smoothly operating. The effect is one of intense worldliness. The narrator is, in a sense, more worldly than the Longs and the Brissendens, the objects of his curiosity, for he has intelligence and an artist's imagination, yet he lives only, so far as we can see, for the exercise of these powers within the narrow world of appearance and conjecture afforded by such people and their goings on.

The novel then is about a particular mode of social life, but also about a particular kind of sensibility that has become involved with it. The narrator reflects aspects of the novelist himself, but with lurid and comic distortions. Though not explicitly an American he shares James's own capacity to lose himself imaginatively in English social life as an exotic phenomenon. He has obsessions akin to an artist's, but apparently no artist's medium. He seems to be unmarried, with no friendships and loves of his own: he is the avid spectator of other people's. Extraordinarily susceptible to emotional and dramatic tension in the pursuit of a vision to which he is totally committed, and for which he suffers a sort of martyrdom, he might be the very emblem of the artist at odds with society, were it not for the grosser aspects of his role.

There is a grossness, which has a flavour of the comic, in the florid literary idiom with which he and his associates refer to love and passion. The erotic is fulsomely acknowledged —this society flaunts its freedoms—but discussion of it is bounded by a heavy decorum. Thus, in conversation with Ford Obert concerning the plight of the "superannuated

---

[43] *S.F.*, p. 5.

youth," Guy Brissenden, and how far he "likes" the process of depletion of which he is the victim:

> I made up my mind on the spot. "If he loves her he must. That is if he loves her passionately, sublimely. . . ."[44]

Mrs Brissenden sees the sacred fount situation, but not that instance of it in which she is the exploiting party, in similar terms. She converses with the narrator:

> "And the relation—to do that sort of thing—must be necessarily so awfully *intimate*."
> "*Intimissima*."[45]

In the same conversation, when the narrator makes a covert allusion to Mrs Brissenden's situation, stopping short of an explicit reference, a similar note is struck:

> "You have the advantage, for your beauty, of being admirably married. You bloom in your husband's presence. . . . If there were nothing else there would be the help given you by your quiet confidence in his lawful passion."[46]

The narrator differs from his interlocutors only in being more fluent and more ingenious in the use of this rhetoric, and more obsessed in his tracing of the finer ramifications of the "laws" it expresses. We relish these passages *as* rhetoric, not for anything they reveal about personal relationships. We relish them all the more for their application to the loves of these country house *habitués*:

> What an intimacy, what an intensity of relation, I said to myself, [in an early part of the book, when the idea is still young] so successful a process implied! It was of course familiar enough that when people were so deeply in love they rubbed off on each other—that a great pressure of soul to soul usually left on either side a sufficient show of tell-tale traces. But for Long to have been so stamped as I found him, how the pliant wax must have been prepared and the seal of passion applied![47]

The sacred fount image is bizarre, macabre: reminiscent of a Spenserian "Masque of Cupid," visible only to the

---

[44] *S.F.*, p. 25.　　　　　　　[45] *S.F.*, p. 28.
[46] *S.F.*, p. 34.　　　　　　　[47] *S.F.*, pp. 14-15.

initiated, in which cruel rites are practised. But the agents of the unspeakable mystery are of a banality! The conversations in which the theme is so freely canvassed are liable, when they are not portentous, to take on a sprightly vulgarity:

> ". . . It's a second wind, another 'go'—which isn't the sort of thing life mostly treats us to. Mrs. Briss had to get her new blood, her extra allowance of time and bloom, somewhere; and from whom could she so conveniently extract them as from Guy himself? She *has*, by an extraordinary feat of legerdemain, extracted them; and he, on his side, to supply her, has had to tap the sacred fount. . . ."[48]

In another passage, Long is referred to as having been "suddenly caught . . . in the act of presenting his receptacle at the sacred fount. . . ."[49] In a later episode the narrator imagines that Mrs Brissenden is "looking her time of life straight *at* him [*i.e.*, her husband] and yet making love to him with it as hard as ever she could" and that "poor Briss," now "thoroughly got back into·hand" is "feeling afresh in his soul, as a response to her, the gush of the sacred fount."[50] In yet another place, where a similar encounter is postulated, the poetry is dispensed with and the situation reduced to one of crude dynamics:

> He had met his wife; she had in some way dealt with him; he had been with her, however briefly, alone; and the intimacy of their union had been afresh impressed upon him. Poor Briss, in fine, looked ten years older.[51]

Transcendental verbiage mingles with the open zest of the scandalmonger. The narrator's manner presents a lavish mixture of components, including the delighted ghoulishness displayed at its best in the passages concerning Guy Brissenden. The relation between "poor Briss" and his beguiled observer is highly flavoured with comedy. It is when they meet, on the evening of arrival, that the intriguing theme first takes on its delicious eeriness, and the prose dances to the measure. The context is perfectly ordinary: the narrator has run into

[48] *S.F.*, p. 24.   [49] *S.F.*, p. 32.
[50] *S.F.*, p. 50.   [51] *S.F.*, p. 122.

Brissenden while they were both looking for their rooms, and
then he reflects on why he has failed to recognise him earlier:

> He had escaped my notice since our arrival, but I had, as a
> much older man, met him—the hero of his odd union—at some
> earlier time. Like his wife, none the less, he had now struck
> me as a stranger, and it was not till, in his room, I stood a
> little face to face with him that I made out the wonderful
> reason.
>
> The wonderful reason was that I was *not* a much older man;
> Guy Brissenden, at any rate, was not a much younger. It
> was he who was old—it was he who was older—it was he who
> was oldest.[52]

The dance is renewed at later stages in the drama, as the victim
advances further and further towards his doom. In one place
the narrator focuses his attention on two contrasting compositional elements—poor Briss's back, and his wife's "fine
retreating person":

> It was when he presented his face that he looked, each time,
> older; but it was when he showed you, from behind, the
> singular stoop of his shoulders, that he looked oldest.[53]

The final encounter, when the narrator (in the middle of a
disquieting talk with Obert) receives Brissenden's message
that Mrs Brissenden awaits him, is the climax of his vision
and of his ecstatic enjoyment. If the narrator's self-indulgence
reaches its most blatant, it is also true that his intelligence
and perception are at their height. In all its inflated, infatuated
grossness, the passage displays superbly the novelist's delight
in drama, boldness of heightening and wealth of *décor*:

> I can't begin to say how the fact of his appearance crowned
> the communication my interlocutor had just made me, nor in
> what a bright confusion of many things I found myself facing
> poor Briss. One of these things was precisely that he had never
> been so much poor Briss as at this moment. That ministered
> to the confusion as well as to the brightness, for if his being there
> at all renewed my sources and replenished my current—spoke

---

all, in short for my gain—so, on the other hand, in the light of
what I had just had from Obert, his particular aspect was
something of a shock. I can't present this especial impression
better than by the mention of my instant certitude that what
he had come for was to bring me a message and that somehow—
yes, indubitably—this circumstance seemed to have placed
him again at the very bottom of his hole. . . . Poor Briss!—
I had asked myself before he spoke with what kindness enough
I could meet him. Poor Briss! poor Briss!—I am not even now
sure that I didn't first meet him by *that* irrepressible murmur.
It was in it all for me that, thus, at midnight, he had traversed
on his errand the length of the great dark house. I trod with
him, over the velvet and the marble, through the twists and
turns, among the glooms and glimmers and echoes, every inch
of the way, and I don't know what humiliation, for him, was
constituted there, between us, by his long pilgrimage. It was
the final expression of his sacrifice.[54]

The sacred fount image, if taken seriously, would be rather
revolting. It both expresses and does not express the idea of
sexual intercourse. The fact that it does and does not, the
mingling of prurience with a sterile, unmeaning aestheticism,
would be intolerable were the strong comic flavour not present.
Many of the passages are richly entertaining because, without
quite inviting us to think in terms of the physical process, they
actually provoke us strongly to do so. Behind the façade of
portentous symbolism we have glimpses of a country-house
life in which, at any hour of the leisurely day (for example,
during the period of dressing for dinner) couples lawful and
unlawful are going to it.

The Sacred Fount is not, in any limited, specific sense, a
satire on the social or sexual attitudes of the Edwardian well-
to-do, or on the myths relating to passion that might belong
to the superstructure of such a world. To describe the book
in this way would be to claim to have solved its riddle, and no
illusion of this kind is entertained here. Whatever it may be,
it is more than this. In any attempted description, it
would be necessary to stress the consistency with which any
elementary human naturalness or value is excluded. It is a

[54] *S.F.*, pp. 175-6.

huis clos world from which everything has been omitted but
the forms of the social game, to which is added for some a
game of curiosity and, for others, a round of obscure man-
oeuvres in a game of sex. In the narrator's fevered imagination
some of the characters are pictured as suffering agonies of
passion, but their pangs, if indeed real, are hidden beneath a
social mask. It is a kind of death-in-life. The air, to adapt
the Jamesian phrase, has been pumped gaspingly dry. This
is a repellent book for anyone who does not see that the author
(the creator, after all, of Maisie and Milly, vessels of goodness
and life and love) has willed these limitations.

The interest is in the private drama of the narrator, and
this proceeds by stages until climax follows climax. The first
page, as we have seen, finds him expectant, but with no idea
of what lies ahead. On his arrival, in the second chapter, his
intenser feelings are still not aroused: he can refer to the next
sequence of encounters as "the happiest little chapter of
accidents."[55] But, at dinner, after he has seen Brissenden,
"positive excitement" develops. The drama enters a further
stage when he wonders whether he has fallen in love with
May Server, so anxious is he that her condition as a victim
should not be detected: "my nervousness had taken an extraordinary stride."[56] James is a master of the idiom of tension
and nervous shock, as of so many other idioms, and he makes
the most of the narrator's mental adventure. A new thought,
gleaned from Mrs Brissenden, comes to him "with a whirr
of wings."[57] He sees himself as "shielding," even "fighting
for" Mrs Server, and in their most romantic encounter he
feels as if he were "trapping a bird or stalking a fawn,"[58]
and then as if he and she together "were in a beautiful old
picture . . . a beautiful old tale."[59] "It was prodigious what,
in the way of suppressed communication, passed in these
wonderful minutes between us,":[60] these are his thoughts
during a scene of which we may be inclined to doubt his
interpretation. His desperate rivalry with fellow-inquirers
is dramatised in some extravagant images: "I had achieved my
flight into luminous ether and, alighting gracefully on my feet,

---

[55] *S.F.*, p. 12.   [56] *S.F.*, p. 48.   [57] *S.F.*, p. 57.
[58] *S.F.*, p. 102.   [59] *Ibid*.   [60] *S.F.*, p. 108.

reported myself at my post"[61] is his description of the situation
as he faces his final bout with Mrs Brissenden. In his conversation with Lady John, a mere bungler in such speculation
and despised as such, we see a touch almost of buffoonery
in his moves: we see him dashing across a field and picking
up a straw.[62] But he has moments when withdrawal from
such absorptions seems the more proper course. In such an
atmosphere as that of Newmarch, what place is there for
imagination and intelligence? He sees these qualities as "the
uninvited reporter in whose face a door is closed."[63] And when
he first realises that Mrs Brissenden's curiosity is busy with
May Server, he experiences "a kind of chill—an odd revulsion,"
and it occurs to him that this concern with the intimate life
of another may be "wanting in taste."[64]

Part of the narrator's personal drama arises out of his
reflexions on his own perceptive and analytic powers, about
which he has some misgivings! Has he seen too much in the
queer phenomena?

> . . . A part of the amusement they yielded came, I daresay,
> from my exaggerating them—grouping them into a larger
> mystery (and thereby a larger "law") than the facts, as
> observed, yet warranted; but that is the common fault of
> minds for which the vision of life is an obsession. . . .[65]

Abstract theorising is indeed one of his leanings. "The agents
of the sacrifice are uncomfortable . . . when they suspect or fear
that you see,"[66] is his formulation in an early exchange with
Obert, and we see in it a premature recourse to something like
a technical vocabulary ("the agents of the sacrifice"), which
has its own rhetoric. Later he arrives at the advanced pro-
position that the effect of the sacrifice on the beneficiary might
be out of proportion to the resources of the victim: "It was as if
these elements might really multiply in the transfer made of
them."[67] Situations begin to look like geometrical theorems,
and at every change in the characters' behaviour a new "law"
suggests itself. Gradually, he feels himself to be a creator,

[61] *S.F.*, p. 199.   [62] *S.F.*, p. 147.   [63] *S.F.*, p. 123.
[64] *S.F.*, p. 37.   [65] *S.F.*, pp. 19-20.   [66] *S.F.*, p. 25.
[67] *S.F.*, p. 43.

not merely an observer. "I found, on my side, a rare intellectual joy," he admits to himself, with reference to Lady
John, ". . . in feeling her begin instantly to play the part I
had attributed to her in the irreducible drama."[68] He has
the delighted sense of "determining, almost of creating results."[69]
The "beauty of having been right"[70] makes for him an element
in which, on a fine late afternoon, he "wanders," "drifts,"
and "securely floats." How well James conveys the enthralled
state! The "charm of the moment and of the place" is so
great, so persuasive, that any event that followed might well
be assimilated to its mood; and, indeed, when May Server
appears, walking alone in the wood, it seems to the narrator
that the whole meaning of his theory and her doom is written
on her beautiful ravaged face. In the passage that follows
his thoughts reveal an egregious mixture of thrilled romanticism
and ogreish satisfaction; while in his exchange with her on the
subject of Guy Brissenden's imminent approach, his manners
are as bad as his speculations are sublime.

The most important relationships in the novel are those in
which the narrator himself is involved with the characters whom
he sees as agents of the mystery: with the hapless May Server,
with poor ageing Brissenden, and with terrible Mrs Brissenden.
They are handled with peculiar power, dominated as they are
by the narrator's vision of the abnormal role (menacing or
menaced) of the other party. There is an emphatic piece of
comedy in the fifth chapter, where the narrator and Mrs
Brissenden meet to consider the question of Long's victim,
whom she has identified as Mrs Server but concerning whom
the narrator has chosen to be provokingly unhelpful. When he
says that it was she, not he, who "jumped" at the name of
Mrs Server, Mrs Brissenden's baulked expression is all the more
shocking to him because of what he knows of her own sacred
fount activities. She looms before him as a monster:

> My interlocutress stared, and I had at this moment, I re-
> member, an almost intolerable sense of her fatuity and cruelty.
> They were all unconscious, but they were, at that stage, none
> the less irritating. Her fine bosom heaved, her blue eyes

---

[68] *S.F.*, p. 81.   [69] *S.F.*, p. 168.   [70] *S.F.*, pp. 100-1.

expanded with her successful, her simplified egotism. I couldn't, in short, I found, bear her being so keen about Mrs. Server while she was so stupid about poor Briss. She seemed to recall to me nobly the fact that *she* hadn't a lover. No, she was only eating poor Briss up inch by inch, but she hadn't a lover. . . .[71]

After a few more words, in which it becomes too apparent that he is lukewarm about the detection of Long's victim, she turns to him "with dreadful gaiety," and says "Weak man, you've been squared."[72] At this stage they are still, more or less, allies. Later, her attitude turns to what can only be described as brutal hatred.

The final episode of the novel is of Richardsonian length, and justifies its length for Richardsonian reasons. Her treatment of him has to be long drawn out. She has very little to reveal—it could have been said in a page or two—but she must delay it and spin it out for the sake of the continued pressure, the attrition, the display of bland, invincible power. As a personality nourished by abnormal supplies of the life-force she is fearfully convincing. The mere keeping up of the dreadful endgame through countless moves in a restricted manoeuvring space gives occasion for formidable technique on James's part.

One might make the elementary point that, in the treatment of Mrs Brissenden, the sacred fount idea operates as a mechanism of artistic exaggeration and distortion. The old *cliché* "larger than life" comes into its own. But, as with all effective exaggeration, it leaves us with the recognition that, after all, real people can be monstrous too. The sacred fount might be taken then as a portentous and humorous way of accounting for the shocking vitality, brazen good looks and unshakeable nerve of some women; just as it might be interpreted as a fancifully excessive explanation for the arid and boring solemnity and listlessness of some young men. Part of the piquancy of "poor Briss" is that he reminds one of some lack-lustre persons in their thirties who have acquired an expression and posture which will serve them in their sixties: victims possibly of insatiable (or hen-pecking) wives, or perhaps

[71] *S.F.*, pp. 56-7.　　　[72] *S.F.*, p. 57.

only of boredom. Such thoughts as these could hardly be offered as interpretations of the novel: but it is part of the drollery of the work that they enter the reader's mind as alternatives to the fabulous imaginings of the narrator.

The reader who is on good terms with *The Sacred Fount* is rewarded in many places by virtuoso effects which only this novel, with its queer *donnée*, could have provided. A charming one occurs in the passage already referred to, where the narrator and Mrs Brissenden have continued further their speculations on Mrs Server and her various male friends. Breaking off the conversation, after one of his hazardous speeches, Mrs Brissenden walks out on to the terrace, from which she can see a couple seated in the shade of the beech tree. There is a lady in blue, clearly identified as Mrs Server, and a companion partly hidden from view. "There!" she triumphantly exclaims, in reference to the narrator's previous testimony that she had been in the library with the Comte de Dreuil. Mrs Brissenden is sure that the half-hidden gentleman must be Long: "It's *he*!" But the narrator insists that she is still with M. de Dreuil, until the sight of a brown shoe in a white gaiter causes him to change his mind: "It must be Lord Lutley." Mrs Server and her friend move slightly, but he is still not fully visible. The watchers gaze attentively, studying her gestures and manner, with further exclamations and a growing sense that here indeed was a "relation"; "It stuck out of her, her part in a relation; it hung before us, her part in a relation; it was large to us beyond the breadth of the glade." With whom could it be, such a relation, but Gilbert Long? The anti-climax follows:

> The question was not settled till she had come on some distance; then the producer of our tension, emerging and coming after her, offered himself to our united, to our confounded, anxiety once more as poor Briss.[73]

Another fine moment occurs after dinner when the assembled company listen to a piano performance. The narrator notes lightly that "when music, in English society . . . is not an accompaniment to the voice, the voice can in general be

[73] *S.F.*, p. 67.

counted on to assert its pleasant identity as an accompaniment to music. . . ."[74] Newmarch however is better "schooled," and the guests are in fact silently listening: a situation which has its own suggestiveness for the narrator. Each listener brings his own thoughts to the music, each with a special secret need to have the imagination flattered or the nerves quieted: but all have in common their acknowledgment of the player's spell. And the narrator is struck with the idea of what might be happening under cover of such a ritual, with the "beauty and terror of conditions so highly organised that under their rule [Mrs Server's] small lonely fight with disintegration could go on without the betrayal of a gasp or a shriek, and with no worse tell-tale contortion of lip or brow than the vibration, on its golden stem, of that constantly renewed flower of amenity which my observation had so often and so mercilessly detached only to find again in its place."[75] The presence of an audience and protagonists in such an atmosphere suggests a grand dramatic climax:

> It was as if there were some last act to be performed before the curtain could fall. Would the definite dramatic signal for ringing the curtain down be then only—as a grand climax and *coup de théâtre*—the due attestation that poor Briss had succumbed to inexorable time and Mrs. Server given way under a cerebral lesion? Were the rest of us to disperse decorously by the simple action of the discovery that, on our pianist's striking his last note, with its consequence of permitted changes of attitude, Gilbert Long's victim had reached the point of final simplification and Grace Brissenden's the limit of age recorded of man?[76]

---

[74] *S.F.*, p. 130.   [75] *S.F.*, pp. 131-2.   [76] *S.F.*, p. 132.

X

The Later Novels: I

A useful point of departure for discussion of *The Ambassadors* (1903)—and of the other late novels, perhaps in a lesser degree—is its allusiveness. James is here dealing with subjects akin to those that had occupied him, off and on, for thirty years, and he treats them as old friends. To a reader unacquainted with the earlier books, or with American themes generally, his oblique and parenthetic approach, in itself delightful, may give difficulty. Such a reader needs something more explicit than allusion. Given the right conditions, passages of this kind may become richly accessible, and may be enjoyed as one enjoys something that is basically familiar and yet new; for the artistic use made of the subjects transforms them. For example, Strether's "first glimpse" of Waymarsh "disconcerted in the porch of the hotel"[1] before they meet in the presence of Maria Gostrey is a slight but unmistakable echo of the passages in earlier novels by James and Howells where busy Americans on vacation cut an awkward figure in hotels: the "vague prostrations on benches of tired heads of American families" in *The Reverberator*; the Laphams lurking helplessly in New England resorts "and not knowing how to put themselves forward," and so on. Readers of the earlier books are aware that one of the few consolations of exiled businessmen in Europe was reading the newspapers at the American banker's. Mr Ruck is dependent on this resource in Geneva. Mr Dosson occupies himself similarly in Paris, but so does the expatriate Mr Luce in *The Portrait of a Lady*, who has been enjoying Parisian life in his peculiar way for fifty years. How gratifying then to find Waymarsh in the same tradition! But the point occurs in a passage the chief interest of which is that Strether, who might have been expected to act similarly, does not do so. This is very much Strether's chapter; it is

---

[1] *Amb.*, I. 21.

devoted mainly to his first golden impressions of Paris: but Waymarsh's conformity to type provides scope for an effective contrast. The two Americans visit the rue Scribe together for letters. Strether, after a "controlled impulse" to read them in the bank, puts them into his pocket "with a sense of the greater felicity of carrying them off":

> Waymarsh, who had had letters yesterday, had had them again today, and Waymarsh suggested in this particular no controlled impulses. The last one he was at all events likely to be observed to struggle with was clearly that of bringing to a premature close any visit to the rue Scribe. Strether had left him there yesterday; he wanted to see the papers, and he had spent, by what his friend could make out, a succession of hours with the papers. He spoke of the establishment, with emphasis, as a post of superior observation; just as he spoke generally of his actual damnable doom as a device for hiding him from what was going on. Europe was best described, to his mind, as an elaborate engine for dissociating the confined American from that indispensable knowledge, and was accordingly only rendered bearable by these occasional stations of relief, traps for the arrest of wandering western airs.[2]

It is no injustice to his earlier portrayal of such types to say that in Waymarsh James achieves a finer virtuosity. As a study in anti-climax Waymarsh's first utterance, in the conversation with Strether in his hotel bedroom, could not be bettered. After pages devoted to the subtle awakening of Strether's susceptibilities his compatriot speaks: " 'I don't know as I quite see what you require it for. You don't appear sick to speak of.' It was of Europe Waymarsh thus finally spoke."[3] His words proceed from the depths of abysmal assumptions: that Europe exists primarily as a rest cure for members of the over-worked race. The contrast between Strether's quickened response to his European adventure, tactfully and quaintly subdued to meet the mood of his friend, and the latter's dreary hollowness becomes a matter for stylistic play. Waymarsh's communication to Strether, later in the novel, that he is joining the Pococks in their trip to

[2] *Amb.*, 1. 69.   [3] *Amb.*, 1. 24.

Switzerland, shows that he acknowledges other American reasons for coming to Europe—reasons more appropriate perhaps to a woman: " 'Mrs. Pocock wants some scenery. She hasn't had much yet'."[4] The announcement that Sarah, whose hands are soon to be covered with Strether's blood, has asserted the need for scenery, is a happy stroke of national portraiture, and Waymarsh's phrasing of it is another; and in their context the words are stylistically most pleasing. These juxtapositions, which are among the delights of the later books, will mean much less to the reader who is unfamiliar with the individual components. In an earlier story each separate point of manners or type could be given a simpler prominence, a more separate treatment. In *The Ambassadors* James is handling many components at once, some inevitably subordinated to others or foreshortened with admirable economy. Not that it is a fatal disadvantage to miss these points. A first reading of *The Ambassadors* may be a little mystifying, and yet enchanting, so authentic is the spell of Strether's adventure. In a letter to Hugh Walpole, James described it as "a very packed production—with a great deal of one thing within another,"[5] and this gives a valuable description of its mode of economy. The opening sections provide some good simple examples. It would have been possible to allow much more space to Strether's enjoyment of English scenes. Any reader familiar with the English sketches knows that James was superlatively equipped to convey the impact not only of Chester but even of Liverpool on the newly-arrived transatlantic visitor. Strether responds as much as any of James's pilgrims. But the emphasis at the opening is not here; and experiences of this kind are placed in a subsidiary relation to more crucial matters. The first page or two are haunted by the name of Waymarsh, whom he is to meet at Chester, where he has now arrived, and whom he is glad, in a guilty way, not to have met at Liverpool. Delighted though he will be to meet his old friend, he cannot suppress the thought that his business would have been "slightly bungled" had the latter's countenance on the quay-side been his "first 'note' of Europe."[6] He has had his "qualified draught of Europe, an afternoon and an

---

[4] *Amb.*, II. 170.   [5] *L.*, II., 253.   [6] *Amb.*, I. 3.

evening on the banks of the Mersey, but such as it was he took his portion at least undiluted."[7]   Liverpool has been left behind; Strether's consciousness is now otherwise occupied, but a brief parenthetic reference a page or two later to "the dreadful delightful impressive streets the night before,"[8] point to what has been omitted, and all that we know of James's unequalled art in depicting English city squalor comes to mind. All that was needed is done in these few words, which are slipped in without stress.   He allows himself rather more words in his account of Strether's walk round Chester with Maria Gostrey, where he refers to "the tortuous wall—girdle, long since snapped, of the little swollen city, half held in place by careful civic hands."[9]   After more charming touches of detail, we read: "Too deep almost for words was the delight of these things for Strether"; yet in the episode where this occurs the emphasis does not fall here: Maria Gostrey is diagnosing his New England psyche, his "failure to enjoy"— the general failure of Woollett and Strether's world.   And later, when they take Waymarsh with them, there are more delightful phrases of expressive description, but it is the lowering un-responsiveness of Waymarsh and his queer behaviour (his "sacred rage") that dominate the passage.   The descrip-tive passages are all that could be wished for, but only as elements in a composition.   They are vivid without being obtrusive.

To return to the first page: Strether has several things on his mind, but it is important that some thoughts—for example, those relating to his mission, Woollett, the Newsomes—should be held back.   And only indirectly, in a reference to "his adventure" and its promise of success, do we become aware on the first page that he has come to Europe on an interesting quest.   The sentence in which we learn it tells us of what his first sense of Europe has in fact meant to him: "such a con-sciousness of personal freedom as he hadn't known for years. . . . such a deep sense of change."   And it is this that is upper-most: other considerations must "keep" until a favourable occasion arises.   He has the opportunity to disclose them in his hotel conversation with Waymarsh, and declines it with a

[7] *Amb.*, I. 4.   [8] *Amb.*, I. 12.   [9] *Amb.*, I. 14.

"not tonight": a postponement which has annoyed some readers. But this method of preparing for explanations later is technically excellent. We sense a reluctance in Strether, a slight anticipation of problems to come, and all this contributes to the rich complexity of the opening sections. The facts are extracted from him eventually, in conversations with Maria Gostrey and Waymarsh, his interlocutor in each case adding something to their enhancement. The dominant note of the early pages is his odd sense of beguilement, the atmosphere of new possibilities. *The Ambassadors*, though a novel of manners and as full of sociology as an egg is of meat, has some of the character of a romance. Maria Gostrey, standing on the threshold of Europe, virtually in waiting for Strether, is almost like an emblematic figure in an old allegory. On his meeting with her he feels that something momentous has started: "Nothing could have been odder than Strether's sense of himself as at that moment launched in something of which the sense would be quite disconnected from the sense of his past and which was literally beginning there and then."[10] She has formalised roles to fulfil. ("I bear on my back the huge load of our national consciousness.")[11] As a woman of enigmas and revelations, she represents new forms of knowledge; she is "the mistress of a hundred cases or categories, receptacles of the mind, subdivisions for convenience, in which, from a full experience, she pigeon-holed her fellow mortals with a hand as free as that of a compositor scattering type."[12] Their exchange might be compared with those long dialogues in medieval poetry, so full of "doctrine." When Strether's trouble (Woollett, Waymarsh, Maule's curse) has been specified, and he shows that he wishes to be helped, she accepts the special magical role ("she took over the job . . . on the spot.")[13] In these pages Strether lives, we live, in a charmed world. And yet, at another level, what is Maria but another intelligent American expatriate spinster? The air of romance in these pages is the air of Strether's bewilderment, the newness of everything: but what he encounters can be seen also as straight social truth.

[10] *Amb.*, I. 8.   [11] *Amb.*, I. 16.
[12] *Amb.*, I. 10.   [13] *Amb.*, I. 18.

The romantic charm is maintained. The house in the rue Malesherbes, with the balcony on which the mysterious young man (Little Bilham) smokes his cigarette, represents for Strether, as he pauses in the street below, strange daunting possibilities:[14] what ways of living will he be confronted with when he enters that dwelling? He does enter it, and what he meets there provides further riddles for Maria Gostrey to solve. Chad's appearance in the box at the theatre is indeed a magic moment; and the chapter that follows, so full of insights for Strether, also has its atmosphere of the glamorously enigmatic. ("Chad raised his face to the lamp, and it was one of the moments at which he had, in his extraordinary way, most his air of designedly showing himself.")[15] The Garden of Gloriani might almost be a place of Spenserian meanings, peopled with strange denizens ("The deep human expertness in Gloriani's charming smile—oh the terrible life behind it!—")[16] And when Jeanne de Vionnet with Chad make their appearance, they have a touch of "faerie" for the captivated Strether. Even the most uninitiated reader need not miss the poetry of Strether's saturated state. And this is conveyed from first to last through the language. The prose of *The Ambassadors* has more weight, but also more lightness, greater rhetorical power but also greater discreetness of implication, a fuller variety of resources in every way than the prose of the early books, admirable though that can be at its best. How well James conveys the impression of sensibility quite flaring up on a casual provocation, in the chapter describing Strether's first days of roaming Paris! The passage is well-known: he is sampling the bookstalls, so much haunted by the young and aspiring:

> He wasn't there for his own profit—not, that is, the direct; he was there on some chance of feeling the brush of the wing of the stray spirit of youth. He felt it in fact, he had it beside him; the old arcade indeed, as his inner sense listened, gave out the faint sound, as from far off, of the wild waving of wings.[17]

---

[14] *Amb.*, I. 85.   [15] *Amb.*, I. 137.

[16] *Amb.*, I. 173.   [17] *Amb.*, I. 83.

There is a considerable amount of rhetoric, expressive of Strether's sense either of the drama or of the fatal oddity of his plight (or of James's sense of these things: the relation of the novelist with the hero, the novelist enhancing and embellishing the latter's awareness, is an area of discussion on which angels might fear to tread!). An element of drollery adds its flavour. During the first days of acquaintance with Chad, the latter's "manner," inscrutable to both Strether and Waymarsh, provokes an image of unplumbable depths: "The fathomless medium held them—Chad's manner was the fathomless medium; and our friend felt as if they passed each other, in their deep immersion, with the round impersonal eye of silent fish."[18] On occasion Strether can strike a note of the portentous ("I feel as if my hands were imbrued with the blood of monstrous alien altars.")[19] It is part of his Americanism—this sense of doing something that constitutes an adventure—that all kinds of little manifestations can take on a quality calling for emphasis. It is not nothing—in fact, "things have come to pass"—that he should, at a time when relations with Mrs Newsome are severed and the reinforcements are due, undertake certain little trips for mere pleasure:

> . . . he went to Chartres and cultivated, before the front of the cathedral, a general easy beatitude; he went to Fontainebleau and imagined himself on the way to Italy; he went to Rouen with a little handbag and inordinately spent the night.[20]

The greater weight of the prose tallies with the greater density of the materials; but it is also a relaxed style because the materials are familiar and so is the narrator's relation with the reader. Everything is presented for enjoyment, Strether being one of those on whom no occasion for a charged or pointed response is lost. Even in the post office, where he pens his little reply to Mme de Vionnet, Strether's "too interpretative innocence" sees in the women, driving steel pens on the sand-strewn table, "arranging, pretexting goodness knew what . . . something more acute in manners, more sinister in morals, more fierce in the national life. . . . He was mixed

---

[18] *Amb.*, I. 152.   [19] *Amb.*, II. 148-9.   [20] *Amb.*, II. 51.

up with the typical tale of Paris."[21]   Whatever takes place at any moment has charm, comedy, mystery, drama, sometimes the highest poetry, for him, and James's range of language encompasses it.

The romantic, poetic aspects of the book are part of its realism as an American novel of manners; for Strether is a romantic in the American way, and his experience is therefore documentary. He has also intense awareness of manners, of the differences between Americans and Europeans, and between Americans and Americans; though his reflexions on them are so assimilated to the peculiar tone of his adventure, that it would be easy for a reader not to appreciate how much "ground" has been "covered," and to have the general impression of less documentation than in the earlier books. There are multitudes of small points, some of which, admittedly, are not treated very explicitly: Waymarsh's breakfast at Chester, for example. Maria Gostrey is accustomed to these situations, and she sees to it that he "breakfasts like a gentleman."[22]   But unhappily no details are given; we know only of the beef and oranges from which she weans him. There is a delightfully documentary little episode, infinitesimally minor, in which Strether is taken by Little Bilham to visit some young artist friends, "ingenuous compatriots," whom he finds "quaint and queer and dear and droll," and who "twanged with a vengeance the aesthetic lyre—they drew from it wonderful airs." But we are left without much knowledge of their "delicate daubs," or of Strether's delicate response to them.[23] In these cases the allusiveness is rather tenuous, though what we lose in specific detail is made up for in ease and lightness. But there are plenty of passages of greater substance than these.

The earlier works are by no means lacking in examples of James's art of juxtaposing his Americans, so that they draw out each other's Americanness. With Newman and Mrs Tristram he does something similar to what he achieves later with Strether and Maria Gostrey: but his art in *The Ambassadors* is altogether more accomplished. It is Maria's function to draw him out about Woollett and the Newsome family

[21] *Amb.*, II. 242-3.   [22] *Amb.*, I. 33.   [23] *Amb.*, I. 112-13.

business, and to supply interpretations which would never have occurred to him:

> "Is there a business?"
>
> "Lord, yes—a big brave bouncing business. A roaring trade."
>
> "A great shop?"
>
> "Yes—a workshop; a great production, a great industry. The concern's a manufacture—and a manufacture that, if it's only properly looked after, may well be on the way to become a monopoly. It's a little thing they make—make better, it appears, than other people can, or than other people, at any rate, do. . . ."
>
> "And what *is* the article produced?"
>
> Strether looked about him as in slight reluctance to say; then the curtain, which he saw about to rise, came to his aid.
>
> "I'll tell you next time. . . ."[24]

Here we have one of the jokes of the novel: he never tells her. But his fastidious reluctance (in itself a piece of New Englandism) comes after a passage in which he has talked about Woollett matters—money and the business acumen that makes it—in a tone that reflects an innocent, mainly unquestioning acceptance of them. It is brought home to us here, obvious though it ought to be, that whatever Strether's "values" have been (for example, the intellectual traffic of his high-toned Review) he has fitted easily enough into the Woollett scheme of things. How indeed could he not, the role of business in the American world being what it is? The curve of this conversation defines most elegantly Strether's relation to his community, with a great saving of tedious detail. (In a later conversation with Waymarsh Strether speaks quite glibly of Chad's importance to the business, and of his own interest in the matter: "Well, I naturally want what my future wife wants. And the thing will be much better if we have our own man in it.")[25]

Maria has her own interpretation of the gentilities of the Newsome world, about which Strether is completely solemn. Mrs Newsome's "large beneficence" becomes "expiation"[26] for the late Mr Newsome's ill-gotten gains: Strether has

---

[24] *Amb.*, I. 52.   [25] *Amb.*, I. 97.   [26] *Amb.*, I. 55.

admitted that there were "practices" and Maria sees "infamies." In his references to her Strether uses the idiom most congenial to American womanhood, and Miss Gostrey explodes it:

"... She's moreover highly nervous—and not at all strong."

"You mean she's an American invalid?"

He carefully distinguished. "There's nothing she likes less than to be called one, but she would consent to be one of those things, I think," he laughed, "if it were the only way to be the other."

"Consent to be an American in order to be an invalid?"

"No," said Strether, "the other way round. She's at any rate delicate, sensitive, high-strung. She puts so much of herself into everything——"

Ah Maria knew these things! "That she has nothing left for anything else? ..."[27]

This might be compared with a passage on a similar theme later in the book where Strether's timid earnestness is contrasted with another kind of bracing idiom, that of Jim Pocock. Whatever else Jim might fail to be, he is an American humorist and we may welcome his contribution to the stylistic repertory. The Pococks have just arrived, but Sarah's manner is inscrutable and Strether applies to Jim for light on the situation:

"Has Mrs. Newsome at all given way——?"

" 'Given way'?"—Jim echoed it with the practical derision of his sense of a long past.

"Under the strain, I mean, of hope deferred, of disappointment repeated and thereby intensified."

"Oh is she prostrate, you mean?"—he had his categories in hand. "Why, yes, she's prostrate—just as Sally is. But they're never so lively, you know, as when they're prostrate."

"Ah Sarah's prostrate?" Strether vaguely murmured.

"It's when they're prostrate that they most sit up."

"And Mrs. Newsome's sitting up?"

"All night, my boy—for *you*! ..."[28]

The artistic economy that excludes Mrs Newsome altogether from the action, and that keeps Sarah away from Strether,

[27] *Amb.*, I. 50.   [28] *Amb.*, II. 76-7.

o

except for the one deferred occasion when he experiences the full impact of her personality, may be seen as, among other things, a charitable arrangement. It is not that the women of Woollett are monsters in their own social environment: Woollett has its points, and Strether has accepted it and them for many years. But a situation has been brought about in which the monstrous has been released in them. James's technique with Sarah is to show us once only how far she can go, and to build up towards this moment mainly with gruesome imagery. Strether's wry imaginings of what the meeting with Sarah will be like are in James's best vein of grotesque and ominous wit:

> One thing remained well before him—a conviction that was in fact to gain sharpness from the impressions of this evening: that if she *should* gather in her skirts, close her eyes and quit the carriage while in motion, he would promptly enough become aware. She would alight from her headlong course more or less directly upon him; it would be appointed to him, unquestionably, to receive her entire weight.[29]

In another place, where Strether thinks he has caught a glimpse of Sarah on Chad's balcony, we have again this muffled rhetoric, the euphemistic phrases being agreeably juxtaposed with the more openly violent:

> . . . If the person were Sarah he might on the spot therefore be served to his taste. He might lead her by a move or two up to the remedy for his vain tension; as to which, should he get nothing else from it, he would at least have the relief of pulling down the roof on their heads. There was fortunately no one at hand to observe—in respect to his valour—that even on this completed reasoning he still hung fire. He had been waiting for Mrs. Pocock and the sound of the oracle; but he had to gird himself afresh—which he did in the embrasure of the window, neither advancing nor retreating—before pro- voking the revelation. It was apparently for Sarah to come more into view; he was in that case there at her service.[30]

But it turns out to be Mamie instead, and Strether, with the reader, is reprieved.

The absoluteness of Sarah's rejection of the whole situation of Chad and Mme de Vionnet must be noted as one of those cases of American behaviour in which intolerance prevails and accommodation has no place. The affront to her sexual and cultural susceptibility represented by Strether's claims for Mme de Vionnet, and also by his view of Chad as changed for the better, is too great. Not only does morality rebel, but Chad is a threat to the supremacy of the New England woman. Among the many aspects of Chad that come home to Strether during their first conversation is his sexual assurance and the note of authority that accompanies it:

> He saw him in a flash as the young man marked out by women; and for a concentrated minute the dignity, the comparative austerity, as he funnily fancied it, of this character affected him almost with awe.[31]

The impression may be contrasted with his realisation, on the arrival of the Pococks, of the status of Jim. It is one of the great strokes of economy in the novel that Strether's Parisian experience gives him the opportunity to see with fresh eyes, for our benefit, areas of the American character that he has known, but without marking, for years. The old familiar fact of the relegation of the male to a merely money-making role comes home to him with a wealth of implication. Jim, for example, has no personal concern with the "moral side" of their mission. He is "nothing compared to Sally, and not so much by reason of Sally's temper and will as by that of her more developed type and greater acquaintance with the world."[32] This gives Strether material for reflexions which culminate in the realisation that "the society over there, that of which Sarah and Mamie—and in a more eminent way, Mrs Newsome herself—were specimens, was essentially a society of women, and that poor Jim wasn't in it."[33]

The same principle of economy operates brilliantly in the presentation of Mamie. Mamie has almost no part to play in the action, but she has great value for contrast—and for respite. The scene where Strether finds her instead of Sarah on the balcony is charmingly contrived, and the niceness of

---

[31] *Amb.*, I. 135.   [32] *Amb.*, II. 70-1.   [33] *Amb.*, II. 71-2.

Mamie is a little oasis of consolation for him at this stage of his perplexing adventure. Strether's experience of the previous months give him a new appreciation of the kind of human phenomenon that Mamie is, and his recognition expresses itself in a flood of insights. James is seldom praised for rapidity of delineation, but the passages embodying Strether's reflexion and recollections of her are remarkable examples of *multum in parvo*:

> What Maisie was like was the happy bride, the bride after the church and just before going away. She wasn't the mere maiden, and yet was only as much married as that quantity came to. She was in the brilliantly acclaimed festal stage. . . .[34]

> Yes, she was funny, wonderful Mamie, and without dreaming it; she was bland, she was bridal—with never, that he could make out as yet, a bridegroom to support it; she was handsome and portly and easy and chatty, soft and sweet and almost disconcertingly reassuring . . . and she had a mature manner of bending a little, as to encourage and reward, while she held neatly together in front of her a pair of strikingly polished hands; the combination of all of which kept up about her the glamour of her "receiving", placed her again perpetually between the windows and within sound of the ice-cream plates, suggested the enumeration of all the names, all the Mr. Brookses and Mr. Snookses, gregarious specimens of a single type, she was happy to "meet".[35]

She has something of Verena, with a touch of Pandora: but she is less "bright" than either, and her version of the usual loquacity has its ominous possibilities for Strether. The "flat little voice" of a girl of fifteen is combined with that "hint of the polysyllabic" which may make her a bore in middle age. The whole American world of female assurance and its usages that she calls to mind is almost as exotic as the world in which he has been living since he came to Europe.

How full of good conversation this novel is, and how amiably the nicer Americans get on with each other! Some of the conversations are openly comic; for example, those in

which the humorous Miss Barrace talks of Waymarsh (Strether's
"splendid encumbrance"), with whom she is giving some help.
Some are relaxed, easy and acute at the same time. In
Gloriani's garden Miss Barrace, Little Bilham and Strether
have a brief exchange, a brief moment of expatriate reflexion
on Paris, and on how in the light of Paris "everything shows":

> "It's the fault of the light of Paris—dear old light!"
> "Dear old Paris!" Little Bilham echoed.
> "Everything, every one shows," Miss Barrace went on.
> "But for what they really are?" Strether asked.
> "Oh, I like your Boston 'reallys'! But sometimes—yes."
> "Dear old Paris then!" Strether resignedly sighed. . . .[36]

He then asks whether this applies to Mme de Vionnet. These
expatriates delight in speculative, humorous talk. It falls to
them to interpret for Strether the situation that so much
concerns him, rather avoiding the cardinal issues (Little Bilham
lies to him on one occasion), but with a wealth of reference,
some of which is enigmatic to him, to such ambiguous matters
as Chad's "goodness."

It falls to Maria Gostrey in their last scenes together to go
over with him again the tale of his misunderstandings, spelling
out some things that still remain for a New Englander to
recognise in what has happened. Theirs is finely tempered
dialogue, grave and yet light, its tensions controlled by a
kindly familiarity. It is much better than the dialogue of
The Awkward Age, if only because of the friendship and understanding between them, and their shared Americanness, which
makes for appreciation, humour and ease.

The Wings of the Dove is, in some places, more difficult than
The Ambassadors. On this question of difficulty we need to be
specific. A certain passage may mystify a particular reader in
particular circumstances; possibly because he lacks some
piece of equipment that the novelist felt he could take for
granted in the audience he was addressing. A gifted reader may
fail here. A genuinely difficult passage can make the reader
lose the thread, or cause him to be impatient or inattentive in
the perusal of passages which in themselves should raise no

[36] *Amb.*, I. 182.

query at all. Sometimes the difficulty is due to one's having
expected a very different kind of writing, and with an adjustment of expectation the problem ceases to exist. All these
remarks may seem elementary, but some misinterpretations
of *The Wings of the Dove* have been very elementary, and the
eminent critic and the common reader have gone astray
together. Nothing in Jamesian criticism is more remarkable
than the widespread failure to appreciate Milly. This may be
partly due to the reader's unpreparedness for so thoroughgoing
a case of Americanism.

A highly illustrative passage is the episode of Milly's visit
to the National Art Gallery. It occurs after her second and
most momentous interview with Sir Luke Strett: she is now
fully aware of the precariousness of her health; and indeed it
is to allow Sir Luke the opportunity to talk to Mrs Stringham
and tell her the worst that she has arranged not to be at home
on this particular morning. She feels by no means well, and
soon sees it as rather symptomatic that she should study the
lady copyists rather than the great originals: she is "too weak
for the Turners and the Titians." And then, a little tired, she
turns her eyes away from pictures and they rest, "in her vagueness, on the vagueness of other visitors." The word "vagueness" is a pointer: we know that there are fellow-Americans
in the offing. And now follows a passage of shrewd, rueful,
whimsical reflexions. This is "the moral of a menaced state
of health—that one should sit in public places and count the
Americans." We come to a most revealing sentence:

> Partly, no doubt, they didn't so much as notice or know her,
> didn't even recognise their community of collapse with her,
> the sign on her, as she sat there, that for her too Europe was
> "tough".[37]

It helps here if the reader remembers the huddled, harassed
Americans on vacation of earlier stories. Milly's identification
of herself with them ("community of collapse . . . for her too
Europe was 'tough' ") is most beautiful, as a stroke of humorous
fancy and as an example of the national resilience.

Milly knows her types, and as three ladies pass, a mother

[37] *W.D.*, I. 255-6.

and her daughters, she feels almost guilty at being able to place them so completely. She knows them "as easily as a schoolboy with a crib on his lap would know the answer in class," and questions her right "so to possess, to dispossess" people who had done her no harm. Some of the particulars that follow would be familiar to a reader of such pieces as "Daisy Miller," "The Pension Beaurepas," "A Bundle of Letters," and so forth, though admittedly there are others that demand a closer awareness of American types and ways than such a person might possess. But an occasional obscure detail need not be disconcerting. What emerges from the passage is: first, that here, rather unexpectedly, in an episode where our attention is very much on the tragic heroine as such, James manages to tuck in a little of the old familiar humorous portraiture of national manners; and secondly, that these impressions come to us as those of the tragic heroine herself.

A page or two later Milly finds herself suddenly in the company of Kate and Densher; a situation calling for rapid adjustment, since Kate and Milly, who both love Densher, have never mentioned him to each other. Everyone behaves perfectly, and Milly quickly sees that her best contribution will be to act as a true American girl. There is humour in her recognition of herself, and of what is expected of American girls: but there is also passion in her living out this role as the highest expedient in a moment of considerable stress. The passage has remarkable vivacity of implication:

> The finest part of Milly's own inspiration, it may further be mentioned, was the quick perception that what would be of most service was, so to speak, her own native wood-note. . . . She still had reserves of spontaneity, if not of comicality; so that all this cash in hand could now find employment. She became as spontaneous as possible and as American as it might conveniently appeal to Mr. Densher, after his travels, to find her. She said things in the air, and yet flattered herself that she struck him as saying them not in the tone of agitation but in the tone of New York. . . .[38]

Here we have one of the features of James's late manner, of which examples were seen in *The Ambassadors*: a compositional,

[38] *W.D.*, I. 260-1.

sometimes dramatic economy.   Part of the secret is in the choice
of context.   The fullness of the moment for the character most
concerned causes whole worlds of familiar meanings to come
rapidly together, lit up with a special significance.   It is, of
course, an allusive technique.

This one chapter tells us enough about the acuteness and
originality of Milly to disprove a world of misconceptions about
her, whether sentimental or anti-sentimental.   It also shows
that James's notation in this late work is sharp and clear-cut,
a fact not sufficiently recognised.   That "Milly isn't there"[39]
is one of the more extraordinary judgments of Dr Leavis, a
critic whose observation of this kind of pointedness can often be
so impressive.

To take another illustration: the previous chapter of the
novel contains an important and moving scene where Kate
calls Milly a dove.   It is moving for a number of reasons, one
being that Kate genuinely wants to say something tender,
near as she is to the first steps in her plot to deceive Milly.
We are moved on Kate's behalf.   But the moment is important
also as a stage in Milly's realisation of her role.   The thought
"lighted up the strange dusk in which she lately had walked.
. . . She was a dove.   Oh, *wasn't* she? . . ."[40]   When Mrs
Lowder returns and speaks to her, she feels it as almost like
"dove cooing to dove."   Milly's answer to her question about
Densher is composed in as dovelike a manner as possible.   She
"studies the dovelike" with Mrs Stringham.   Here we have
only another example of Milly's continual need to compose
her relations with the world into some bearable and acceptable
shape.   It is easier for everyone concerned when Milly *is*
dovelike and accepts the sweetened version of her fate which
Sir Luke Strett and Mrs Stringham offer her, but she has a
habit of saying little unnerving things which threaten to spoil
their game.   During her last visit to Sir Luke before she leaves
for Venice she realises that she must be careful.   If she goes
too far he will be quite ready to hate her for "heading him off"
and embarrassing him "in the exercise of a kindness that, no
doubt, rather constituted for him a high method."   She even
has the fantastic little thought that their roles are reversed:

---

[39] *The Great Tradition* (1948), p. 158.   [40] *W.D.*, I. 249.

he is the patient, she the physician. She must not alarm him with her subtlety, she must leave the subtlety to him: "he would enjoy his use of it; and she herself, no doubt, would in time enjoy his enjoyment."[41]

These are not unduly difficult passages. There is no reason whatever why one should not, in reading them, recognise Milly for what she is: intelligent, ironical, self-reliant. But these facts do not fit in immediately with the elementary conception, with which readers tend to begin, of Milly as primarily a gentle person, deceived and deeply hurt, and sublimely forgiving. Milly *is* deceived, in one respect: but otherwise we may include her among those on whom little or nothing is lost. She is indeed loving and subject to tremulous feeling, and yet also the kind of person whom Henry James's brother would have called "toughminded." An admirable example of what Milly can digest—but this *is* a difficult passage and would call for lengthy analysis—may be found in her long scene with Lord Mark in Venice.[42] Lord Mark's motives as a suitor are suspect enough, and it is deplorable that he does not retire sooner from a position which becomes gradually more untenable; yet, with her realisation of all this, she can be good-humoured, and enjoy his social gifts—she laughs at him, and he is not put out—and this keeps unpleasantness at bay. She is an American girl, and he is an English lord. When Milly confides in him and makes it so easy for him to go from bad to worse (but this she regrets in the later stages) it is as an example of American tolerance, in one of its quainter forms, that we must understand her.

[41] *W.D.*, II. 112.   [42] *W.D.*, II. 129 f.

XI

The Later Novels: II

SOME of the difficulties in *The Wings of the Dove* seem to be due to James's desire, in his later phase, to grapple with difficult material for its own sake, not out of perversity but rather perhaps with a sense of *noblesse oblige*. Where life is inherently intractable the great artist has his opportunity: not to simplify, but to compel the difficulty itself to work for him; or even to intensify the difficulty, provided that some fine stroke of truth may be thus enhanced. The cultivation of difficulty should not be dismissed as mere aesthetic exclusiveness. If we obey Arnold's injunction to "let our minds rest upon that great and inexhaustible word *life*," we can easily see how much of common experience eludes artistic treatment how much of it is lost to any kind of interpretation.

American quaintness is one of these elusive materials. "Quaintness" may serve as a term for a number of things; the tendency not to "connect," to be tangential, to improvise, to be helpless being among them. James immerses himself more thoroughly in American quaintness in the later books than in the earlier, sometimes setting himself the formidable problem of using it as a medium for conversations intended to be expository, with results that to many readers must be almost unintelligible. Strether has a certain amount of it, and so has Milly; the Ververs in *The Golden Bowl* have more. Mrs Stringham is a case not only of American quaintness but also of American "nerves." The scene[1] in which she tries to tell Mrs Lowder of Sir Luke Strett's report on Milly is a virtuoso piece: she just cannot bring herself to formulate a straight statement in answer to the most obvious question. She talks "in the air," she is tangential, she is helpless. It must be

---

[1] *W.D.*, II. 97 f.

remembered, of course, that she is emotionally stricken: the "darkness" had "suddenly descended" with the doctor's visit.[2] Poor Mrs Stringham's nerves are also much taxed at the awful dinner party given by Mrs Lowder (a passage of grisly comedy), where all the wrong things are said about the absent Milly: "They quivered . . . they hummed and drummed, they leaped and bounded. . . ."[3] All this is noticed by the observant Densher, who knows his American types. In the chapter later in the novel where Mrs Stringham visits Densher's rooms in Venice, some parts of the conversation have proved impenetrable to at least one reader. The artistic principle, of entrusting a precious point to speakers who, for one reason or another, fail persistently to achieve common ground, so that meaning comes through, if at all, only after trial and error, and perhaps in some kind of verbal disguise, is excellent, and the result can be beautiful. This is what so much of life is like. James makes a stylistic exercise of devising a dialogue composed of imprecisions; even exaggerating the characters' vagueness, partly to offset the precision that he himself can always bring to bear when needed, partly to help situations to escape the commonplace summing-up that renders them lifeless. The imprecise is organically part of the manoeuvring between the characters concerned. (This is sometimes true, of course, of dialogues where the characters are not American, though the idiom of American quaintness has special possibilities.)

Quaintness, as one of the aspects of a Strether, a Milly or a Maggie, may be seen as a compositional resource, effective in its relation to other elements. It ranks as an intimate aspect rather than an heroic one: the heroic is perhaps provided for elsewhere. James's treatment of Milly in the chapters where she first appears affords a good example of these juxtapositions. It is only after the passage in which Mrs Stringham sees Milly perched on the rock overlooking the Alpine precipice, "looking down on the kingdoms of the earth"[4]—a passage that does everything to place her as a figure of tragic beauty—that we have a taste of her personal idiom (together

---

[2] *W.D.*, ii. 95.   [3] *W.D.*, ii. 34.   [4] *W.D.*, i. 111.

with that of Mrs Stringham!) in the conversation in which she raises the question about her health:

> Mrs. Stringham at this flared into sympathy. "Are you in trouble—in pain?"
> "Not the least little bit. But I sometimes wonder . . .!"
> "Yes,"—she pressed: "wonder what?"
> "Well, if I shall have much of it."
> Mrs. Stringham stared. "Much of what? Not of pain?"
> "Of everything. Of everything I have."
> Anxiously again, tenderly, our friend cast about. "You 'have' everything; so that when you say 'much' of it . . ."
> "I only mean," the girl broke in, "shall I have it for long? That is if I *have* got it."
> She had at present the effect, a little, of confounding, or at least of perplexing her comrade, who was touched, who was always touched, by something helpless in her grace and abrupt in her turns, and yet actually half made out in her a sort of mocking light. "If you've got an ailment?"
> "If I've got everything," Milly laughed.
> "Ah, *that*—like almost nobody else."
> "Then for how long?"
> Mrs. Stringham's eyes entreated her; she had gone close to her, half-enclosed her with urgent arms: "Do you want to see some one?" And then as the girl only met it with a slow headshake, though looking perhaps a shade more conscious: "We'll go straight to the best near doctor." This too, however, produced but a gaze of qualified assent and a silence, sweet and vague, that left everything open. Our friend decidedly lost herself.
> "Tell me, for God's sake, if you're in distress."
> "I don't think I've really *everything*," Milly said as if to explain —and as if also to put it pleasantly.[5]

Mrs Stringham varies between a tender or helpless evasiveness and an occasional urgent directness. Milly is evasive in her trouble, but capable also of making a game of it.

One of the frequent difficulties of this novel lies in the decorum whereby characters are made to show so little of what they think they are doing. Even when their thoughts are accessible to us, we see them making mental detours.

[5] *W.D.*, I. 117-18.

Thus, when Densher catches sight of Lord Mark at Florian's, he is sure that his descent upon Venice has been a piece of brutality, wounding to Milly and also directed against himself, and that it explains the fact that Milly has ceased to receive visits. But the particular kind of harm is not stated. If it had been stated—if some explicit phrase relating to "fortune-hunting" had actually appeared as the content of Densher's suppositions—his complacent comparison of himself with Lord Mark would have been too much compromised. What we note here is his odd sense of relief that Lord Mark, by intervening in this brutal way, should have made his own behaviour look relatively decent. He, Densher, has acted with delicacy. If Milly has been upset, "it wasn't a bit his act,"[6] and this thought gives him something like "exhilaration." A little later Densher can even reflect, with self-pity, "on what he is doing for Milly"[7]—a man of his parts, reduced to hanging about in such a state of uncertainty; though, admittedly, there are also moments—the words are slipped in without emphasis—when "he felt no straighter than another man."[8] It is a considerable feat on James's part to present a Densher, highly intelligent and yet capable of so much self-deception. Densher is morally fastidious. To do him justice, we must admit that he is not preoccupied with money. He has come into the fortune-hunting scheme at the instigation of Kate, with encouragements from others: but, although Kate has paid her share of the bargain by coming to bed with him, he has maintained a kind of moral aloofness from the plot. He has visited Milly every day, but only as a friend. Or, to put it another way, he has procrastinated, so far as his own fortune-hunting involvement is concerned. And he can cherish the difference between this and the behaviour of Lord Mark, not realising—he has the self-protective male psychology *par excellence*—that not Lord Mark but only he has the power to hurt Milly, and that what he is doing commits him enough.

When Mrs Stringham brings her news that Milly is dying, together with the disclosure of what Lord Mark's visit really meant, Densher does not readily recognise, though he cannot escape the thought, that a sameness exists between Lord

[6] *W.D.*, II. 237.   [7] *W.D.*, II. 239.   [8] *Ibid.*

Mark's attitude to Milly and his own. But what disturbs him most is the challenge, presented by Mrs Stringham, to deny the truth about his relationship with Kate; that is, to tell the supreme lie that may yet save Milly. One might argue that the telling of this lie is included in his share of the bargain with Kate, and that in his insistence on Kate's performing her share—the one occasion in the whole sequence of events when he acts in his own interest, but how crucial!—he has forfeited his freedom to contract out. He feels immense relief when Sir Luke Strett does not renew this suggestion. After all that he now knows of Milly's condition, and of the circumstances that have caused it, it may seem extraordinary that Densher's chief concern is that he should be "let off." The reader may feel that the time has come for remorse, sheer crude remorse at what he has done to Milly: but the irony of Densher's character is that his very fineness, and his overpowering need to believe in himself as a person of sensibility—the intense egoism that can accompany fineness—produce in him something like obtuseness. Crude remorse is for people who have behaved crudely, and Densher has felt from the outset that he is doing only what he has been unavoidably let in for. The need to be considerate to Milly, who loves him, has made it impossible for him not to become more and more involved in the projects of Kate, Mrs Lowder, Mrs Stringham and Sir Luke Strett. He cannot see himself as guilty in any ordinary crude sense. When Sir Luke seeks his company for the last part of his stay in Venice, Densher actually experiences with him an easing of his tension. Sir Luke "did him good. There had been in all the case too many women. A man's sense of it, another man's, changed the air. . . ."[9]

The beauty of this lies in Densher's being preserved unshaken, as it were, until and for his last meeting with Milly. It is immensely enhancing, it is Densher's privilege, that the penetration of his moral being which he must suffer should happen to him only in this way and at this level. But it involves an elaborate contrivance on James's part, and some readers may have to exert their imagination to accept it. The propriety of it is clear. The Densher upon whom Milly will

[9] *W.D.*, II. 271.

bestow her final blessing must still, in a certain sense, retain the beauty for which he has been so loved; just as she, though desperately ill, makes the supreme effort of being completely herself, at this final moment, for him.

A greater compositional artistry has already been noted as a quality distinguishing the later from the earlier work of James. He achieves it as markedly in *The Wings of the Dove* as in *The Ambassadors*, but in different ways. The organisation of the narrative is incomparably poetic in its variety, for reasons that become apparent as we reflect on the central subject. James gives a vivacity and a special range of colour and interest to Milly's story which, at another level, but not at the level at which she appears or desires to appear, can only be one of gradual physical restriction and defeat.

Milly's first notable appearance, the portentous moment in the mountain solitude, is followed, as we have seen, by the conversation in the hostelry with Mrs Stringham. This chapter is beautifully shaped. How admirably, in less than a page, during the interval between this exchange and Milly's re-appearance, does James sketch in the little details of the Alpine evening! Milly on her return comes suddenly to the point: she wants to go to London, and we eventually realise—Mrs Stringham's tact fails her here—that somehow Densher is in her mind. We become aware for the first time of their having met in New York. Milly does not wish to appear to be running after him and, indeed, his return from the United States is still not due: but her sudden wish to be in London, her pre-ference for "people" rather than scenery, has an obscure connexion with this preoccupation. What with her bringing up the theme of her health earlier in the evening, it is as if we now knew the whole burden of her meditation as she sat alone above the Alpine precipice. In this chapter we see a nervously agitated Milly, a little incoherent, making plans and changing them: but the poetic design achieved by the two phases of her talk with Mrs Stringham, separated by the quiet descriptive interlude, and the placing and timing of her outbursts, gives order and grace to the portrait.

At the beginning of the next episode we are plunged *in medias res*: Milly is in London, talking to Lord Mark at Mrs

Lowder's dinner table, and she has now become the "centre of consciousness." Milly at Matcham, in tears before the Bronzino portrait; and then digesting her fate on a seat in Regent's Park, after the interview with Sir Luke Strett; and then in the National Art Gallery, "counting the Baedekers," but unexpectedly running into Kate and Densher; and finally in her Venetian palace: this is a beautiful and moving sequence. No early novel by James, perhaps no other novel by anyone, leaves the reader with such a finely variegated succession of images of the places where the great events occur. The James of *Italian Hours* was supremely equipped to make the subtlest, most varied use of the Venetian setting for the last stage of her pilgrimage. Her palace is very much a piece of contrivance, an expensive makeshift, one of the many ways in which wealth enables her to fulfil her dual role. She needs a palace to support her aspiration to "live" in the eyes of others: but, as one of the mortally sick, she also needs seclusion. The Palazzo Leporelli, obtained by acts known only to the practised Eugenio, provides the ideal solution: a handsome arena for the flocking of visitors, but also a large-scale retreat, a place of spacious privacy.

Apart from the central fact that Milly's money operates as an incentive to fortune-hunters, the role it plays in her life is benign. It bestows protection; it gives human importance, if only the rather sombre importance measured by the amount of time a great London doctor can spend away from his practice to treat her. This is not a case where a socialist's point about the difference between rich and poor invalids would be very relevant. Miss Dorothea Krook makes a very interesting comparison between James's rich characters and the kings and queens of Shakespeare's plays:[10] wealth enables them to stand out as figures of exemplary significance. The immense consideration that is shown to Milly, what with Mrs Stringham's "Byzantine" view of her, and the elaborate way in which her resources can be used to give all possible decorum to her precarious existence: all this somehow heightens her relation to the ordinary human lot. Like a Shakespeare king or queen, Milly is both more privileged and more exposed than ordinary

[10] *The Ordeal of Consciousness in Henry James*, p. 13.

people. She can take an ironical view of her special opportunities: "She was more prepared than ever to pay enough,
and quite as much as ever to pay too much. What else . . .
was the use of being, as the dear Susies of the earth called you,
a princess in a palace?"[11] The "high florid rooms," "splendid
ceilings," with cherubs, medallions and so forth,[12] are all
present in the first introductory account of Milly's new home.
This points the transition from London to Venice, achieved
since the previous chapter. What is described here is her
"apartment of state," but the chapter opens with the stress
on her solitude: there have been people around her for weeks,
but now she needs to be by herself, and she sees her palace less
in terms of its splendour than as "the ark of her refuge," which
she will never leave. Or, to cite the image that occurs to her
later, as a fortress: "The romance for her . . . would be to sit
there for ever." She dreams of "never going down, of remaining aloft in the divine dustless air, where she would hear but
the plash of the water against stone."[13] That Milly, in very
low spirits, thus romanticises her plight, is a point which may
perhaps bring a gleam into the eyes of certain critics. Poignantly conveyed at certain moments in the scene that follows
(her conversation with Lord Mark) is the sense of Venice as a
world of enchantment outside and away from Milly's enclosed
existence.

By way of contrast, the first conversation in Venice between
Kate and Densher takes place "in the middle of Piazza San
Marco, always as a great social saloon, a smooth-floored,
blue-roofed chamber of amenity, favourable to talk . . . the
splendid Square, which had so notoriously, in all the years,
witnessed more of the joy of life than any equal area in Europe."[14]
No evocation of Venice could be more glowingly simple.
Kate and Densher enhance it, as it enhances them. But a
sense of the place hovers also about the more ominous
aspects of their situation. The great space provides "remoteness from earshot," so that they are free to say secret things:
but this freedom creates an anxiety in each concerning what the
other wants to say. It is as if "this very quantity, seated on

[11] *W.D.*, II. 128.   [12] *W.D.*, II. 119.
[13] *W.D.*, II. 133.   [14] *W.D.*, II. 171, 174.

P

their lips in the bright, historic air, where the only sign for their ears was the flutter of the doves, begot in the heart of each a fear."[15]

The boldest contrast—and only an artist of supreme eloquence could have brought off this great stroke of the obvious—is produced by the sudden storm, the first sea-storm of autumn, that sweeps over Venice after Milly has received the blow delivered by Lord Mark and Densher finds himself denied access to the palace. This kind of effect had not been achieved with such poetic authority since Shakespeare:

> It was a Venice all of evil that had broken out for them alike . . . a Venice of cold lashing rain from a low black sky, of wicked wind raging through narrow passes, of general arrest and interruption, with the people engaged in all the water-life huddled, stranded and wageless, bored and cynical, under archways and bridges.[16]

In this Venice all the familiar places and features have lost their meaning. For Densher the cheerless and desolate scene is in some way connected with the sinister presence of Lord Mark:

> The vice in the air, otherwise, was too much like the breath of fate. The weather had changed, the rain was ugly, the wind wicked, the sea impossible, *because* of Lord Mark.[17]

With equal obviousness, but with the same poetic warrant, the calm comes with the arrival of Sir Luke Strett:

> The weather changed, the stubborn storm yielded, and the autumn sunshine . . . came into its own again and, with an almost audible paean, a suffusion of bright sound that was one with the bright colour, took large possession. Venice glowed and plashed and called and chimed again; the air was like a clap of hands, and the scattered pinks, yellows, blues, sea-greens, were like a hanging-out of vivid stuffs, a laying-down of fine carpets.[18]

Sir Luke indeed enters upon the scene like a great natural force. Some critics exalt him into a symbol of ineffable moral significance: for Quentin Anderson he represents Divine

[15] *W.D.*, II. 174.   [16] *W.D.*, II. 232.
[17] *W.D.*, II. 236.   [18] *W.D.*, II. 262.

wisdom, just as Milly represents Divine love.[19] Without en-
dorsing anything so explicit as this, without even conceding
that Sir Luke embodies anything more august than the distinction, tact and kindness which he clearly possesses, one must
grant that James builds up his role into something of extraordinary poetic force. The actual moving in of Sir Luke
Strett is, to Densher's imagination, an inescapable portent.
He represents *truth* taking over, where all have conspired to leave
it unspoken. Milly's condition has been ringed round with
"expensive vagueness . . . smiles and silences and beautiful
fictions and priceless arrangements." From this fool's paradise
the "specified had been chased like a dangerous animal,"
but now the "specified" stands at the gate, "in Sir Luke Strett's
person, and quite on such a scale as to fill out the whole pre-
cinct."[20] Certain facts "of incurable pain, of the chance
grimly narrowed,"[21] are now acute and manifest, and the only
thing left to be thankful for is the breadth of his shoulders.
Portentous again for Densher is Sir Luke's re-appearance
after an unheard-of lapse of time, during which his own
miserable suspense has reduced him to his lowest level of de-
pression, and he has almost convinced himself that the great
doctor must surely have returned to London. The sight of him
in his doorway is a vision that "for an instant cut like a knife."[22]
Yet, shaken as he is by the thought of the sheer magnitude
of Milly's "case" and of the sacrifice of so much of Sir Luke's
time, it is a relief to him when the latter makes no mention
of her. The easing of tension in the few days that follow—
days during which Venice is normal again, a place for relaxa-
tion and desultory visiting—could be interpreted in more
ways than one. Sir Luke is inscrutable. We do not know how
much he knows of Densher or what he thinks of him. As for
Densher's feeling that "he was large and easy . . . he knew
what mattered and what didn't: he distinguished between . . .
the just grounds and the unjust for fussing,"[23] this does not seem
to point directly to a presence embodying supernatural values,
or to anything conducive to better moral understanding on
Densher's part; though an advocate of the theory of Divine

[19] *The American Henry James* (1958), pp. 271-2.   [20] *W.D.*, ii. 266.
[21] *W.D.*, ii. 266.   [22] *W.D.*, ii. 269.   [23] *W.D.*, ii. 271.

wisdom might accept the point that what Densher now needs is a companion who will not judge him, and a respite before the supreme moment of his final visit to Milly. Going to the opposite extreme, however, one could make out a case for something much nearer to mere worldly urbanity and tact on Sir Luke's part. It is not important to make up one's mind on this. Whatever Sir Luke's attitude may be, we are not to know it. We must accept him in the terms in which James gives him to Densher and to us.

The last phase of the novel, after we have done with Milly, has no less beauty in its placing and timing of events: but there is less variety—indeed, not much occasion for it. It is a time of waiting for Densher. Winter comes on as Milly's death approaches. Her letter to him arrives as a Christmas gift. It would be difficult by quotation or recapitulation to suggest the unobtrusive arts by which James conveys the impression of a mild, somewhat blank London Christmas, and of Densher's feelings in their subdued relation to the season.

The Golden Bowl will be discussed more briefly and selectively than the other two late novels. It is for me the most difficult of the group and, in certain important respects, unsatisfying. But it has suffered more than any other of James's novels from the tendency in readers to judge by the wrong criteria; that is, not to consider a book on its own terms. Perhaps it will be useful to begin with a defence of aspects which have been somewhat maligned.

No passage in the novel is better known that that with which the second volume begins, where the pattern of relationships threatening Maggie's happiness is depicted as a great ivory pagoda with tinkling bells. The image has been viewed as a gross example of sterile aestheticism, a symptom of decadence in James's art: but surely a more sympathetic reading can be found. Maggie, a person of unsophisticated sensibility, living in a world of costly *objets d'art* and intimidating appearances generally, is confronted with what might be referred to as another of her father's purchases. But whereas his other treasures are passive, this one behaves in a mysterious manner. (When one acquires human beings, as the Prince and Charlotte have been acquired . . .!) The passage conveys most effectively the impression of a huge expensive aberration on the collector's part. Different elements of feeling are present. The words, "she had carried on her existence in the space left for circulation, a space that sometimes seemed ample and sometimes narrow," are quite touching. We are reminded of Isabel Archer's constricted world. The behaviour of the strange object is sinister; Maggie senses danger: but there is also an Alice in Wonderland quality about the whole situation, with Maggie as the puzzled child looking for the clue to some new outlandish phenomenon. The exotic edifice would be engagingly absurd, were it not decidedly unpleasant.

This aspect should be kept in mind when we turn to the next notable passage in which Maggie sees her position in terms of imagery. Here there is certainly a humorous element. The image is of a spaniel that has scrambled out of the stream, shaking the water from its ears and pretending that nothing has happened—or trying to maintain this pretence, while wondering whether it might not perhaps have caught cold! Maggie's position gives her no cause for levity; yet, in her state of tension, she can think of the new preoccupation as a "high pastime." The problem of concealing her attitude makes it something of a game. But then the note changes:

> The ingenuity was thus a private and absorbing exercise, in the light of which, might I so multiply my metaphors, I should compare her to the frightened but clinging young mother of an unlawful child.[24]

So the situation *is* painful; the mother-child image is all the more effective coming after that of the spaniel. ("Might I so multiply my metaphors" reminds us of the presence of the novelist, and of the fact already stressed that in the late work of James we are confronted not with impersonality but with the more or less covert intervention of the novelist.) In a later chapter Maggie sees herself "in a bath of benevolence . . . over the brim of which she could but just manage to see by stretching her neck."[25] They (that is, Charlotte and the Prince) have got her into the bath and are keeping her there. In the same passage we see her also as a captive bird, flapping her wings in her desire for escape, "not merely as a plea for a more gilded

[24] *G.B.*, II. 6-7.   [25] *G.B.*, II. 39.

cage or an extra allowance of lumps of sugar." Much later,
during a phase of great strain for Maggie and others, "company" at their country dwelling, Fawns, is seen as "a kind of
renewed water-supply for the tank in which, like a party of
panting goldfish, they kept afloat."[26]

Here we have then the familiar Jamesian (and American)
habit of seeing a far from comic predicament in something
near to comic terms. Particular images may be approved or
not, according to personal taste, but there is no question of
such imagery's being a lapse from Jamesian decorum. The
grotesque and the droll in such contexts are entirely Jamesian.
They seem to tell us something about Maggie: that she is
humble, that she does not see herself as an impressive or tragic
victim, that her plight has for her an element of the absurd
as well as of the agonising.

When Maggie thinks of the Prince and Charlotte, the
imagery is often strikingly rhetorical. *They* are impressive,
and Charlotte sometimes tragic. In an early stage of her
struggle, when she reflects on the effect of a separation of these
lovers, the paragraph ends with extraordinarily baleful words:

> And say they accepted this account of their situation as a
> practical finality, acting upon it and proceeding to a division,
> would no sombre ghosts of the smothered past on either side
> show across the widening strait pale unappeased faces, or raise
> in the very passage deprecating, denouncing hands?[27]

This might be taken to express Maggie's awed sense of the
guilty pair as totally beyond her in style and range. The second
book of *The Golden Bowl* is full of such effects. The most
splendid passage is that in which Maggie imagines, with compassion and something like self-abasement, the agony of the
defeated Charlotte. She sees Charlotte as no ordinary person.
With her generosity of mind she makes her wonderful in her
grief, and even in her scorn and resentment. The passage is
great as a monument to the recognition by one woman of the
sufferings of another who has been her enemy:

> Charlotte was hiding neither pride nor joy—she was hiding
> humiliation; and here it was that the Princess's passion, so

---

[26] *G.B.*, II. 254.   [27] *G.B.*, II. 66.

powerless for vindictive flights, most inveterately bruised its tenderness against the hard glass of her question.

Behind the glass lurked the *whole* history of the relation she had so fairly flattened her nose against it to penetrate—the glass Mrs. Verver might, at this stage, have been frantically tapping from within by way of supreme irrepressible entreaty. . . . She could thus have translated Mrs. Verver's tap against the glass, as I have called it, into fifty forms; could perhaps have translated it most into the form of a reminder that would pierce deep. "You don't know what it is to have been loved and broken with. You haven't been broken with, because in *your* relation what can there have been worth speaking of to break? Ours was everything a relation could be, filled to the brim with the wine of consciousness; and if it was to have no meaning, no better meaning than that such a creature as you could breathe upon it, at your hour, for blight, why was I myself dealt with all for deception? why condemned after a couple of short years to find the golden flame—oh, the golden flame!—a mere handful of black ashes?" Our young woman so yielded at moments to what was insidious in these foredoomed ingenuities of her pity, that for minutes together sometimes the weight of a new duty seemed to rest upon her—the duty of speaking before separation should constitute its chasm, of pleading for some benefit that might be carried away into exile like the last saved object of price of the *émigré*, the jewel wrapped in a piece of old silk and negotiable some day in the market of misery.[28]

In another place Charlotte awakens in her "some echo of an ancient fable—some vision of Io goaded by the gadfly or of Ariadne roaming the lone sea-strand."[29] Her romanticism— another national trait not to be forgotten—pictures Charlotte and the Prince as "high Wagnerian lovers . . . interlocked in their wood of enchantment."[30] These "poetic" passages, had we the whole of James's text laid out for inspection, would be seen to provide striking contrast with the homeliness of the Ververs, who really are, to apply a Jamesian turn of phrase, of a quaintness! It is appropriate that, in the mind of Maggie, these formidably initiated beings should appear in terms reminiscent of the Old World tradition of fulfilled love and

[28] *G.B.*, II. 290-1.　　[29] *G.B.*, II. 271.　　[30] *G.B.*, II. 247.

romantic desolation.   Hers is a haunted imagination, compelled to live with fantasies, so much of the truth being kept
from her.

There have been many complaints about the style of *The
Golden Bowl*, but if we are willing to accept the novel on its own
terms, which often means seeing situations as Maggie sees
them, at a distance from what is "really happening"—the
desire for immediacy, in this case, may be a sign of narrowness
in readers—these objections evaporate.   Example after example can be cited of virtuosity with language: especially of
James's gift of bringing together the contrasting values of
imagery and abstract formulation, so that situations intellectually stated glow or reverberate, or find expression in
portentous gesture:

> . . . the thick air that had begun more and more to hang, for our
> young woman, over her accumulations of the unanswered.[31]

> . . . this air of beatific reference, less subdued in the others
> than in Amerigo and Charlotte, lent them, together, an
> inscrutable comradeship against which the young woman's
> imagination broke in a small vain wave.[32]

> . . . the pathless wild of the right tone. . . .[33]

> . . . there had appeared beforehand no reason why she should
> have seen the mantle of history flung, by a single sharp sweep,
> over so commonplace a deed.[34]

> To say anything at all would be in fine to have to say *why* she
> was jealous;   and she could in her private hours but stare
> long, with suffused eyes, at that impossibility.[35]

One of the pleasures of reading the late James—let us be frank
and let the detractors of this style make what they will of it—
is a pleasure in words used with the fullest rhetorical effect
that words are capable of.   No one can equal James's capacity
to make a situation terrific:

> They stood in the centre of the immense room [*i.e.*, Maggie and
> Charlotte at the outset of the great challenge scene], and Maggie

---

[31] *G.B.*, II. 13.   [32] *G.B.*, II. 44.   [33] *G.B.*, II. 187.
[34] *G.B.*, II. 9.   [35] *G.B.*, II. 31.

could feel that the scene of life her imagination had made of it twenty minutes before was by this time sufficiently peopled. These few straight words filled it to its uttermost reaches. . . .[36]

She saw, round about her, through the chinks of the shutters, the hard glare of nature—saw Charlotte, somewhere in it, virtually at bay. . . .[37]

The Golden Bowl is also rich in passages of bland and polished levity. The visit to the Gutermann-Suess household, *àpropos* of the Damascene tiles, provides a well-sustained example. The description of Mr Crichton, the British Museum official ("this perhaps most flower-loving and honey-sipping member of the great Bloomsbury hive")[38] is in this vein, and also the pleasant passage about Mr Crichton's rueful but good-humoured view of Mr Verver's purchases:

He carried his amiability to the point of saying that since London, under pettifogging views, *had* to miss from time to time its rarest opportunities, he was almost consoled to see such lost causes invariably wander at last one by one with the tormenting tinkle of their silver bells, into the wondrous, the already famous fold beyond the Mississippi.[39]

James can be light and, to use an epithet that has already been applied to his late style, *relaxed*, without any loosening of the fine verbal texture. The word helps to express the supreme ease which accompanies an almost limitless art in the adjustment of means to ever-varying ends. This style, like no one else's, allows one effect to flourish under cover of another or in defiance of another, almost any combination or transition being possible. A good example of his lighter manner, with other elements accompanying but not clashing, is the paragraph introducing Father Mitchell, the London priest who has luncheon with the Ververs on an especially hot afternoon. The "viands artfully iced" and the "slow circulation of precious tinkling jugs," a comic reference to Fanny Assingham's prostration, and a friendly humorous description of the priest himself, go together with such words as "a consensus of languor, which

---

[36] *G.B.*, ii. 218.   [37] *G.B.*, ii. 267.
[38] *G.B.* ii. 130.   [39] *G.B.*, ii. 129.

might almost have been taken for a consensus of dread." The good priest chats amiably, but there is a pointed hint that he is "urbanely filling up gaps," by no means unaware of the tensions among his hosts. The paragraph concludes with Maggie's reasons for not using him as a confessor; and, what with the imagery of the drinking glass, and an easy turn of phrase in the references to divine things, the transition comes about with perfect continuity of idiom:

> . . . Some day at some happier season she would confess to him that she hadn't confessed, though taking so much on her conscience; but just now she was carrying in her weak, stiffened hand a glass filled to the brim, as to which she had recorded a vow that no drop should overflow. She feared the very breath of a better wisdom, the jostle of the higher light, of heavenly help itself; and, in addition, however that might be, she drew breath this afternoon as never yet, in an element heavy to oppression.[40]

The closing words prepare us for a grimmer theme in the paragraph that follows.

Rich passages are to be found in abundance—some of the great familiar ones have been ignored here—and it is important that this fact should be recognised before questions are broached concerning the more doubtful features of the novel. It is fatally easy to describe *The Golden Bowl* in such a manner as to make it seem basically unsatisfactory, its actual quality passage by passage never having been tested.

In spite of so much to be praised in James's treatment of Maggie, she poses awkward problems. The reader is expected to admire her, it seems, on certain occasions when she is more likely either to embarrass or to alienate. When she begins to discover what is happening to her marriage she makes a series of moves to alter the pattern of relationships and routines which Charlotte and the Prince are using to facilitate their intrigue: but the reader cannot help being acutely aware that this pattern has been of the Ververs' making in the first instance. In their unimaginative good faith they have cast their respective spouses for roles that bring them frequently together, so that

[40] *G.B.*, II. 263.

they, father and daughter, can also be together in their blissful domesticity. This shows a defect of intelligence. And Maggie seems to have no awareness of the boredom—Charlotte's, at least, had reached the point of desperation—which has been partly responsible for the adultery. Some of the attempts she now makes to seize the initiative socially are, frankly, of a kind that might well produce more boredom or, rather, acute discomfort. She lacks the right touch for these matters, while Charlotte possesses it supremely. It is typical of her that she has no taste in dress, just as she lacks her father's feeling for *objets d'art*, and she has other limitations that make it better that she should not try to be a brilliant hostess. The fact is that Maggie, with all her substantial virtues, lacks some of the gifts that would seem to be indispensable for such an enterprise as she is engaged in: the winning back of her dazzling husband. She lacks charm, distinction, personal style. It becomes difficult in the end to accept the fact that she really has won him back. What can one make of a passage like the following?:

> Maggie's way tonight was to surprise them all, truly, by the extravagance of her affability. She was doubtless not positively boisterous; yet, though Mrs. Assingham, as a bland critic, had never doubted her being graceful, she had never seen her put so much of herself into being what might have been called assertive.[41]

But the scene that raises most problems is that in which the Prince is confronted with the broken bowl and with Maggie's knowledge of his past association with Charlotte. There is a long passage describing Maggie's desire, as she turns away from him to pick up the pieces, to spare him the indignity and embarrassment of appearing to be taken aback: but when finally she speaks ("So there it is—in its three pieces . . .")[42], some of her words might be described as unsparing. She refers to the Prince's having had "two relations" with Charlotte, and he, rather helplessly, queries the word "two"; whereupon she says: "Oh, you may have had fifty—had the same relation with her fifty times! Its of the number of *kinds* of relation

---

[41] *G.B.*, II. 132.   [42] *G.B.*, II. 167.

with her that I speak . . ."—a speech which would depend for its impact, no doubt, on the tone of voice, but nothing is done here to prevent its seeming quite crushing.[43] The Prince tries to explain about Charlotte's proposed wedding-gift, and Maggie then asks what in the end *was* given. Nothing was given, and Maggie does not let this point go: "Yes; it comes round after all to your having got me the bowl."[44] And later, when the Prince speaks of her getting her money back, she has another cutting remark ready: "Oh, I'm far from wanting it back—I feel so that I'm getting its worth," and she adds: "The great fact about the day we're talking of seems to me to have been quite remarkably that no present was made to me."[45] The scene ends with Maggie's refusal to tell him how much the others, especially her father, know about the new situation: "Find out for yourself!"[46] What effect could all this be expected to have on a man of taste, conscious of guilt though he is? Something has gone wrong here, either with the scene itself and James's conception of Maggie, or with my interpretation.

Her relation with her father is more moving than her relation with the Prince. In one of the most beautiful chapters in the novel she imagines her father arriving at the recognition of their need to separate and actually putting it into words: a poignantly appealing fantasy which she has to put away from her, because if he came to that it could only be through his discovering what he must not discover. She imagines him saying: "Sacrifice me, my own love; do sacrifice me, do sacrifice me!" She virtually hears him "bleating it at her, all conscious and accommodating, like some precious spotless exceptionally intelligent lamb." And as she joins him, realising with a pang the impossibility of it, nothing could be lighter or easier on the surface, or more in keeping with her generosity and courage, than her morning endearments: the smile, the "slightly smarter twist" she gives to his necktie, and then "to make up to him for her hidden madness . . . [her] rubbing her nose into his cheek according to the tradition of their frankest levity."[47]

In brief, *The Golden Bowl* is brilliant in many of the parts,

[43] *G.B.*, II. 168.   [44] *G.B.*, II. 172.   [45] *G.B.*, II. 175.
[46] *G.B.*, II. 179.   [47] *G.B.*, II. 73.

but rather perplexing as a whole. The end for which Maggie so bravely and so triumphantly strives is the keeping intact of two marriages, her father's and her own, neither of which is shown in a very convincing light. The stages of her struggle, the great dramatic scenes, are rightly praised: but as we move towards the solution, in what state of mind do we contemplate the prospect that lies before the four central figures? Mr John Bayley, in a most interesting essay on this novel, refers to the ending as "a victory for anti-romanticism, an abolition of Paterian intensities,"[48] but did James really intend nothing happier than this?

Whatever the reader makes of these problems, the important thing is that the novel should not be spoilt for him by the kind of deflating generalisation that has been all too current in recent criticisms. *The Ambassadors* and *The Wings of the Dove*, in their different ways, are more successful as wholes; and their central characters make a more intelligible appeal to one's imagination and sympathy. In *The Golden Bowl* the reader may sometimes have to accept situations for their sheer vividness, tension and splendour of *décor* without being completely sure of their human content. It helps if one can take James's work as a whole, recognising that in some books the nature of the artistic experiment may involve the deliberate forgoing of values that in other books are abundantly present. It would be unreasonable to expect every book to satisfy in the same way or to satisfy completely. A writer so eager to accept hazards needs generous and imaginative readers, who will risk a little time and effort on what may sometimes prove to be insoluble problems, but in the hope that a fine solution may emerge. The greatness of James entitles him to such consideration.

[48] *The Characters of Love* (1960), p. 135.

Appendix

Standard edition of the Novels and Stories of Henry James,
edited by Percy Lubbock (1921-3)

Almost all quotations from the novels and stories are from this
edition, (see p. 229). References to novels contain the title of the
novel, or its abbreviation. References to short stories contain the
volume number in the series as shown below. Novels in two volumes
are referred to by the volume number of the novel itself, not the
number in the total series.

CONTENTS

1. *Roderick Hudson.*
2. *The American.*
3. *The Europeans.*
4. *Confidence.*
5. *Washington Square.*
6-7. *The Portrait of a Lady.*
8-9. *The Bostonians.*
10-11. *The Princess Cassamassima.*
12-13. *The Tragic Muse.*
14. *The Awkward Age.*
15. *The Spoils of Poynton. A London Life. The Chaperon.*
16. *What Maisie Knew. In the Cage. The Pupil.*
17. *The Aspern Papers. The Turn of the Screw. The Liar. The Two Faces.*
18. *The Reverberator. Madame de Mauves. A Passionate Pilgrim. The Madonna of the Future. Louisa Pallant.*
19. *Lady Barbarina. The Siege of London. An International Episode. The Pension Beaurepas. A Bundle of Letters. The Point of View.*
20. *The Lesson of the Master. The Death of the Lion. The Next Time. The Figure in the Carpet. The Coxon Fund.*
21. *The Author of Beltraffio. The Middle Years. Greville Fane. Broken Wings. The Tree of Knowledge. The Abasement of the Northmores. The Great Good Place. Four Meetings. Paste. Europe. Miss Gunton of Poughkeepsie. Fordham Castle.*
22. *The Altar of the Dead. The Beast in the Jungle. The Birthplace. The Private Life. Owen Wingrave. The Friends of the Friends. Sir Edmund Orme. The Real Right Thing. The Jolly Corner. Julia Bride.*
23. *Daisy Miller. Pandora. The Patagonia. The Marriages. The Real Thing. Brooksmith. The Beldonald Holbein. The Story In It. Flickerbridge. Mrs Medwin.*

24. *Watch and Ward. Longstaff's Marriage. Eugene Pickering. Benvolio. The Impressions of A Cousin.*

25. *The Diary of A Man of Fifty. A New England Winter. The Path of Duty. A Day of Days. A Light Man. Georgina's Reasons. A Landscape Painter. Rose-Agathe. Poor Richard.*

26. *The Last of the Valerii. Master Eustace. The Romance of Certain Old Clothes. A Most Extraordinary Case. The Modern Warning. Mrs. Temperly. The Solution. Sir Dominick Ferrand. Nona Vincent.*

27. *Lord Beaupré. The Visits. The Wheel of Time. Collaboration. Glasses. The Great Condition. The Given Case. John Delavoy. The Third Person. The Tone of Time.*

28. *Maud Evelyn. The Special Type. The Papers. The Velvet Glove. Mora Montravers. Crapy Cornelia. A Round of Visits. The Bench of Desolation.*

29. *The Sacred Fount.*

30-31. *The Wings of the Dove.*

32-33. *The Ambassadors.*

34-35. *The Golden Bowl.*

Bibliography

I. HENRY JAMES

Fuller information may be found in *A Bibliography of Henry James* by Leon Edel and Dan H. Laurence, 1957 (2nd edn. revised, 1960), to which I am much indebted in the compilation of the following lists.

The New York and Standard editions. In 1907-09 the New York edition of James's Novels and Tales appeared in twenty-four volumes, published by Charles Scribner's Sons, New York. James made extensive revisions for this edition, and also wrote eighteen Prefaces, one for each novel and one for each volume of stories. *Watch and Ward, The Europeans, Confidence, Washington Square, The Bostonians, The Other House, The Sacred Fount* and a considerable number of stories were excluded. In 1921-3 Percy Lubbock's edition of the Novels and Stories appeared in thirty-five volumes, published by Macmillan and Co. Ltd., London. This is here referred to as the Standard edition. It is based on the New York edition, using the same text, but it also contains works which had been excluded from the latter, *e.g.*, the novels listed above, with the exception of *The Other House*, and a number of stories. It does not include the unfinished, posthumous books, *The Ivory Tower* and *The Sense of the Past*, which had been added to the New York edition. *The Outcry* is also excluded.

Many of the stories excluded from both the New York and Standard editions were reprinted in various collections, but now all the stories are available in *The Complete Works of Henry James* in twelve volumes, published by Rupert Hart-Davis, 1962-4.

Quotations from the novels and stories, so far as possible, will be taken from the Standard edition. A plan of the contents of the thirty-five volumes is given on p. 227.

I. NOVELS

Abbreviated titles used in references are given in square brackets.

Watch and Watch, in *Atlantic Monthly*, XXVIII, 1871. Book publication: Boston 1878.

Roderick Hudson [= *R.H.*], in *Atlantic Monthly*, XXXV-XXXVI, 1875. Book publication: Boston 1875; first Eng. edn. London 1879.

The American [= *Amer.*], in *Atlantic Monthly*, XXXVII-XXXIX, 1876-77. Book publication: Boston 1877; London 1877.

The Europeans [= *Eur.*], in *Atlantic Monthly*, XLII, 1878. Book publication: London 1878; Boston 1878.

Confidence, in *Scribner's Monthly*, XVIII-XIX, 1879-80. Book publication: London 1879; Boston 1880.

Washington Square [= *W.S.*], in *Cornhill Magazine*, XLI-XLII, and Harper's *New Monthly Magazine*, LXI-LXII, 1880. Book publication: New York 1880; London 1881.

The Portrait of a Lady [= *P.L.*], in *Macmillan's Magazine*, XLII-XLV and *Atlantic Monthly*, XLVI-XLVIII, 1880-81. Book publication: London 1881; Boston and New York 1881.

The Bostonians [= *B.*], in *Century Magazine*, XXIX-XXXI, 1885-86. Book publication: London 1886; New York 1886.

The Princess Cassamassima, in *Atlantic Monthly*, LVI-LVIII, 1885-86. Book publication: London and New York 1886.

The Reverberator, in *Macmillan's Magazine*, LVII-LVIII, 1888. Book publication: London and New York 1888.

The Tragic Muse [= *T.M.*], in *Atlantic Monthly*, LXIII-LXV, 1889-90. Book publication: Boston and New York 1890; first Eng. edn. London 1890.

The Other House, in *Illustrated London News*, CIX, 1896. Book publication: London 1896; New York 1896.

The Spoils of Poynton [= *S.P.*], in *Atlantic Monthly*, LXXVII-LXXVIII, 1896, with title *The Old Things*. Book publication: London 1897; Boston and New York 1897.

What Maisie Knew [= *W.M.K.*], in *Chap Book*, VI-VII, and *New Review*, XVI, 1897. Book publication: London 1897; Chicago and New York 1897.

The Awkward Age [= *A.A.*], in *Harper's Weekly*, XLII-XLIII, 1898-99. Book publication: London 1899; New York 1899.

The Sacred Fount [= *S.F.*]. New York 1901; London 1901.

The Wings of the Dove [= *W.D.*]. New York 1902; London 1902.

The Ambassadors [= *Amb.*], in *North American Review*, CLXXVI-CLXXVII, 1903. Book publication: London 1903; New York 1903.

The Golden Bowl [= *G.B.*]. New York 1904; London 1905.

The Outcry. London 1911; New York 1911.

The Ivory Tower. London 1917; New York 1917.

The Sense of the Past [= *S.P.*]. London 1917; New York 1917.

STORIES REFERRED TO IN THE TEXT

In *The Collected Tales of Henry James*, ed. Leon Edel [= *C.T.*], these stories appear either in the magazine text or in that of the first book publication. Many of them are included in the Standard edition [= St.Edn.], those which James revised for the New York edition being in the revised text. The relevant volume numbers of these collected editions are given here.

"The Story of a Year,' in *Atlantic Monthly*, XV, 1865. *C.T.*, I.

"A Landscape Painter," in *Atlantic Monthly*, XVII, 1866. *C.T.*, I. St.Edn., XXV.

"A Day of Days," in *Galaxy*, I, 1866. *C.T.*, I. St.Edn. xxv.

"Poor Richard," in *Atlantic Monthly*, xix, 1867. *C.T.*, I. St.Edn. xxv.

"Osborne's Revenge," in *Galaxy*, vI, 1868. *C.T.*, I.

"Travelling Companions," in *Atlantic Monthly*, xxvi, 1870. *C.T.*, II.

"A Passionate Pilgrim," in *Atlantic Monthly*, xxvII, 1871. *C.T.*, II. St.Edn., xvIII.

"The Madonna of the Future," in *Atlantic Monthly*, xxxi, 1873. *C.T.*, III. St.Edn., xvIII.

"Madame de Mauves," in *Galaxy*, xvII, 1874. *C.T.*, III. St. Edn., xvIII.

"Four Meetings," in *Scribner's Monthly*, xv, 1877. *C.T.*, IV. St.Edn., xxi.

"Daisy Miller," in *Cornhill Magazine*, xxxvII, 1878. *C.T.*, IV. St.Edn., xxIII.

"An International Episode," in *Cornhill Magazine*, xxxvIII-xxxIX, 1878-9. *C.T.*, IV. St.Edn., xix.

"The Pension Beaurepas," in *Atlantic Monthly*, xLIII, 1879. *C.T.*, IV. St.Edn., xix.

"A Bundle of Letters," in *Parisian*, 38, 1879. *C.T.*, IV. St.Edn., xix.

"The Point of View," in *Century Magazine*, xxv, 1882. *C.T.*, IV. St.Edn. xix.

"Lady Barbarina," in *Century Magazine*, xxvIII, 1884. *C.T.*, v. St.Edn. xix.

"The Author of *Beltraffio*," in *English Illustrated Magazine*, I, 1884. *C.T.*, v. St.Edn., xxi.

"Georgina's Reasons," in *New York Sun*, 20 (27 Jul., 3 Aug.), 1884. *C.T.*, v. St.Edn., xxv.

"A New England Winter," in *Century Magazine*, xxvIII, 1884. *C.T.*,v. St.Edn., xxv.

"The Liar," in *Century Magazine*, xxxvI, 1888. *C.T.*, v. St.Edn. xvII.

"A London Life," in *Scribner's Magazine*, III-IV, 1888. *C.T.*, v. St.Edn., xv.

"The Pupil," in *Longman's Magazine*, xvII, 1891. *C.T.*, v. St.Edn., xvI.

"The Marriages," in *Atlantic Monthly*, LxvIII, 1891. *C.T.*, v. St.Edn., xxIII.

"The Chaperon," in *Atlantic Monthly*, LxvIII, 1891. *C.T.*, v. St.Edn., xv.

"Lord Beauprey," in *Macmillan's Magazine*, Lxv-LxvI, 1891. Reprinted under title of "Lord Beauprè". *C.T.*, vIII. St.Edn., xxvII.

"The Wheel of Time," in *Cosmopolitan Magazine*, xiv, 1892-3. *C.T.*, vIII. St.Edn., xxvII.

"Owen Wingrave," in *Graphic*, Christmas number, 1892. *C.T.*, Ix. St.Edn., xxII.

"The Death of the Lion," in *Yellow Book*, I, 1894. *C.T.*, Ix. St. Edn., Ix.

"The Coxon Fund," in *Yellow Book*, II, 1894. *C.T.*, Ix. St.Edn., xx.

"Europe," in *Scribner's Magazine*, xxv, 1899. *C.T.*, x. St.Edn., xxi.

"Miss Gunton of Poughkeepsie," in *Cornhill Magazine*, vIII; *Truth* (N.Y.), xix, 1900. *C.T.*, xi' St.Edn., xxi.

"The Beldonald Holbein," in *Harper's New Monthly Magazine*, cIII, 1901. *C.T.*, xi. St.Edn., xxIII.

"Fordham Castle," in *Harper's Magazine*, cx, 1904. *C.T.*, xII. St.Edn., xxi.

"Crapy Cornelia," in *Harper's Magazine*, VII, 1909-10. *C.T.*, XII. St.Edn., XXVIII.

"The Bench of Desolation," in *Putnam's Magazine*, VII, 1909-10. *C.T.*, XII. St.Edn., XXVIII.

3. PLAYS

The Complete Plays of Henry James, ed. Leon Edel, New York 1949; London 1949.

4. TRAVEL SKETCHES

The following are referred to in the text.
  "Saratoga," in *Nation*, XI, 1870.
  "Newport," in *Nation*, XI, 1870.
[Quotations from the above are in the revised version of the first book publication in *Portraits of Places*, 1883.]
"Chester," in *Nation*, 4 Jul. 1872.
"From Chambéry to Milan," in *Nation*, 21 Nov. 1872.
"Roman Rides," in *Atlantic Monthly*, Aug. 1873.
"Roman Neighbourhoods," in *Atlantic Monthly*, Dec. 1873.
"The Old Saint Gothard," with the title "An Autumn Journey," in *Galaxy*, Apr. 1874.
"London at Midsummer," in *Lippincott's Magazine*, Nov. 1877.
"In Warwickshire," in *Galaxy*, Nov. 1877.
"Italy Revisited," first appeared as two essays "Italy Revisited" and "Recent Florence," in *Atlantic Monthly*, Apr. and May 1878.
"Venice," in *Century Magazine*, Nov. 1882.
"London," in *Century Magazine*, Dec. 1888.

These English and Italian sketches were revised for book publications. Quotations are from *English Hours* [*E.H.*], London 1905; and *Italian Hours* [*I.H.*], London 1909.

  Other travel books are:
A Little Tour in France, in *Atlantic Monthly*, LII-LIII, 1883-4, with title "En Province." Book publication: Boston 1884; first Eng. edn. London 1900.
The American Scene, London 1907; New York 1907. Most of it had appeared in periodicals.

5. CRITICISM

The Art of the Novel. Critical Prefaces by Henry James, with introd. by R. P. Blackmur. New York 1934; London 1935.
The Scenic Art. Notes on Acting and the Drama 1872-1910, ed. with introd. and notes by Allan Wade. New Brunswick, N.J., 1948; London 1949.

The American Essays, ed. with introd. by Leon Edel. New York 1956.

The Painter's Eye. Notes and Essays on the Pictorial Arts, selected and ed. by John L. Sweeney. London 1956; Cambridge, Mass. 1956.

The House of Fiction, ed. with introd. by Leon Edel. London 1957.

Literary Reviews and Essays on American, English and French Literature, ed. Albert Mordell. New York 1957. Includes more than sixty essays and reviews from the first twenty years of James's literary life.

6. BIOGRAPHY

Hawthorne. London 1879; New York 1880.

William Wetmore Story and his Friends. Edinburgh and London 1903; New York 1903.

7. AUTOBIOGRAPHY

A Small Boy and Others. New York 1913; London 1913.

Notes of a Son and Brother. New York 1914; London 1914.

The Middle Years. London 1917; New York 1917.

Henry James: Autobiography, ed. with introd. and notes by F. W. Dupee [= *A.*]. London 1956; New York 1956. The three autobiographical works listed above are here published together.

8. LETTERS

The Letters of Henry James, selected and ed. by Percy Lubbock, 2 vols. [= *L.*]. London 1920; New York 1920.

Theatre and Friendship. Some Henry James Letters with a Commentary by Elizabeth Robins. London 1932; New York 1932.

Henry James and Robert Louis Stevenson. A Record of Friendship and Criticism, ed. with introd. by Janet Adam Smith. London 1948.

The Selected Letters of Henry James, ed. with introd. by Leon Edel. New York 1955; London 1956.

Henry James and H. G. Wells. A Record of their Friendship, their Debate on the Art of Fiction and their Quarrel, ed. with introd. by Leon Edel and Gordon N. Ray. London 1958.

9. NOTEBOOKS

The Notebooks of Henry James, ed. with introd. by F. O. Matthiessen and Kenneth B. Murdock. New York and London 1947.

10. MISCELLANEOUS

Within the Rim and Other Essays. London 1919.

II. OTHERS

This list of books and articles dealing with James's life and writings is a mere sample of the immense body of work that has appeared. Some pieces have been included because they are specifically referred to in the text, and others because they illustrate viewpoints or tendencies which are of particular interest. For fuller materials Lyon N. Richardson's bibliographical list in *The Question of Henry James*, ed. by F. W. Dupee, 1945 [= *Q.H.J.*], and that of Maurice Beebe and William T. Stafford in *Modern Fiction Studies*, III, 1 (Spring 1957) may be recommended.

ALLOTT, MIRIAM: "Symbol and Image in the Later Work of Henry James," in *Essays in Criticism*, III (Jul. 1953), pp. 321 ff.

——: "Henry James and the Fantasticated Conceit: *The Sacred Fount*", in *The Northern Miscellany*, 1953, pp. 76 ff.

ANDERSON, QUENTIN: *The American Henry James*. New Brunswick, N.J. 1957; London 1958.

AUDEN, W. H.: Introduction to *The American Scene*, 1946 edn. New York and London, pp. v-xxvi.

BARZUN, JAQUES: "Henry James, Melodramatist," in *Q.H.J.*, pp. 254 ff.

BAYLEY, JOHN: *The Characters of Love*. London 1960.

BEACH, JOSEPH WARREN: *The Method of Henry James*. New Haven 1918; London 1918.

BEWLEY, MARIUS: *The Complex Fate*. London 1952; New York 1954.

——: *The Eccentric Design. Form in the Classic American Novel*. London 1959; New York 1959.

BLACKMUR, R. P.: "Henry James," in *Literary History of the United States*, ed. R. E. Spiller and others. New York 1948, II, pp. 1039 ff.

——: "In the Country of the Blue," in *Q.H.J.*, pp. 191 ff.

——: "The Loose and Baggy Monsters of Henry James," in *The Lion and the Honeycomb*. London 1955, pp. 268 ff.; New York 1955.

BROOKS, VAN WYCK: *The Pilgrimage of Henry James*. New York 1925.

CARGILL, OSCAR: *The Novels of Henry James*. New York 1961.

CHASE, RICHARD: *The American Novel and its Tradition*. New York 1957; London 1958.

DUPEE, F. W.: *The Question of Henry James: A Collection of Critical Essays*, ed. F. W. Dupee. New York 1945; London 1947.

——: *Henry James*. New York 1951; London 1951.

EDEL, LEON: *Henry James: The Untried Years, 1843-1870*. New York and Philadelphia 1953; London 1953.

——: *Henry James: The Conquest of London. 1870-1883*. New York and Philadelphia 1962; London 1962.

——: *Henry James: The Middle Years. 1884-1894*. New York and Philadelphia 1962; London 1963.

——: "Henry James: The Dramatic Years." Introduction to *The Complete Plays of Henry James*, ed. Leon Edel. New York 1949; London 1949.

EDEL LEON: Introduction to *The Sacred Fount*. New York 1953; London 1959.

ELIOT, T. S.: "Henry James." First pub. 1918; in *Q.H.J.*, pp. 123 ff.

FIREBAUGH, J. J.: "The Ververs," in *Essays in Criticism*, IV (Oct. 1954), pp. 400 ff.

GIFFORD, HENRY: "Henry James: The Drama of Discrimination," in *Pelican Guide to English Literature*, VII. London 1961, pp. 103 ff.

GOSSE, SIR EDMUND: "Henry James," in *Aspects and Impressions*. London 1922, pp. 28 ff.

GREGOR, IAN: "The Novel of Moral Consciousness: 'The Awkward Age,' " Chapter 5 of *The Moral and the Story* by Ian Gregor and Brian Nicholas, London 1962, pp. 151 ff.

HAGOPIAN, JOHN V.: "Seeing Through 'The Pupil' Again," *Modern Fiction Studies*, V (Summer, 1959-60), pp. 169 ff.

HOLLOWAY, JOHN: " 'Tess of the D'Urbervilles' and 'The Awkward Age,' " in *The Charted Mirror*. London 1960, pp. 108 ff.

JEFFERSON, D. W.: *Henry James*, in *Writers and Critics*. Edinburgh and London 1960; New York 1961.

KELLEY, CORNELIA P.: *The Early Development of Henry James*. Univ. of Illinois Studies in Language and Literature, XV, 1930.

KETTLE, ARNOLD: *An Introduction to the English Novel*, II. London 1953; New York 1960.

KROOK, DOROTHEA: *The Ordeal of Consciousness in Henry James*. London 1962; New York 1962.

LEAVIS, F. R.: *The Great Tradition* [= *G.T.*]. London 1948; New York 1948.

——: "The Novel as Dramatic Poem: *The Europeans*," in *Scrutiny*, XV (Spring 1948), pp. 209 ff.

——: "*What Maisie Knew*: A Disagreement by F. R. Leavis," in Marius Bewley: *The Complex Fate* (*q.v.*).

LUBBOCK, PERCY: *The Craft of Fiction*. London 1921; New York 1921.

MARTIN, TERENCE: "James's 'The Pupil': The Art of Seeing Through," *Modern Fiction Studies*, IV, 4, Winter 1958-9, pp. 335 ff.

MATTHIESSEN, F. O.: *American Renaissance: Art and Expression in the Age of Emerson and Whitman*. New York 1941.

——: *Henry James: The Major Phase*. London and New York 1944.

NOWELL-SMITH, SIMON: *The Legend of the Master*, compiled by Simon Nowell-Smith. London 1947; New York 1948.

POIRIER, RICHARD: *The Comic Sense of Henry James*. London 1961; New York 1961.

POUND, EZRA: "Henry James." First pub. 1920; in *Literary Essays of Ezra Pound*, ed. with introd. by T. S. Eliot. London 1954, pp. 295 ff.

PUTT, S. GORLEY: *Scholars of the Heart. Essays in Criticism*. London 1962.

RAHV, PHILIP: "The Heiress of All the Ages," in *Image and Idea*. New York 1949, pp. 51 ff.

——: "Attitudes towards Henry James," in *Image and Idea*. New York 1949, pp. 77 ff. Also in *Q.H.J.*, pp. 280 ff.

ROURKE, CONSTANCE: *American Humour*. New York 1931.

SHORT, R. W.: "The Sentence Structure of Henry James," in *American Literature*, XVIII, Mar. 1946, pp. 71 ff.

SPENCER, JAMES L.: "Symbolism in James's *The Golden Bowl*," in *Modern Fiction Studies*, III, 4 (Winter 1957-8), pp. 333 ff.

TRILLING, LIONEL: "The Princess Cassamassima," in *The Liberal Imagination*. New York 1950; London 1951, pp. 58 ff.

——: "*The Bostonians*", in *The Opposing Self*. New York 1955; London 1955, pp. 104 ff.

WALSH, WILLIAM: "Maisie in *What Maisie Knew*," in *The Use of Imagination*, London 1959, pp. 148 ff.

WARD, J. A.: *The Ambassadors*: "Strether's Vision of Evil," in *Nineteenth Century Fiction*, XIV, 1, June 1959, pp. 45-58.

WATT, IAN: "The First Paragraph of *The Ambassadors*: An Explication," in *Essays in Criticism*, Jul. 1960, pp. 250 ff.

WEGELIN, CHRISTOF: "The Internationalism of *The Golden Bowl*," in *Nineteenth Century Fiction*, XI (Dec. 1956), pp. 161 ff.

WHARTON, EDITH: *A Backward Glance*. New York 1934; London 1934.

WILSON, EDMUND: "The Ambiguity of Henry James." First pub. 1934; with revisions in *The Triple Thinkers*, London 1952, pp. 89 ff.

WINTERS, YVOR: "Maule's Well, or Henry James and the Relations of Morals to Manners," in *Maule's Curse*, 1938; reprinted in *In Defence of Reason*, New York 1947, pp. 300 ff

Index A

The Works of Henry James

"Abasement of the Northmores, The": 4.

Ambassadors, The: vii, viii, 23, 37, 65, 67, 68, 77, 91, 103, 109, 115, 167, 188-201, 211, 225.

American, The: 7, 65, 89-90, 98, 104, 116, 132, 195.

"Art of Fiction, The": 21.

Art of the Novel, The (James's Prefaces): 3-10, 135, 137, 165, 174.

"Aspern Papers, The": 5, 11.

"Author of Beltraffio, The": 3, 118, 122.

Awkward Age, The: 4, 20, 72, 134, 164-76, 201.

"Beldonald Holbein, The": 163.

"Bench of Desolation, The": 141-2.

Bostonians, The: vi, 38, 65, 88, 90-92, 95, 100, 103, 134.

"Bundle of Letters, A": 65, 67-68, 78, 79, 123, 203.

"Chaperon, The": 7, 118, 119.

"Chester," in *English Hours:* 41, 43.

Confidence: 99-100.

"Coxon Fund, The": 150-55, 162.

"Crapy Cornelia": 140.

"Daisy Miller": 70-72, 77, 78, 88, 165 (stage version), 203.

"Day of Days, A": 72-73.

"Death of the Lion": 120, 122.

"Emile Zola," in *Notes on Novelists:* 18-19.

English Hours: 18, 43, 46, 118.

"Europe": 155-58.

Europeans, The: v, 25-37, 38, 59, 66, 67, 82, 91, 102.

"Figure in the Carpet, The": 122.

"Fordham Castle": 158-62.

"Four Meetings": 62.

"From Chambéry to Milan," in *Italian Hours:* 51.

"Georgina's Reasons": 108.

Golden Bowl, The: viii, 9, 11, 24-25, 137-39, 206, 216-25.

Hawthorne: 101.

Henry James and H. G. Wells: 12-17, 22.

"Honoré de Balzac," in *Notes on Novelists:* 18.

"In Warwickshire," in *English Hours:* 43, 46.

International Episode, An: 59, 70, 75, 82-85, 97-98, 139.

Italian Hours: 46-54, 212.

"Italy Revisited," in *Italian Hours:* 49, 52.

"Landscape Painter, A": 42, 72.

"Lady Barbarina": 3, 7, 115-16, 119, 139, 175.

Letters of Henry James, The (ed. Lubbock): 3, 7, 11, 190.

"Liar, The": 36, 118.

"London," in *English Hours:* 46.

"London in Midsummer," in *English Hours:* 118.

"London Life, A": 7, 114.

"Lord Beaupré": 119.

"Madame de Mauves": 58-59, 85-86, 139.

"Madonna of the Future, The": 43, 63, 66, 139.

"Marriage, The": 118-19.

"Middle Years, The": 3.

Middlemarch, Review of: 41.

"Miss Gunton of Poughkeepsie": 78.

"New England Winter, A": 61, 66, 68, 69, 75-76, 123.

"New Novel, The": 12, 20.

"Newport," in *Portraits of Places*: 42, 74.

"Next Time, The": 120-21.

Notebooks of Henry James, The: 165.

Notes of a Son and Brother (see *Autobiography*).

"Old Saint Gothard, The": in *Italian Hours*: 50.

"Osborne's Revenge": 42, 73.

Other House, The: 165.

Outcry, The: 11, 165.

"Owen Wingrave": 117-18, 162-63.

Painter's Eye, The: 54-55.

"Passionate Pilgrim, A": 43.

"Pension Beaurepas, The": 32, 66, 76-78, 86, 93, 95, 98, 101, 138, 203.

"Point of View, The": 65-68, 70, 75, 76, 86-87.

"Poor Richard": 73.

Portrait of a Lady, The: v, vii, 7, 28, 38, 88, 89, 92, 95, 107, 108-13, 116, 133-34, 135-36, 139, 175, 188.

Princess Casamassima, The: 9, 105, 125.

"Pupil, The": vi-vii, 71, 146-50, 158.

Reprobate, The: 165.

Reverberator, The: 66, 68, 72, 88, 92, 93, 96-102, 115, 188.

Roderick Hudson: 5, 7, 64-65, 68, 81-82, 87, 89, 102, 147.

"Roman Rides," in *Italian Hours*: 50.

"Roman Neighbourhoods," in *Italian Hours*: 49-51.

"Saratoga," in *Portraits of Places*: 42, 70, 74.

Sacred Fount, The: 107, 146, 158, 176-87.

Sense of the Past, The: 140-41.

"Siege of London, The": 92, 98.

Small Boy and Others, A (see *Autobiography*).

Spoils of Poynton, The: 6, 7, 8, 142, 143, 162.

"Story of a Year, The": 72.

"Story-teller at large, The: Mr Henry Harland": 41.

Tragic Muse, The: 114, 116-17, 122-25, 129-32, 139, 175.

"Travelling Companions": 43, 58, 73.

"Tree of Knowledge, The": 4.

"Venice," in *Italian Hours*: 52, 54.

Washington Square: 92, 106-7, 133.

What Maisie Knew: vi, 8, 136-37.

"Wheel of Time, The": 119.

Wings of the Dove, The: 142, 144-45, 201-16, 225.

Index B

James's critics, and a selection of other authors

Anderson, Quentin: 214.
Arnold, Matthew: 116, 206.
Austen, Jane: 22, 121.

Balzac, Honoré de: 18, 63.
Bayley, John: 225.
Blackmur, R. P.: 5.
Brontë, Emily: 139.

Conrad, Joseph: 20-21, 28.

Dickens, Charles: 15, 105, 121.
Dreiser, Theodore: 63.
Dumas, Alexandre (*fils*): 174.

Edel, Leon: 12, 17, 22.
Eliot, George: 15, 28, 83, 89, 102, 116, 121, 139.
Emerson, R. W.: 37.

Faulkner, William: v.
Fielding, Henry: 121.
Forster, E. M.: 23, 102.

Gissing, George: 121.
Gregor, Ian: 175.

Hardy, Thomas: 121.
Harland, Henry: 41.
Hawthorne, Nathaniel: 41, 44-49, 53, 56-57, 101, 105.
Holloway, John: 175.
Holmes, Oliver Wendell: 123.

Howells, W. D.: 3, 7, 41, 46-48, 53, 57-58, 79-81, 93-96, 98-99, 100, 101, 188.

Irving, Washington: 44-46.

James, William: 205.
Jewett, Sarah Orne: 17.
Joyce, James: v.

Kinglake, A. W.: 47.
Kingsley, Charles: 41.
Kipling, Rudyard: 121.
Krook, Dorothea: 133, 139, 175, 212.

Lawrence, D. H.: 47.
Leavis, F. R.: 25, 32, 204.
Lewis, R. W. B.: 23.

Martin, Terence: vi.
Melville, Herman: 63, 113.
Moore, George: 121.

Norris, Frank: 63.

Pater, Walter: 123.
Poe, Edgar Allen: 73.
Poirier, Richard: 35.

Ray, Gordon N.: 12.
Richardson, Samuel: 132, 185.
Ruskin, John: 47, 51-52.
"Rutherford, Mark": 121.

239

Scott, Sir Walter: 121.
Shakespeare, William: 212.
Smollett, Tobias: 121.
Spencer, James L.: 24.
Spiller, Robert E.: 43.
Sterne, Laurence: 121.
Stevenson, Robert Louis: 47.
Swift, Jonathan: 11.

Thackeray, W. M.: 14, 15, 83, 121.
Trollope, Anthony: 102, 122.

Twain, Mark: 53, 63.

Walpole, Hugh: 19-20, 190.
Ward, J. A.: 23.
Wells, H. G.: 12-17.
Wharton, Edith: 11, 93, 95-96, 100, 101, 103, 158.
Wilde, Oscar: 123.

Zolà, Emile: 18-19.

PRINTED IN GREAT BRITAIN BY OLIVER AND BOYD LTD., EDINBURGH